Praise for the author as a disruptive leader

Matthew is a deeply experienced leader who has consistently shown outstanding leadership in demanding and rapidly evolving environments. Matthew's values-based leadership style, combined with unwavering ethics, has helped him navigate diverse, complex situations resulting in consistently outstanding outcomes. Matthew sees every challenge as an opportunity for growth and improvement and adopts an innovative and disruptive approach to problem solving. Through years of leading teams across different industries and geographies, Matthew has developed the ability to build diverse, empowered and accountable teams that outperform in rewarding and inclusive environments. Matthew's journey as leader is never-ending, with a continuous hunger to learn and adapt to our ever-changing world.

DAVID MATHESON, Managing Director DM Insights (formerly Chief Operations Officer, Kmart Group, Wesfarmers), Melbourne, Australia

The world of management has two types of leaders: those who point and say 'do it because', and those who: roll up their sleeves and engage across all levels; are educated in processes and detail; and are able to challenge, mentor and progress through collaboration. It is easy to rule by fear, but do those who are ruled really follow? Does a team really become a team because of a title? Leadership is partnership, fellowship, mentoring and education, and getting down into the detail while being open to adaptation, manoeuvring and learning through trial and error. In a world of 'leaders', it is good to see that people like Matthew Webber still exist and thrive on collaborative partnership with the broadmindedness to always grow—both personally and with his team.

WADE THOMPSON, Global Chief Commercial Officer/Senior Vice President, DSV 4PL Solutions, France

Matthew's transformational leadership has set the benchmark of what it is to be a leader and lead organisations on transformational journeys in 2024 and beyond. There is no more of the set and forget style of servient leadership (where leaders were often asked to sit back and become servants for their organisations). Replacing this style with a transformational leadership journey of mentoring, listening and activation allows leaders to lead and grow organisations whilst remaining authentic to achieving the best possible outcomes—those of growth, sustainability and ensuring an organisations long term strategy is aligned to its values and ultimately its people who they serve both internally and externally through leading and leadership.

SHARON LEE, Legal & Compliance Lead (Asia Pacific), US listed healthcare company

Matt, firstly, is a friend. He has also been a work colleague, a sounding board and business coach to me. Matt's strong network connects him to varying industries, markets and opportunities for interaction, which has provided me with situational examples. These examples have proved to be helpful and resilient during these recent business-disrupted years. Furthermore, Matt's many experiences through work, education and life have enabled him to be the consummate leader and professional we see today. I thoroughly appreciate Matt's structured discussions, insights and friendship, which I have used to influence and implement into my management style and roles.

BILL HARRIES, Supply Chain Manager APAC Region— Graphics and Intelligent Labels, Avery Dennison, Australia

I had the privilege of meeting Matt during our time at Stanford, and it was an instant connection, both intellectually and through our shared experiences. In Manila, our first encounter sparked a friendship rooted in deep discussions and a shared passion for analysis. Matt's insights have been invaluable to me in navigating complex business challenges, providing clarity in issues I was grappling with. His strength lies not only in his analytical prowess but also in his remarkable ability to build relationships and identify opportunities. Matt's unwavering support and expertise have been instrumental in my personal and professional growth. His impact is undeniable.

JENNIFER TONGCO, CEO Netrust Philippines, Mania Philippines

Matthew Webber is an experienced and insightful teacher and facilitator who has conducted numerous workshops for our network of CEOs, General Directors and Country Managers in Vietnam. Matthew knows his content and material very well and also uses stories, examples, and metaphors to help learners understand the concepts thoroughly.

VICTOR BURRILL, CEO Business Executive Network, Vietnam

Working with Matt as my executive leadership coach, as part of a course at Stanford LEAD on Foundations of Leadership Immersion, was a transformative experience. Matt's deep-seated wisdom and individualised tactics allowed me to confront intricate situations with renewed assurance and insight. Rather than typical coaching, my experience with Matt felt like a comprehensive exploration of both personal introspection and career development. Through stimulating conversations and bespoke action plans, Matt played a pivotal role in amplifying my leadership acumen, bolstering team synergy and driving notable achievements. The consistent encouragement and insightful critiques he provided were instrumental in creating an affirming and uplifted setting. Matt's skills did more than just bolster my leadership potential; they reshaped my entire perspective on success. Professionally, I was able to advance my career to the next level with his support.

JEAN MATTHEWS, Learning Lead—Business Transformation Services, IBM, Delhi, India

Matt's coaching elevated my leadership skills to challenge the status quo and take bold, innovative actions. He gave me tips and challenged me to go outside of my comfort zone in fearlessly pursuing the truth, becoming a lifelong learner, and being adaptable so that I could inspire confidence in my team. While he listened patiently to my ideas, he was motivating me to adapt my leadership style and manage the conditions that drive team performance. Matt's coaching has equipped me with skills to navigate the complexities of businesses in an ever-changing business environment. Thank you so much Matt; you have appreciated that leadership coaching plays an important role in disruption.

ROSALIA DE GARCIA, Managing Director Sage Publishing Asia Pacific & CIS, Singapore

Working with Matt as my executive leadership coach, as part of a course at Stanford LEAD on Designing Organisations for a Culture of Innovation, was a transformative experience. His profound insights and personalised approach enabled me to navigate complex challenges with newfound confidence and clarity. His guidance went beyond conventional coaching; it was a holistic journey of self-discovery and professional growth. Through insightful discussions and targeted strategies, he helped me enhance my leadership skills, improve team dynamics and achieve remarkable results. His unwavering support and constructive feedback fostered a positive, empowering environment. His expertise not only elevated my leadership abilities, but also significantly impacted the way I thought about my success. I wholeheartedly recommend his services to any leader aspiring for excellence and sustainable growth.

RAJ SHIVA, JP Morgan Chase & Co, Market Conduct and Regulatory Compliance, New York, USA

I highly recommend Matt as a leadership coach. I had the pleasure of working with him for several months at Stanford LEAD, and I was consistently impressed by his ability to help me unlock my leadership potential. Matt is a gifted listener. He takes the time to understand my unique needs and challenges, and he tailors his coaching accordingly. He is also very skilled at asking thought-provoking questions that help me to see things from new perspectives. One of the things I appreciate most about Matt is his ability to give specific guidance. He doesn't just tell me what to do; he helps me to develop a plan for achieving my goals. He also provides me with actionable steps that I can take to improve my leadership skills and performance. As a result of working with Matt, I have become a more confident and effective leader. I am better able to build relationships with my team members and customers, and achieve our shared goals.

VIKRAM BANDARUPALLI, Principal Solutions Engineer, Tableau Software, California, USA

Matthew, my coach during the Stanford LEAD program, has had a transformative impact on my leadership style. He expertly guided me in collecting feedback from peers, superiors, partners, and customers. His insights and tailored career guidance were exceptional. I'm now perceived as more focused and result-driven, benefiting not only me but also my team and organisation. I've improved in understanding diverse perspectives and making inclusive decisions. I extend my heartfelt gratitude to Matthew for his unwavering support and guidance. Thank you for making me a better leader and contributor to my organisation's success.

ASHISH CHINTHAL, Napino Digital Solutions, Head of Strategy & Business Operations, Mumbai, India

My journey with Matthew Webber, my Stanford Business School storytelling coach, has been nothing short of transformative. Matthew has not only been a mentor but also a source of inspiration on my storytelling path. Through his patient guidance and unwavering support, I've discovered the art of weaving stories that reflect my unique voice and perspective. I can't thank him enough for the gift of storytelling he's shared with me. If you're looking to find your storytelling voice and make it truly personal, I wholeheartedly recommend Matthew's coaching.

AMITABH DAS GUPTA, KPMG, Director, Melbourne, Australia

Matthew's mentorship has been an invaluable asset in my journey. Matthew's unwavering encouragement has pushed me to delve into thinking creatively and exploring innovative perspectives. When it comes to strategies, navigating early-stage development, and crafting compelling pitches for seed funding, his insights have been a guiding light, providing clarity and direction in what can often be a complex landscape. Matthew's wealth of knowledge and experience is a beacon of support, propelling me forward with confidence and purpose. I am deeply grateful for his guidance and mentorship, which have undoubtedly played a pivotal role in my growth and success.

DEEPA P MANI, Entrepreneur & Creative Director, Melbourne, Australia

Matt is a beacon of empathy, always ready to lend an ear and offer his heartfelt understanding. He doesn't just listen; he engages and uplifts with actionable and realistic advice. During a particularly challenging project, Matt was my pillar of support. He advised me to focus on the small, achievable steps I could take, instilling in me the belief that these minor efforts could culminate in substantial success. His unwavering support was indispensable; I couldn't have completed the project without him. Additionally, Matt has played a pivotal role in my journey towards self-improvement. He taught me the invaluable lesson of striving for a better version of myself, all while embracing and acknowledging my existing strengths and worth. His guidance has been instrumental in fostering a new-found sense of self-confidence. Thank you, Matt, for your incredible support and wisdom.

AYANO FUJITO, EU-Japan Centre for Industrial Cooperation, Manager, Training and Business Support Services, Kawa-saki, Japan

Matthew is truly passionate about driving change for a better world, particularly in the realm of innovation. His tireless dedication and unwavering enthusiasm to promote these values within industries and communities are commendable. I have no doubt that his passion and commitment will continue to make a positive impact on the lives he touches.

PAUL LENNEN, Managing Director, Weave, Hong Kong

DISRUPTIVE LEADERSHIP

DISRUPTIVE LEADERSHIP

How to create a
powerful legacy in a rapidly
changing world

MATTHEW WEBBER

GRAMMAR
FACTORY
— EST. 2013 —

Published by Grammar Factory Publishing, an imprint
of MacMillan Company Limited.

Grammar Factory Publishing
MacMillan Company Limited
25 Telegram Mews, 39th Floor, Suite 3906
Toronto, Ontario, Canada
M5V 3Z1

www.grammarfactory.com

Webber, Matthew.
Disruptive Leadership: How to create a powerful legacy
in a rapidly changing world / Matthew Webber.

Paperback ISBN 978-1-998756-76-6
eBook ISBN 978-1-998756-77-3

1. BUS071000 BUSINESS & ECONOMICS / Leadership. 2.
BUS008000 BUSINESS & ECONOMICS / Business Ethics. 3.
BUS041000 BUSINESS & ECONOMICS / Management.

Production Credits
Cover design by Designerbility
Interior layout design by Setareh Ashrafologhalai
Book production and editorial services by
Grammar Factory Publishing

Grammar Factory's Carbon Neutral Publishing Commitment
Grammar Factory Publishing is proud to be neutralizing the carbon
footprint of all printed copies of its authors' books printed by or
ordered directly through Grammar Factory or its affiliated companies through the purchase of Gold Standard-Certified International
Offsets.

Disclaimer
The material in this publication is of the nature of general comment
only and does not represent professional advice. It is not intended
to provide specific guidance for particular circumstances, and it
should not be relied on as the basis for any decision to take action
or not take action on any matter which it covers. Readers should
obtain professional advice where appropriate, before making any
such decision. To the maximum extent permitted by law, the author
and publisher disclaim all responsibility and liability to any person,
arising directly or indirectly from any person taking or not taking
action based on the information in this publication.

Dedication

To my heartbeats, Rhylee, Abbey, Noah and Emmerson: every day, you remind me of the kind of leader I aspire to be. Your dreams, innocence and kindness fuel my drive. Always dream grandly, and let kindness be the light that guides your steps.

The family circle has expanded in 2023 with the arrival of two precious souls, Banks Reign and Parker Joshua, born to Rhylee and Abbey. To these newest members of our lineage, and all the tiny footprints that will follow, I dedicate this work. My deepest wish is to mould a world for you that is abundant in opportunities and where kindness isn't just a virtue, but a way of life.

To Kelly: in every sense, you are my anchor, my inspiration and my guiding star. You complete my world. I love you.

CONTENTS

ACKNOWLEDGEMENTS

N LIFE'S JOURNEY, I've been both guided and challenged by many. In penning this piece, I'm deeply
indebted to several individuals for their candid
feedback and persistent encouragement. Kelly Smith,
Simon Murphy, Alissa Knight, Gerard Paganoni, Adam
Noakes and Sarah Halaseh-Russo: your invaluable
insights and thorough reviews of the manuscript were
instrumental in shaping its final form.

To some of the most awe-inspiring leaders I've
had the privilege of crossing paths with: Kelly Smith,
Terry McGrath, Conor O'Malley, Adam Noakes, David
Matheson, Simon Murphy, Professor Sarah Soule and
Professor Jennifer Aaker: I'm humbled. Your leadership, anchored in compassion and integrity, has been
a beacon for me. Thank you for demonstrating that the
true essence of leadership lies in first being remarkable human beings.

I extend gratitude to the leaders whose actions
proved challenging. From you I've learned lessons

the hard way, lessons that became stepping stones, reinforcing my belief in authentic and transformative leadership.

To Scott, Carolyn and the entire Grammar Factory team: your meticulous patience and unwavering honesty encapsulate the very essence of the principles I've tried to convey in this book. And to Anna White, of White Creative, your artistic genius breathed life into abstract concepts, making them tangible and relatable.

To each of you, and to many others who've been part of this journey, from the bottom of my heart, thank you.

INTRODUCTION

EVERYWHERE I LOOK, I see disruption. The stable, prosperous post-war decades are now well behind us. Modern corporate businesses, severed from the lifeline of a protectionist, tariff-heavy trading paradigm, must navigate treacherous waters. In a world of increased competition, not everyone will flourish.

In my corporate career, I have often been confronted with stark reminders of global inequities. One such instance occurred during a business trip to Bangladesh. On the drive to our warehouse I was immersed in a different world: a path riddled with potholes wove through bustling markets, we passed men breaking bricks on the side of the road and people wandering aimlessly, seemingly without purpose. Walking into the warehouse (operated by a third party) the air and the floor were thick with black dust. It felt much dimmer than it actually was. This was a typical warehouse—much like any warehouse I would expect to see in an emerging economy like Bangladesh. But one element of the scene shocked me to the core. I looked at the workers loading and unloading shipping containers and trucks, and was horrified to see that they were children.

These children were young—very young. Their tiny hands, blackened with grime, worked methodically. They displayed a level of maturity one wouldn't expect from children their age. They were more like miniature adults, carrying out tasks that appeared routine to them. I found it unsettling that there was a hum of normalcy in their actions; none of them showed any overt signs of distress. Yet, the weight of their circumstances pressed down on me, making my heart heavy. Where was the whimsy and delight of a carefree childhood? I couldn't help but think of my own children, safely ensconced in the comfort of their school, worlds away from the reality before me.

The sight of these children had stopped me in my tracks. Here I was, a corporate professional dedicated to finding ways to help my organisation flourish in the cut-throat world of business. But at what price?

Horrified, I found myself grappling with the weight of the situation. My instinctive reaction was immediate—to halt operations at the warehouse and relocate our cargo to another facility. And from a business and moral standpoint, it seemed like the only viable option; a swift action to mitigate the explicit exploitation unfolding before me. It was a disruptive act, but I was not afraid to take a stand and make some waves. I thought I had done the right thing, but had I?

A subsequent conversation with my Executive Leader presented a side of the issue I hadn't fully considered. His reaction mirrored my horror, but his approach was different—he was stoic in his accountability for the situation as a whole, while I was focused on the immediate needs of the business. I had shut down operations because I wanted to protect the reputation of the business and make sure that it was not party to any unethical conduct, while taking action to ensure that goods would still flow. But my leader drew attention to the personal implications for these children and their families.

'Matthew, where are the children now? How will they eat tonight?' he asked. His words landed heavily. Suddenly, the reality of my actions and their consequences dawned on me. I hadn't considered either the immediate or the long-term effects on the very individuals I sought to protect. My intentions, though noble, were a stark reflection of a blinded perspective— these children were working for their survival, and in my haste to end their exploitation, I had unwittingly jeopardised them.

Faced with this sobering insight, the conversation with my leader turned into a pivotal reflection on the broader responsibilities of our organisation. It became clear that intervening was not merely a gesture of immediate aid; it was about sustaining a meaningful change.

The organisation, upon understanding the full scope of the issue, did not hesitate to extend their hand. Their action was not a reactionary patch to a sudden problem; it was a considered strategy to mend a broken system—a system that had allowed such situations to persist. Although the company did not directly operate the warehouse or employ those children, they refused to be bystanders to their own indirect involvement. They took accountability for what could have been argued was not their responsibility. The leadership's commitment to go beyond the call of duty emerged from a recognition of their position within a global ecosystem where their choices had ripple effects, reaching far into the lives of individuals they might never meet.

As I watched and learned from the leaders of this organisation, my own understanding of disruptive leadership crystallised. What unfolded in the reality of that warehouse was not just a test of corporate responsibility, but a defining moment in my own journey, as the faces marked by hardship taught me the profound lessons of empathy and action in leadership.

The connection between this incident and disruptive leadership lies in the understanding that our actions as leaders in the era of disruption are not just about innovating or pivoting strategies; they're about the humanity that guides our decisions, the vision that reaches beyond profit margins, and the legacy we leave when we dare to disrupt the status quo for the greater good.

The disruptive era is now

Our world today is confronted with a constantly shifting landscape. This extends far beyond mere change; its defining characteristic lies in the speed and unpredictability of such transformations. Unsettling economic upheaval, geopolitical tensions and technological advancements have caused traditional industries and economic powers to lose footing, ushering in a new world order.

Consider the recent global pandemic, which continues to reshape our economies, our ways of working and societal norms. Or the war in Ukraine, which has not only inflicted immense human suffering but also disrupted global energy markets and spurred a realignment of global power dynamics. In between drafts of this very book, the Israeli-Palestinian conflict escalated into all-out war. These events ripple through our lives, morphing our realities and confronting leaders with challenges of a magnitude we've never seen before.

Then there's the economic landscape. The once dependable framework of supply chains was thrown into disarray when a single ship blocked the Suez Canal, an incident that highlighted our interconnected vulnerability. Simultaneously, previously dormant markets, like Africa, and South and Southeast Asia, are starting to assert their global influence, creating new pathways and potential blind spots for existing leadership.

Equally disruptive is the meteoric rise of novel business models, with companies like Uber and Airbnb overthrowing established sectors. The sheer scale of blockchain's potential, the disruptive power of artificial intelligence, and the burgeoning implications of quantum computing are demanding leaders to continually re-evaluate their strategies and understandings.

The disruptive era is a testing ground for leaders. Traditional leadership—once firmly rooted in established practices and predictable trends—is being severely tested. Outdated approaches not only risk irrelevance but can be the precursor to the downfall of entire organisations. The scale of Blockbuster's collapse, in the face of Netflix's rise, serves as a stark reminder of the destructive potential of clinging to the status quo.

Yet, among the chaos is unparalleled opportunity. The very disruptions that upend the old order are catalysts for innovation, gateways to new frontiers of growth and positive societal impact. For leaders attuned to this era's demands and capable of anticipating and shaping the course of disruption, the potential for crafting revolutionary changes in their industries, organisations and communities is immense.

The hope at the heart of disruption

The global impact of disruptive leadership is likely to be vast. Imagine a world where businesses are not merely concerned with survival, but are actively thriving amidst chaos. This is a world where disruption is harnessed to innovate, to rethink our social systems and industries, and to find solutions to the critical problems plaguing our planet. This is a world where leaders steer their organisations towards success while creating positive societal impact, becoming stewards for a more equitable and sustainable future.

As we delve into disruptive leadership, we are not only equipping ourselves to survive the disruptive era, but also positioning ourselves to utilise its potential for positive transformation. This is an outlook not grounded in naive optimism, but in reality—a reality with hope. Hope that we can pivot amidst challenges, that we can find opportunities in crises, and that we, as leaders, can become catalysts for meaningful change.

We'll discover throughout this book that disruptive leadership can significantly shift the trajectory of not just businesses, but entire communities, nations, and potentially the globe. It holds the promise of contributing to a more inclusive and sustainable world, where leaders do better.

We live in a world desperate for positive change. If you're among those who dare to dream, you will see in every challenge an opportunity for growth and innovation. This book is designed for you—emerging leaders, entrepreneurs, intrapreneurs—who dare to redefine the future and spearhead change.

In the coming pages we will explore, dissect and construct the new model of leadership—one that thrives on disruption rather than wilting under it. This model won't be a regurgitation of theoretical concepts, but an organic construct derived from lived experiences, and the experience of leading organisations through transformative change. The journey will be as enlightening as it will be empowering. By the end of it, you'll not just understand the disruptive leadership paradigm, but you'll be well on your way to embodying it—creating positive change in your organisations and communities, and leading them with courage, empathy and an entrepreneurial spirit that drives our world forward.

The disruptive leadership toolkit

To successfully navigate leadership in today's high-speed era, a comprehensive toolkit is required that encapsulates the nuances of disruptive leadership. This toolkit, made up of the Disruptive Leadership Framework and the Maturity Models, serves this very purpose.

Disruptive Leadership Framework

The Disruptive Leadership Framework forms the foundation of our exploration, providing the central structure of the book. It is composed of five segments, each emphasising a unique perspective on leadership: Contemporary Leadership, Influential Leadership, Future-Ready Leadership, Legacy-Oriented Leadership and Transformational Leadership. Each segment

delves into a unique aspect of leadership, introducing the fundamental principles required to navigate through disruptive times.

- **Part 1: Contemporary Leadership** introduces the basic disciplines of disruptive leadership accountability and resilience, and the importance of diversity and inclusion in modern organisations.

- **Part 2: Influential Leadership** zeroes in on the interpersonal dynamics of leadership, detailing how to foster trust, negotiate and influence change, and use storytelling as a motivation tool.

- **Part 3: Future-ready Leadership** explores practical skills for modern leadership, addressing competencies such as leading remote teams, promoting cultural intelligence, and encouraging entrepreneurial thinking within teams.

- **Part 4: Legacy-Oriented Leadership** investigates how leaders can have a lasting, positive impact on their organisations and broader society, with a focus on adaptability, ethical leadership and legacy creation through positive influence.

- **Part 5: Transformational Leadership** examines the importance of being action-oriented and reflective. It delves into personal disruption and self-transformation, emphasising the need for continuous learning and adaptability.

Maturity Models

The second compartment of the toolkit contains the Maturity Models, which offer a detailed exploration of each leadership principle. Each of the fifteen chapters is based on one of the fifteen models and concentrates on two pivotal leadership traits.

You will see these models come to life at the end of each chapter. Two axes represent the two leadership traits discussed in the chapter, creating four quadrants that show differing levels of maturity that a leader may possess. These models enable leaders to scrutinise their leadership style and pinpoint areas for growth and development.

The fifteen models are:

1   The **Modern Leader**, centring on embracing disruption and driving innovation. The key learning is the evolution of leaders into change agents, harnessing disruption for innovation and growth.

2   The **Accountable and Resilient Leader** underscores accountability and resilience; critical qualities required for accountability, for successful change navigation, and for legacy creation.

3   The **Inclusive Leader** champions diversity and inclusion. This chapter emphasises that fostering diversity and inclusivity results in more-effective disruption navigation.

4   The **Trustful Leader** explores self-trust and team trust. It illustrates the paramount importance of trust in leadership for impactful outcomes.

5   The **Influential Leader** focuses on negotiation skills and influence. Proficiency in negotiation and influence is pivotal to leading through disruption.

6   The **Master Storyteller** advocates storytelling and communication skills. Mastering communication is crucial for team engagement and disruption navigation.

7   The **Omni Leader** promotes remote and in-office leadership skills. Mastery of these skills enables leaders to thrive in diverse and fragmented environments.

8   The **Global Leader** values global awareness and local responsiveness. Balancing global and local perspectives is key to navigating global disruptions.

9   The **In/Entrepreneurial Leader** focuses on intrapreneurship, entrepreneurship and business acumen. These skills are vital to fuel innovation and strategic thinking.

10 The **Legacy Leader** highlights ethical leadership and personal-professional alignment. Maintaining ethics and alignment is essential to navigate disruption while creating a meaningful legacy.

11 The **Adaptable Leader** explores individual and team adaptability. Cultivating adaptability is crucial for building a resilient culture in times of uncertainty.

12 The **Vulnerable and Humble Leader** focuses on vulnerability and humility. Fostering these traits is key to building trust and resilience, driving effective change.

13 The **Action-Oriented Leader** zeroes in on action-orientation and balanced decision making. Acting decisively and making informed decisions are critical for thriving in disruptive times.

14 The **Reflective Leader** delves into reflection depth and reflective insight application. Enhancing these traits aids in informed decision making and successful leadership.

15 The **Disruptive Leader** spotlights personal and organisational disruption. Embracing disruption at all levels is key to fostering dynamic leadership for legacy creation.

These models provide a solid blueprint for disruptive leadership. Individually, they allow leaders to zoom in on individual aspects for targeted growth or zoom out to view the leadership journey holistically, driving deep insights and transformative action. Collectively, they guide you on a comprehensive journey of understanding, reflection, and evolution, empowering you to harness disruption as an opportunity for innovation and to forge a legacy.

My story

The toolbox I present to you in this book is the culmination of my story.

Each page in this book reflects my life's journey—my experiences, lessons and insights. Like the stories of many, mine is peppered with challenges and triumphs, all of which have carved out the beliefs I now hold. At its core, my narrative has always revolved around one fundamental idea: the undeniable power and responsibility of leadership. I firmly believe that the wellbeing of our planet, the success of our organisations and the quality of our individual lives are deeply intertwined with the calibre of our leadership.

Between these lines, however, is an unspoken truth. My journey wasn't just shaped by successes, but also by failures, missteps and broken dreams. These moments, while challenging, brought forward the importance of humility and accountability. They taught me that true leadership isn't just about steering a ship through calm waters, but taking responsibility when storms arise and navigating through them with grace. Every setback was a lesson, every challenge an opportunity to grow.

From innocent childhood days, when I set up lemonade stands in my driveway or tried to convince neighbours to let me mow their lawn for a fee, to navigating the intricate corridors of corporate powerhouses, my heart has always pulsed with a drive for entrepreneurship and transformative leadership. My early ventures were not just about making money; they instilled in me a sense of enterprise that has never faded. They were my first foray into understanding the essence of leadership—its challenges, its rewards and its profound impact.

Later I stepped into the world of corporate leadership in some of the largest and most recognised global organisations, where my roles have been vast yet united by an undercurrent of steadfast commitment. Whether it was as a graduate accountant, a Chief Executive Officer, or one of the many roles in between, each was an opportunity, a responsibility, and a platform to foster positive change.

My association with the Stanford Graduate School of Business, as a Course Facilitator (Contract) and as a full-time coach in the Stanford Seed program, has only deepened my dedication to mentoring and guiding emerging leaders.

However, beneath all these achievements lies a deeper, personal story. One rooted in resilience and determination. The economic challenges faced by my family in the late 1980s and early 1990s deeply impacted me. Watching my parents grapple with the hardships of business during a recession instilled in me a drive to help others rise above adversity.

Alongside this drive, I became a passionate advocate of transformative power—of leadership, business and entrepreneurship—wholeheartedly believing in its potential to sculpt prosperous, harmonious and thriving societies. I've witnessed the consequences of missteps in leadership and celebrated the positive effects of getting it right—benefits that extend to individuals, families, organisations, communities, and the world at large. Deep-rooted belief and commitment have driven me; they stem from humble beginnings and a promise to make a lasting, positive difference.

Leadership, in my eyes, is more than accolades or positions. It's about the footprints we leave behind and the souls we inspire. In this book, I hope to share my experiences, offering a beacon for those aspiring to leave a meaningful imprint on this ever-shifting world.

Let's get to work!

Welcome to your journey into disruptive leadership. As you travel through this book and grapple with the challenges and opportunities of disruptive leadership, remember the privilege that you hold as a leader and the positive change that you have the power to instigate. Embrace the responsibility, step boldly into the challenges that lie ahead, and be the transformative force that paves the way to a future abundant with possibilities—that are in fact probabilities if you apply sound leadership.

I invite you to immerse yourself in the messages that I share in this book, to reflect on your own experiences, and to envision the kind of leader you aspire to be. I hope that this exploration sparks your curiosity, fuels your passion for change, and empowers you to embark on your own journey of leadership and transformation.

CONTEMPORARY LEADERSHIP

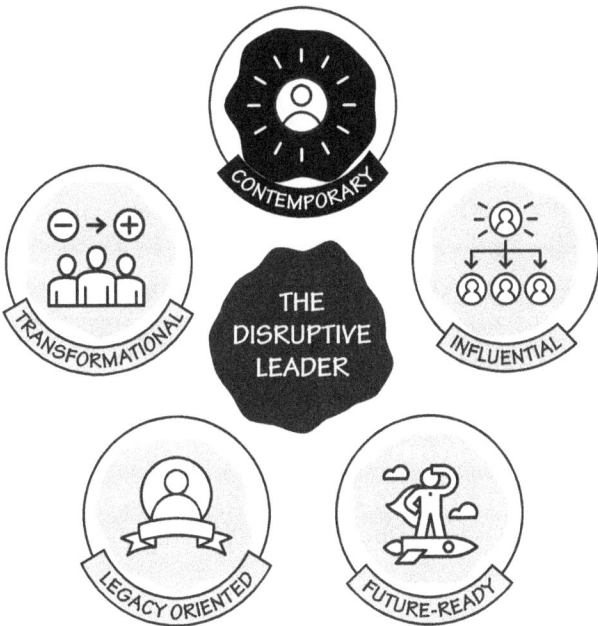

CONTEMPORARY

TRANSFORMATIONAL

THE DISRUPTIVE LEADER

INFLUENTIAL

LEGACY ORIENTED

FUTURE-READY

Part 1: Contemporary Leadership commences with an exploration of the transformation occurring within leadership frameworks and strategies. This evolution is crucial to navigate our current era, which is hallmarked by rapid innovation, escalating competitive forces and an environment filled with unpredictability. Such a landscape calls for an innovative approach to leadership known as disruptive leadership.

The core ethos of disruptive leadership runs counter to the principles of traditional leadership. Traditional leadership primarily emphasises maintaining established norms and perpetuating organisational order, preferring the safety of the known and tried. Conversely, disruptive leadership endorses a spirit of exploration and the willingness to venture into new arenas in the business world.

It is crucial to understand that disruptive leadership does not advocate indiscriminate change. It champions the initiation of the right changes at the most opportune times. This approach calls when to uphold current practices and when to push for innovation. It involves understanding how to exploit disruption as a driving force, propelling superior solutions and helping organisations to be more resilient and robust.

Contemporary leaders must not only understand disruption but embrace it as a catalyst for innovation and growth. Leaders who successfully navigate this disruptive landscape are those who view change not as a hurdle but as an opportunity to evolve and inspire transformation within their organisation. **Chapter 1: Disruption and the Modern Leader** investigates the differences between traditional and disruptive leadership. It underscores the urgency for contemporary leaders to perceive disruption not as a stumbling block but as a gateway to innovation and growth.

Leaders who demonstrate accountability and resilience establish a robust foundation to thrive amidst disruption. By taking responsibility for their actions and displaying resilience in the face of challenges, they inspire confidence and loyalty within their teams. **Chapter 2: Embodying Accountability and Resilience** unravels the importance of these two baseline traits. We discuss in depth how these characteristics can be cultivated and demonstrated effectively, and how they impact team performance and the potential for disruptive leadership.

Diversity and inclusion are critical in fuelling innovation and resilience during disruptive times. Leaders who champion these values ensure a culture where diverse perspectives are welcomed, respected and valued, which drives creative problem solving and fosters an environment of growth and learning. **Chapter 3: Leading with Diversity and Inclusion in Disruptive Times** offers actionable strategies for leaders to harness the power of diverse perspectives and cultivate an inclusive environment.

By embodying the principles of disruptive leadership, championing accountability and resilience, and promoting diversity and inclusion, you will prepare yourself for the disruptive era.

DISRUPTION AND
THE MODERN LEADER

*We always overestimate the change that will
occur in the next two years and underestimate
the change that will occur in the next ten.*

BILL GATES

THIS CHAPTER will guide you through this new
leadership approach. Our exploration will take us
through the role of the disruptive leader in fostering
innovation and driving change, and how this new leadership style is different from traditional forms. We will
unpack why embracing disruption as both a challenge
and opportunity is key, and how to find the delicate
balance between creating disruption as a leader and
managing it within an organisation. By the end of this
chapter, you will have a clearer idea of how to position
yourself in this landscape, ready for transformation.

As I walked into the meeting room, armed with my spreadsheets and a PowerPoint presentation that gleamed with charts and graphs, I felt a subtle surge of anticipation. Today, I was meeting Adam, the new supply chain senior executive, and I was ready to impress. We were both newcomers to a business gasping for survival, struggling to breathe in an environment of relentless competition and disruption.

I expected an introductory meeting. Exchange pleasantries, share the numbers, discuss strategies, and then agree on the next steps. Nothing extraordinary, just business as usual. But what transpired over the next thirty minutes was anything but usual. It was a whirlwind that completely shifted my understanding of leadership and altered the trajectory of my career.

Adam's arrival was unassuming, his smile friendly, his handshake firm. We settled in, and I launched into my usual routine. But before I could even reach the end of my spiel, Adam burst out laughing.

I froze, my mind racing. Was this a joke? A test? Adam's eyes sparkled with amusement, but there was something else in them—a spark of challenge, a hunger for something more profound.

'How are you going to transform the business?' Adam asked, his voice dancing between jest and seriousness. 'How will you build others and lead them to success?'

I blinked, caught off guard. These were not the questions I was expecting. My spreadsheets seemed suddenly irrelevant; my PowerPoint slides insignificant. Before I could grasp the meaning behind his words, Adam reached across the table and ripped them up, tearing through my carefully laid plans.

'We are not in the business of making spreadsheets or PowerPoints,' he said, his voice now filled with a passion that resonated deep within me. 'We are in the business of helping people, giving value to our customers, and making money. That's your accountability.'

I sat there, bewildered, but also intrigued. Was this madness, or was it brilliance?

'You're a leader,' Adam continued, leaning in. 'Act like this was your own business. Take charge, inspire action, lead the leaders.'

His words weren't just declarations; they were a call to action. It was a challenge I hadn't even realised I was craving. Adam wasn't just a superior demanding obedience; he was a visionary pushing me towards greatness. In that meeting room, amid the torn remnants of my former approach, I found a new path. It was a path paved with disruption, agility, collaboration and innovation. It wasn't about hierarchy or ego; it was about impact, accountability and a shared goal.

Adam wasn't a nutcase; he was a catalyst. His laughter was the melody of change, his words the symphony of disruptive leadership.

I walked out of that room not with a list of tasks but with a renewed sense of purpose. I wasn't just a cog in the machine; I was a disruptor, a leader, a visionary. I was ready to embrace uncertainty, to convert challenges into opportunities, and to champion a new era of leadership.

The journey had just begun, and I was leading the way.

Defining disruptive leadership

What exactly is disruptive leadership? Perhaps the best way to answer that question is to examine how it differs from traditional leadership. Traditional leadership styles were often rooted in hierarchical structures, where a leader's authority was unquestioned, and their directives were to be followed without dispute. Leaders were seen as the supreme knowledge bearers and decision makers, while employees were expected to execute orders and conform to established procedures. Leadership was largely about maintaining control and preserving the status quo. Innovation, if it occurred, was typically a top-down process, initiated and directed by leaders. Today hierarchical structures have given way to more fluid and collaborative arrangements, and the command-and-control style of leadership has lost its relevance.

In this new landscape, disruptive leadership emerges as modern leadership. It is a style that shuns rigidity and embraces agility, forsakes dominance and promotes collaboration, and swaps the certainty of control for the dynamism of empowerment. Disruptive leaders don't merely manage teams; they inspire and enable individuals to be their best selves. They don't dictate change; they cultivate a culture where change is a collective endeavour.

Disruptive leadership is also about fostering a growth mindset, both at an individual and organisational level. It's about viewing failures not as setbacks, but as learnings for success. It's about learning from mistakes and continuously seeking ways to improve and grow. This is a stark departure from traditional leadership styles, where failures were punished severely and often seen as pitfalls to be avoided.

Unlike traditional leadership styles, which often prioritise business outcomes over human connections, disruptive leadership recognises the importance of fostering meaningful relationships. It is deeply rooted in empathy and emotional intelligence. Disruptive leaders understand that their teams are not just numbers in the corporate machine, but unique individuals with their own aspirations, challenges and potentials. They strive to create a work environment where everyone feels valued, heard, and motivated to contribute their best.

Disruptive leadership embodies a vision-driven approach. It's not just about responding to changes in the present, but also about anticipating and shaping the future. Disruptive leaders are forward thinkers; visionaries who are constantly scanning the horizon for new trends, opportunities and challenges.

The gravity of disruptive leadership

When many people hear the term 'disruptive leadership', their minds might wander to Silicon Valley start-ups filled with bean bags, ping pong tables and free-flowing snacks. It's an alluring image: the idea that the epitome of innovation is a relaxed environment where employees don flip-flops and brainstorm while munching on tacos from the food truck parked outside. But if you find yourself reading this chapter in the hopes of learning about these superficial trappings, you're in for a wake-up call.

Disruptive leadership isn't about aesthetics or fringe benefits. It's about a radical shift in mindset and an unwavering commitment to both purpose and people. At its core, disruptive leadership demands courage. Courage to stand against the tide, to make decisions that might be unpopular in the moment but transformative in the long run. Neuroscience tells us that our brains are wired for validation and acceptance by our peers. Going against this hardwiring, against our very nature, is what sets disruptive leaders apart.

Let's consider an event from the late 1990s in Australia. After the tragic Port Arthur massacre, Prime Minister John Howard took a bold step that many would have shied away from. Recognising the dangers of unregulated gun ownership, he introduced a stringent gun buyback scheme. The decision was far from popular; many of his staunchest supporters felt betrayed, and there were significant protests. But Howard was convinced that this was a necessary step for the greater good of the country. The result? Australia has had remarkably few mass shootings since.

It's crucial to comprehend that the true disruptors in leadership are not those who opt for style over substance or jump onto every trendy bandwagon. They are the ones who, even in the face of adversity, remain steadfast in their commitment to innovation, integrity and, most importantly, their responsibility towards those they lead.

While the trappings of modern start-up culture—the bean bags, taco trucks and foosball tables—might offer temporary motivation or a break from the daily grind, they don't define disruptive leadership. A disruptive leader isn't swayed by these adornments, but rather is deeply engrossed in nurturing an environment of trust, growth and long-term vision.

If there's one thing you take away from this section, let it be this: disruptive leadership isn't for the faint of heart. It's for those brave souls willing to navigate the murky waters of uncertainty, armed with empathy, vision and an unyielding dedication to leaving a legacy of positive, transformative change in a rapidly evolving world.

The 'why' and 'who' of contemporary leadership
Neuroscience has shown us that the human brain isn't a static entity but rather an ever-evolving powerhouse that thrives on purpose and connection. At the core of this intricate system is our brain's reward centre. When we act in ways that resonate with our purpose, our

brain releases dopamine. This isn't just a fleeting feeling; it's a deeply embedded system designed to propel us towards actions that align with our innate purpose.

Now, bring this understanding into the world of contemporary leadership. When a leader aligns with their 'why'—their profound reason for leading, the purpose behind their actions—they not only experience this dopamine-driven motivation, but also become a beacon of inspiration for others. They exude an authenticity that can't be replicated by simply going through the motions.

However, understanding our 'why' is only half of the equation. The second, equally critical component, is the 'who'.

Adam, the disruptor, challenged the conventional notion of leadership in our first encounter. His questions weren't about profits or statistics, but rather centred on the people impacted by the decisions made. 'How are you going to transform the business? How will you build others and lead them to success?' These questions are about the 'who'.

Every decision, strategy and action taken in leadership has an impact. Sometimes, it's direct and tangible; other times, it's subtle yet still profound. In the context of the modern leader, understanding the 'who' means recognising the ripple effect of their choices.

Contemporary leadership demands that leaders remain acutely conscious of the lives they touch. Every email sent, every meeting conducted, every strategy devised doesn't just affect numbers on a spreadsheet. It affects people—their hopes, their fears, their aspirations.

Consider a CEO deciding to implement a new technology. From a business perspective, it might streamline processes and increase efficiency. But from a human perspective, it may mean employees need to upskill, some roles might become redundant, while others emerge. The 'who' perspective ensures that the CEO doesn't just see the technological advancement, but the faces of every individual affected by it. This modern leader understands the breadth of disruption—the ripples that spread from the core and have the potential to displace the humans caught in the surge.

Our brains are wired for social connection. The same circuits that light up with dopamine when we find purpose also activate when we experience social connection. When leaders make decisions that positively impact others, when they acknowledge the 'who' in their leadership equation, they're not just fulfilling a moral duty. They're tapping into a deeply seeded neural pathway that associates leadership with social bonding.

In an age of disruption, where change is the only constant, the 'why' provides the anchor, and the 'who' determines the direction. The modern leader doesn't exist in isolation. Their purpose intertwines with the lives of every individual they touch.

Emotional intelligence in disruptive leadership

While hard skills and knowledge are vital, they aren't the only determinants of a leader's success. A disruptive leader's effectiveness hinges significantly on understanding, interpreting and acting upon emotions—

their own and those of others. This is where emotional intelligence enters the scene.

At the core of emotional intelligence lies a profound understanding of the intricate dance of human emotions. This isn't merely about recognising when someone is happy, sad or frustrated; it's about delving into the nuances of these emotions, understanding their origins, their impact, and the ripples they create in the broader context of human interaction.

Often, when we think of intelligence, we default to thinking about solving complex mathematical equations, or understanding intricate theories. But the intelligence of emotions—the ability to decipher, respond to, and even predict human reactions—is equally intricate and, arguably, even more vital in leadership. This understanding allows a leader to foresee potential conflicts, repair divisions before they widen, and build bridges where others see only gaps.

Consider a time when you encountered someone who genuinely 'got' people. Their knack wasn't just intuition or chance; it was an ability to read between the lines, hear the unspoken words, and feel the undercurrents of emotion that many might overlook. It's an art and a science. When someone speaks, they're not just conveying information; they're also revealing a wealth of emotions, motivations, fears and aspirations. An emotionally intelligent individual hears all these layers, giving them a richer understanding of the human experience.

This understanding becomes even more crucial in disruptive leadership. Disruption, by its very nature, unsettles the status quo. It challenges established norms, shakes foundations and introduces uncertainty. In such an environment, the human psyche can naturally lean towards resistance or even fear. Herein lies the challenge and opportunity for disruptive leaders. They aren't just battling market dynamics or competitors; they are navigating the complex world of human emotions.

Emotional intelligence fosters genuine connections. In the world of business, relationships are everything. Leaders who can connect authentically with their teams, peers and stakeholders possess a considerable advantage. They can create environments where trust flourishes, collaboration is second nature, and shared goals are pursued with enthusiasm.

Then there's decision making. Effective decisions aren't just logical; they are emotionally intelligent. A leader can have all the data in the world, but without understanding the emotional implications of their choices, they may face unforeseen challenges. An emotionally intelligent leader weighs not just the tangible outcomes, but also considers the intangible effects their decisions might produce.

As the business landscape becomes more complex, the need for emotionally intelligent leadership becomes paramount. Disruptive leaders, with their focus on innovation and transformation, especially stand to gain from honing this skill. Emotional intelligence is not just a desirable trait; in today's world, it's a non-negotiable asset. For those aspiring to lead change, investing in understanding the human heart and mind is as crucial as any strategy or plan.

A vital ingredient: the entrepreneurial spirit

At the crux of disruptive leadership lies a fundamental trait: the entrepreneurial spirit. The entrepreneurial mindset is not merely a state of mind but a way of acting, a manner of approaching the world. It's grounded in action and substance, not just theory or aspiration.

Entrepreneurs have a unique lens through which they view challenges. For them, every problem is a puzzle waiting to be solved. This proactive stance doesn't wait for solutions to appear; it seeks them out, relentlessly. It's about being hands-on, about diving into the issue, understanding its intricacies, and then actively crafting a solution.

Risk? It's part and parcel of the entrepreneurial journey. But it's not reckless risk taking. It's calculated, measured. Entrepreneurs are not scared of failing. For them, failure is just another data point, another learning opportunity. They recognise that sometimes the most valuable insights come from what didn't work rather than what did. They take these lessons, iterate, refine, and then dive back in with renewed vigour.

Then comes optimism. This isn't about wearing rose-tinted glasses but about a genuine belief in possibilities. Entrepreneurs believe in potential—theirs, their team's, and their ideas'. This optimism fuels them, drives them to push boundaries and to continually seek better, more innovative solutions. It's an optimism rooted in reality, grounded in action, and always aimed at tangible results.

Let's discuss collaboration. Entrepreneurs, contrary to the lone-wolf image sometimes portrayed, are supreme collaborators. They know the value of diverse thought, of pooling together different skills, experiences and perspectives. They actively seek out partnerships, networks and synergies. For them, the sum is always greater than its parts. It's this collaborative spirit that allows them to bring together disparate elements, crafting something unique, effective and often groundbreaking.

Innovation is another non-negotiable in the entrepreneurial playbook. Not innovation for the sake of it, but meaningful, purpose-driven innovation. Entrepreneurs often start with a blank slate, but they aren't daunted by it. They see it as an opportunity, a canvas to craft something new, something better. They aren't just content with tweaking the existing; they aim to redefine it. They question, challenge, and then create.

So, what does all this mean for leaders? Why should they care about the entrepreneurial spirit?

Disruptive leadership, when infused with the entrepreneurial mindset, becomes a force multiplier. It combines vision with action, strategy with execution, and ambition with empathy. For leaders, embracing this mindset is not just beneficial: it's essential. It's what will allow them to lead with impact, drive meaningful change, and create a lasting legacy in a dynamic world.

Designing the future:
cultivating genuine innovation

Innovation isn't accidental. It doesn't just happen because you've hired bright people. No, innovation must be intentional. It must be designed. Every leader's role, whether they acknowledge it or not, is to be an architect.

Leaders are responsible for crafting teams, processes and structures that not only support, but actively encourage innovative thinking. By placing individuals with diverse skill sets and perspectives at the core of operations, leaders ensure not just a continuous stream of fresh ideas, but also the creation of value, effective problem solving, enhanced performance, and the identification of new opportunities.

A leader must create an environment where ideas aren't just tolerated, but celebrated. A place where out-of-the-box thinking isn't seen as a challenge to the status quo, but as an enhancement. Think about it. How often are ideas stifled because they aren't 'how things are done here'? Or innovative solutions shelved because they were too unorthodox? Leaders need to be proactive, dismantling these barriers and encouraging free thinking.

This approach is complemented by an adaptable framework, which delineates clear roles yet remains receptive to change. Established routines should emphasise collaboration, open dialogue and continuous feedback loops. The linchpin is a thriving culture: one that values every voice, rewards experimentation, and perceives challenges as gateways to opportunities. When leaders ensure that these elements are in harmony, they transform the organisation, making innovation less of an isolated occurrence and more of a deep-rooted ethos. This holistic approach underpins the financial health and sustainability of the organisation and of the communities it operates and serves.

But to champion innovation, leaders must first understand it. Innovation isn't about seismic shifts; it's often the subtle changes, the small tweaks that cumulatively make a vast difference. A culture that waits for the next big thing misses out on the myriad 'small things' that can redefine its course. These micro-innovations, these incremental shifts, can often be the catalysts for exponential growth.

Moreover, a genuine culture of innovation recognises that failures aren't setbacks, but valuable feedback. It's a system where every misstep is a learning opportunity, where teams are not afraid to pivot, refine, and try again.

In essence, leaders need to design their organisations as innovation engines. This is not about one-off initiatives but a continuous journey where innovation is routine, where it's the norm, not the exception.

The MODERN LEADER Maturity Model

Disruption and innovation have become vital components of enduring leadership. As we advance, we find a model that represents the modern leader and underscores these components, evolving beyond conventional leadership theories. This model rests on the twin axes of driving innovation and embracing disruption. When leaders occupy the optimal quadrant of this model, they are empowered with agility, foresight and an innovation-oriented mindset, enabling them to confidently navigate their industries' uncharted domains. By mastering this model, leaders can turn the tide of disruption from being a threat to becoming a catalyst for propelling their organisations towards impactful results.

The MODERN LEADER

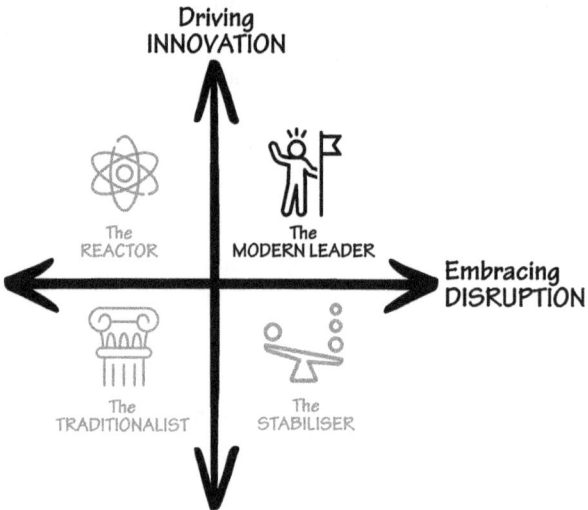

Driving
INNOVATION

The
REACTOR

The
MODERN LEADER

Embracing
DISRUPTION

The
TRADITIONALIST

The
STABILISER

Let's now examine each quadrant in detail to determine which one you currently occupy, and how to move into the ideal sector.

The Traditionalist: This quadrant signifies leaders who exhibit low levels of both embracing disruption and driving innovation. Leaders in this quadrant may be more comfortable with the status quo and resistant to change. They can struggle to identify or capitalise on disruptive opportunities. For development, these leaders should START acknowledging the presence and inevitability of disruption, and the potential opportunities it presents. This can spur transformation. Furthermore, they should START fostering an innovative mindset, encouraging new ideas and novel problem-solving approaches within their teams.

The Reactor: Leaders falling into this quadrant display low disruption-embracing capabilities but are high in driving innovation. They are skilled at fostering innovation but may be more reactive than proactive when it comes to disruption. To grow, these leaders should START viewing disruption as an opportunity rather than a threat and actively seeking out disruptive trends and developments in their industry. They should STOP avoiding disruptions and START integrating them into their innovative efforts.

The Stabiliser: This quadrant represents leaders who embrace disruption but struggle to drive innovation. These leaders understand the importance of disruption but may lack the creativity or agility to leverage these disruptions effectively. For advancement, these leaders should START promoting a culture of innovation, encouraging curiosity, exploration and risk taking. They should STOP sticking to tried and tested methods and START embracing novel and unconventional solutions.

The Modern Leader: This quadrant is the ideal maturity level, representing leaders who excel in both embracing disruption and driving innovation. These leaders see the potential in disruptive trends and use them as catalysts for innovation. To improve even further, they should START sharing their experiences and insights to build a culture of disruptive leadership within their organisations.

Modern leadership in action

The era of disruption is upon us. There is no time to waste. Here are five actions to begin your disruptive leadership.

Embrace disruption as a catalyst: Define and communicate a clear organisational strategy that treats disruption as an opportunity rather than a threat. Drive this mindset throughout all levels of the organisation, encouraging teams to seek out disruptive trends and leverage them for innovation and growth.

Cultivate a culture of continuous innovation: Actively promote a culture where unconventional thinking is celebrated and rewarded. Facilitate regular brainstorming sessions, support cross-functional collaboration, and ensure that resources are allocated for experimentation and development of new ideas.

Strengthen emotional intelligence and empathy: Implement training and development programs that prioritise emotional intelligence as a core leadership skill. Model empathy and effective communication in all interactions, thus building a culture of trust and collaboration that resonates throughout the organisation.

Build resilience through strategic alignment and risk management: Guide the organisation in aligning strategies with the ever-changing market dynamics and ensuring that routines, such as weekly cross-functional team meetings to review progress and adapt strategies, are in place for rapid adaptation. Encourage leaders to view failures as stepping stones and promote meaningful risk taking, all while maintaining a prudent approach to risk management.

Develop leaders across all quadrants: Assess current leadership using the Modern Leader Maturity Model and create targeted development plans. This should include coaching Traditionalists to acknowledge disruption, guiding Reactors to integrate disruption, helping Stabilisers embrace unconventional solutions, and encouraging Disruptive Leaders to share their insights.

As we close the initial exploration of disruptive leadership, we acknowledge the breadth and depth of this new leadership paradigm. It isn't simply about catalysing innovation or enabling change; it's about efficiently navigating the intricacies that come along with disruption. Moving forward, we will delve deeper into two integral qualities that underpin disruptive leadership: personal accountability and resilience. These elements lay the groundwork for our journey into the heart of disruptive leadership.

CHAPTER INSIGHTS

- Disruptive leadership, a paradigm shift from traditional models, champions innovation and change, closely aligning with the entrepreneurial spirit.

- Unlike traditional models focusing on control, disruptive leadership endorses agility, encourages collaboration and empowers individuals, nurturing their potential.

- Amidst global competition and evolving demands, disruptive leaders inspire their teams to challenge norms and convert challenges into opportunities, propelling change.

- These leaders, visionaries in their own right foster continuous innovation, turning creative ideas into tangible changes, demonstrating leadership amidst uncertainty.

- The approach to disruptive leadership adapts according to unique organisational contexts, leading to groundbreaking products or novel disruptive strategies.

- The adoption of a growth mindset is integral to disruptive leadership; it views failures as stepping stones to success and promotes meaningful relationships.

- Modern leaders should view disruption as an opportunity for growth, leveraging it as a catalyst while judiciously managing associated risks.

- Disruptive leaders create a culture where disruption equates to learning and growth, utilising strong communication, empathy and emotional intelligence to build trust.

2

EMBODYING ACCOUNTABILITY AND RESILIENCE

*I have not failed. I've just found
10,000 ways that won't work.*
THOMAS EDISON

B UILDING UPON the introduction to disruptive
leadership in Chapter 1, we will now explore the
role of personal accountability and resilience in
shaping disruptive leaders. In this chapter, we will discover strategies for fostering personal accountability, a
trait that allows us to accept our failures and learn from
them. We will investigate the concept of resilience, an
essential quality for thriving amidst disruption. By
uncovering the relationship between accountability,
resilience and successful leadership, we will learn how
to mould these traits within ourselves.

The air was thick with anticipation as I stepped out of the corporate building and onto the streets of Bangladesh. As a senior executive in supply chain for a multibillion-dollar retailer, I had been invited to one of the most infamous places in the shipping world—a ship-wrecking beach. These beaches in Bangladesh are the final resting places for ships from all over the world, where massive vessels are brutally dismantled. They are notorious, not just for the visual spectacle they offer, but also for the dark forces that lurk beneath the surface.

I had heard rumours about these beaches but had never given this industry much thought until the day of my visit. And nothing could have prepared me for what I was about to see. My host, a stern-faced local businessman, began to reveal the reality of the place as he delivered a briefing. Our phones were confiscated, and strict warnings were issued against leaks. I felt the gravity of the situation tightening its grip on me.

As we walked towards the beach, the stench of metal grinding filled the air. Shrapnel littered the ground, and local men walked about in flip-flops, seemingly oblivious to the danger. My disbelief grew with every step. When the beach finally stretched before us, I was met with a sight that sent chills down my spine.

Mostly uncontracted, workers toiled in an environment polluted by oil, asbestos and toxic chemicals. There were no safety regulations. Later I learned that workers died and lost limbs daily. The method of wrecking the ships seemed to echo the cruelty with which the workers were treated—engines at full throttle, ships rammed onto the shore, men jumping off before impact.

I looked on in horror. Broken-down ships lined the horizon, their decaying bodies testament to the global commerce system we have all created that prioritises profits over both human lives and the environment that supports us. Trust me, as a commercial animal, this is a big statement for me. But this was the moment when I realised that the commercial drive cannot go unchecked.

The notorious reputation of these ship-wrecking beaches was no longer a distant news headline. It was real, tangible, and overwhelmingly present. Two images from that day are seared into my memory: the metallic, silver water—a symbol of environmental degradation—and the name on the ship closest to the shore—*Australia*. This was a piercing reminder of my home country's complicity.

In that moment, accountability weighed on me like a millstone. It wasn't just about this beach; it was about the ripple effects of our choices in every corner of our lives. I questioned our collective failure as consumers, retailers, politicians and global citizens. It wasn't just about acknowledging the wrongdoing, but owning the responsibility to make it right. This beach was a glaring manifestation of our collective irresponsibility; our failure to acknowledge our roles in this mess.

But amidst the despair, there was hope. Something in me refused to accept this situation. I could either be crushed under the weight of guilt or use this heavy realisation as a catalyst. That something was resilience—the quality that allows us to renew our efforts when all seems lost. Accountability and resilience are essential attributes of transformative leadership. Witnessing firsthand the devastating consequences of overlooked responsibility drove home the importance of these traits. Accountability is not limited to addressing monumental challenges, but extends to ensuring that at every level—from interactions with my teams to strategic decisions for the broader organisation—I uphold a high standard of conscious decision making, rooted in integrity and clarity.

That day, I pledged to become part of the solution, not part of the problem. To embody disruptive leadership by challenging norms and leveraging setbacks into growth opportunities. It was about setting the standard, not just adhering to it. I engaged my team to foster trust and respect and promote a culture where failure was part of learning.

The notorious ship-wrecking beach remains a constant reminder of what can happen when we abandon responsibility. But it also stands as a beacon of transformation and hope—a testament to the power of leadership. And while the ship-wrecking beaches continue to exist, there have been improvements. Slowly but steadily, change is occurring as the world awakens to the true cost of our choices.

Accountability begins with the leader

The moment I set foot on the ship-wrecking beaches of Bangladesh, my perception of leadership transformed forever. As an executive in a vast supply chain world, I saw the haunting heart of global commerce. These shores bore testament to our collective negligence—our penchant for prioritising short-term profits over the long-term wellbeing of our planet and its inhabitants.

In the face of such glaring, tangible proof of our lapses, the weight of accountability gripped me. It wasn't just about acknowledging this dire situation. It was about asking the tough questions: what role had I played in this? How could we, as individuals and entities, allow such an imbalance in the scales of commerce and humanity?

Leadership, particularly disruptive leadership, is not merely about pioneering change. It's about recognising when we've gone astray, having the courage and accountability to steer the ship in a different direction, and rallying others to join in this shared responsibility. To disrupt is to challenge the status quo, but it's also to remain answerable to the impact of those disruptions. This is the point—the ship-wrecking beach brought to my attention that in every decision, and every action, there is a flow-on effect, so we need to work hard to ensure that the effect is positive. This is now not about the ship-wrecking beach—this is about understanding the humanity in our leadership.

While personal accountability is a cornerstone of leadership, there are problems so intricate, so intertwined in the fabric of society, that their resolution cannot lie on the shoulders of one. Some of the challenges we face are like tangled webs, woven over generations, demanding collective effort and accountability to unravel. The magnitude of these challenges might seem daunting, and the path to resolution long, possibly spanning generations; but every massive shift starts with an individual—the 'power of one'.

Accountability can be a profound catalyst. It's easy to be overwhelmed by the sheer number of issues and challenges at play, and one person or entity can't rectify every problem. But the power of individual accountability is immense. Just imagine the ripple effect if every leader took ownership of their actions, acknowledged their missteps, and actively sought solutions. Then imagine these ripples converging into waves of collective action, ushering transformative change.

The scope of accountability

Accountability is more than just a term frequently bandied about in leadership seminars, boardrooms or business schools; it often remains superficially explored. While many talk about taking responsibility for one's actions or decisions, for a disruptive leader, accountability is layered. It is intricate behaviours and actions of integrity, foresight and compassion, together with meticulous attention to detail.

Organisations don't just operate in markets; they operate in societies, in neighbourhoods, amidst real people with real challenges. An accountable leader sees beyond profit margins and stock prices. They see the faces of people in the community and understand their aspirations and acknowledge their challenges. This broader vision of accountability means ensuring that the organisation's actions lead to a better quality of life for these communities. Whether it's by supporting local businesses, initiating community development programs, or simply ensuring minimal environmental disruption, the leader's accountability lens is wide, encompassing not just the immediate, but the extended ecosystem. It's about making decisions with a heart that cares and a mind that's aware of its broader societal responsibilities.

A leader's accountability extends not just without, but within. The human stories intertwined with the company's metrics are paramount. The dreams, challenges and aspirations of every team member aren't mere side notes; they are central to the narrative of disruptive leadership. Ensuring the holistic wellbeing of the team, from providing the necessary tools to do their work to ensuring emotional and psychological support, is critical for them to thrive, innovate, and grow.

Disruptive leadership is rooted in a unique blend of vision and action. A disruptive leader's unwavering commitment to seeing through promises and expectations, no matter how daunting the challenge, is what sets them apart. Owning the outcomes, both the successes and missteps, is easy when sailing is smooth. The true test, however, comes in times of adversity. That's when disruptive leaders stand firm, not just acknowledging responsibility, but actively searching for ways to course-correct and learn.

Consider the leadership of Satya Nadella, who took over as CEO of Microsoft in 2014. Under his guidance, Microsoft made a drastic shift from a know-it-all culture to a learn-it-all culture. Faced with the company's previous failures in the mobile market, Nadella embraced accountability by openly acknowledging past missteps and refocusing the company's strategy towards cloud computing and AI. This pivot not only showcased his resilience, but also revitalised Microsoft's growth, re-establishing it as a tech powerhouse. Nadella's approach to accountability, which fostered a culture of learning from failures, and his steadfast focus on innovation became a textbook example for disruptive leaders.

Accountability is more than just caring. The notion of 'All care, no responsibility,' references individuals or leaders who radiate concern, even passion, but are conspicuously absent when challenges arise. Such behaviour erodes trust, curtails enthusiasm and impedes genuine innovation. When people sense no genuine ownership or responsibility from leadership, they question their roles and the integrity of their leaders, leading to an environment that hampers initiative.

But when a leader stands at the forefront, owning a difficult situation, understanding the root causes and, most importantly, learning from it, their actions foster an environment of trust and openness. When team members witness their leaders stand up, take responsibility, and not play the blame game, they feel secure and are more willing to acknowledge their missteps and actively seek improvement. Such a culture is a fertile ground for innovation, nurturing risk taking and boundary-pushing, knowing that failures are but stepping stones to growth.

The spectrum of a leader's accountability is broad, and it does not operate in isolation. It has a critical relationship with resilience. Resilience is deeply rooted in accountability. When leaders practice unwavering accountability, they cultivate an ethos where setbacks are not deterrents but catalysts for growth. This environment is where resilience flourishes. By confronting, learning from and leveraging failures, leaders not only build their resilience but inspire the same in their teams. This mutual resilience, borne from a culture of accountability, prepares both leaders and their teams to adapt, innovate and overcome.

How disruption and accountability build our resilience 'muscle'

Understanding resilience in the space of disruptive leadership requires us to first acknowledge when and why our resilience might falter. Often, it's not the magnitude of challenges but the cumulative weight of numerous small setbacks that diminishes our resilience. Picture it as an endurance run: every individual raindrop or gust of wind might seem insignificant, but together they can make the journey much longer and harder than it would otherwise be.

Our brains are wired for efficiency, often leaning towards familiar paths and comfort zones. Venturing into the unknown or facing continuous challenges can be exhausting, mentally and emotionally. This, combined with societal pressures to constantly succeed, can create a perfect storm that puts our resilience at risk. The fear of failure or judgement can sometimes overshadow our intrinsic ability to adapt and learn.

However, this is where the beauty of resilience shines through, particularly when intertwined with accountability in leadership. Just as a runner builds endurance by pushing through adverse conditions, leaders can fortify their resilience by consistently showing up, taking responsibility, and learning from each experience. By recognising the moments when resilience falters, leaders can consciously focus on developing it. The very act of showing up—be it confronting challenges head on, learning from mistakes, or simply ensuring consistent effort regardless of external conditions—can significantly bolster resilience.

Integrating this understanding with the previous discussion, it's evident that resilience is not a fixed trait. It's dynamic, shaped by our experiences and our responses to them. A resilient leader acknowledges setbacks, learns from them, and remains accountable to their vision, team and stakeholders. This blend of resilience and accountability not only safeguards against the pitfalls that erode resilience, but also builds a leader's credibility and trustworthiness.

The demonstration of such resilience has a cascading effect on teams. It promotes an environment where resilience is celebrated and intertwined with accountability, creating a basis for groundbreaking ideas and innovation. Resilience, then, is more than just a buzzword; it's a foundational trait that, when combined with accountability, adds to the foundation of contemporary leadership. By consciously building resilience, leaders not only navigate the challenges of disruption but also pave the way for others, igniting a leadership style that thrives even in adversity.

How health and wellbeing enhance personal accountability and resilience

The demanding role of a disruptive leader, while rewarding, can also be overwhelming. Health and wellbeing can be pushed to the back seat. However, neglecting these factors can destabilise the foundations of effective leadership.

Health and wellbeing form the bedrock that underpins personal accountability and resilience. Here, 'health' encapsulates physical wellness and mental, emotional and social wellbeing. The degree to which a leader can hold themselves accountable can be severely compromised when dealing with physical or mental health issues. Similarly, resilience, an essential quality for a disruptive leader, is cultivated in the ground of robust health.

A leader's role extends to caring for their team's health and wellbeing. The output of a team reflects its collective health. Leaders who place their wellbeing as a priority tend to foster an environment where team members do the same, creating a healthier, more productive and resilient team—all critical elements in the face of disruption.

Health and wellbeing, along with accountability and resilience, are dynamic processes. They require continuous nurturing, regular evaluations and persistent adjustments. Leaders cannot afford to consider these factors as peripheral to their roles. They form an integral part of a leader's identity, influencing their ability to remain accountable and resilient, shaping their decision-making processes and determining their reactions to disruption.

Now that we have a deeper understanding of how accountability and resilience are embodied in disruptive leadership, let's turn to the second of our Maturity Models to understand how these concepts are reflected in different leadership styles.

The ACCOUNTABLE AND RESILIENT LEADER Maturity Model

The rapidly changing dynamics of the modern world necessitate the evolution of leadership. During this constant flux, two qualities have emerged as critical—accountability and resilience. Together, they form a fundamental leadership matrix that expresses varying degrees of ownership and adaptability. The importance of these traits cannot be overstated, as they lie at the core of a leader's ability to navigate challenges, maintain the team's trust and thrive amidst disruption. By seeking to occupy the ideal quadrant of this accountability-resilience matrix, leaders empower themselves and their teams to turn adversity into an avenue for growth, cultivating an environment that is both robust and responsive to change.

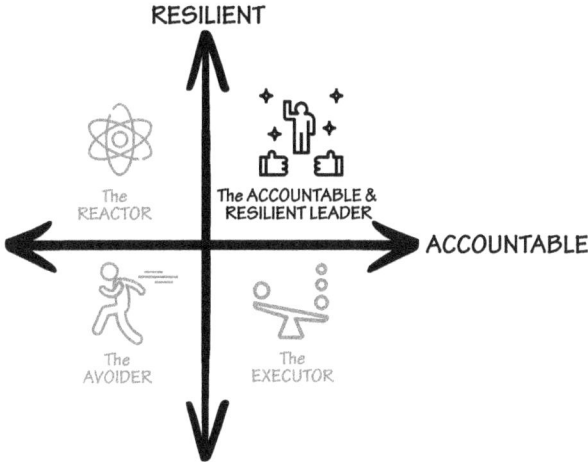

The ACCOUNTABLE & RESILIENT LEADER

Let's consider the four leadership types expressed by this matrix. Where do you fall as a leader? And how can you leverage your knowledge of the matrix to amplify your strengths and pinpoint areas that require further enhancement?

The Avoider: Leaders in this quadrant are characterised by low levels of both accountability and resilience. They may exhibit a reactive leadership style, shying away from taking responsibility and finding it difficult to recover from adversities. These leaders might be prone to shifting blame and may struggle with maintaining morale and performance under pressure. Their lack of accountability can lead to a breakdown of trust, and their low resilience could impact the team's overall capability to recover from setbacks. The evolution for these leaders should START with embracing responsibility for their decisions and actions and exploring effective coping mechanisms to bolster resilience. They need to STOP avoiding ownership and blaming others when faced with challenges.

The Reactor: This quadrant is home to leaders who possess robust resilience but fall short on the accountability front. Their high resilience enables them to navigate through difficulties and recover quickly from setbacks. However, their lack of accountability can result in a lack of ownership, which could impact their credibility as leaders. To foster growth, these leaders should START reflecting on their decisions and actions and consider their alignment with their leadership responsibilities and objectives. They should STOP deflecting blame and START treating mistakes as opportunities for learning and growth.

The Executor: Leaders in this quadrant demonstrate high levels of accountability, but grapple with resilience. They readily accept responsibility for their actions, but their struggles with adversity might lead to harsh self-criticism and inability to bounce back quickly. While their high accountability boosts their credibility, their low resilience might affect the team's morale and productivity in challenging times. These leaders should START fostering resilience, perhaps by reshaping their perspective on failure, viewing it as an opportunity for growth rather than a personal shortcoming. They should STOP being overly critical of themselves when faced with setbacks and focus on learning and enhancing their skills. They should learn to perceive setbacks not as personal failings, but as temporary obstacles on the path to success.

The Accountable and Resilient Leader: These leaders exemplify both high accountability and resilience. They not only take responsibility for their actions but also effectively rebound from adversity, using it as a stepping stone for growth. Their leadership style is proactive, inspiring and robust, contributing to a high-performing and resilient team culture. These leaders should START sharing their strategies and insights to nurture a culture of accountability and resilience within their teams. They should CONTINUE leveraging adversity as a catalyst for growth.

Accountable and Resilient leadership in action

Hopefully by now I've convinced you that accountability and resilience are key ingredients in disruptive leadership. I also hope that you're keen to get the ball rolling. Let's now look at five ways to put these theories into action.

Lead by example in personal accountability: Set clear expectations around personal responsibility, honesty and reliability. Model these values through your actions and communication, making them a standard within the organisation. Acknowledge and analyse mistakes openly, turning them into opportunities for learning and growth.

Develop a resilience training program: Create a specific training program focusing on resilience. Incorporate workshops, real-life case studies, scenario planning and stress-management techniques. Encourage the sharing of personal stories where challenges were turned into growth opportunities. This will create a culture where setbacks are seen as learning experiences.

Implement a comprehensive wellbeing initiative: Establish a wellbeing program that addresses both physical health and mental wellness. Recognise the direct link between wellbeing and effective leadership, and ensure the initiative supports building resilience and accountability. Regularly evaluate the program, making necessary adjustments to align with the leadership needs of the organisation.

Foster a culture of open communication and continuous learning: Encourage open dialogue about successes, failures and lessons learned. Create regular forums where leaders can discuss their experiences and challenges, and strategies for overcoming them. Implement a mentoring program where more-experienced leaders guide others in developing accountability and resilience, promoting a continuous learning environment.

Utilise the accountability-resilience leadership matrix for capability uplift: Integrate the quadrant model into leadership assessments and development. Identify where leaders fall within the quadrants, and provide actionable steps tailored to their specific needs. For instance, help Avoider leaders embrace responsibility, and assist Executor leaders in building resilience. Use the insights gained from this model to create individualised development plans that enhance accountability and resilience across the organisation.

With a firm understanding of the importance of accountability and resilience in leadership, we appreciate their role in leading disruption. However, we're just scratching the surface. The next chapter introduces us to another vital dimension of leadership—the embrace of diversity and inclusion. We'll uncover how valuing a multitude of perspectives can ignite the spark of innovation and further strengthen a leader's resilience amid disruption.

CHAPTER INSIGHTS

- Personal accountability, a key aspect of disruptive leadership, involves taking responsibility for one's actions, successes and failures, and leveraging mistakes as learning opportunities.

- By demonstrating personal accountability, and embodying honesty and reliability, leaders foster trust and respect within teams and create a culture of integrity.

- In disruptive leadership, personal accountability goes beyond task ownership; it's about challenging norms, acknowledging errors, recovering from failures and instilling trust.

- Resilience is about using challenges and setbacks as opportunities for growth and transformation, making it a crucial attribute of disruptive leadership.

- By promoting a culture where failure is part of learning, leaders encourage innovation and risk taking, with resilience as the foundation.

- Leaders can enhance accountability by understanding their roles, encouraging self-evaluation, promoting transparency, and fostering a learning-from-failures culture.

- To cultivate resilience, leaders must foster a growth mindset, engage in scenario planning and nurture supportive relationships, sharing experiences and strategies along the way.

- The health and wellbeing of leaders and teams significantly influence accountability and resilience, making it imperative for leaders to prioritise these factors to build a productive and resilient workforce.

3

LEADING WITH DIVERSITY AND INCLUSION IN DISRUPTIVE TIMES

*In diversity there is
beauty and there is strength.*

MAYA ANGELOU

RAWING FROM our exploration of personal accountability and resilience, we venture into another
critical aspect of disruptive leadership. This chapter focuses on the imperative of diversity, explaining
the value of different perspectives in decision making
and innovation. We'll explore effective strategies for
leading and integrating misfits into a team and delve
into the importance of taking inclusion to the next
level by fostering a culture of belonging.

The room buzzed with the excitement of a new
beginning as I looked out at the vibrant cityscape of
a third-world country. The opening of our new office
was a milestone filled with promise and uncertainty.

This was a land of contrasting values, where cultural traditions were held dear, and the power dynamics between men and women were deeply entrenched. A country where women were expected to follow, not lead. But I knew that true leadership leveraged diversity, celebrated differences and championed innovation.

I had a clear task to complete while I was there and that was to appoint a Country Supply Chain Manager. After a rigorous selection process, I found the perfect candidate. Brilliant, resourceful and committed. There was only one catch, according to some. She was a woman.

I'll never forget the moment another senior executive, a Westerner who should've known better, told me, 'Matthew, she is female. It won't work.' His words were coated in a misguided concern for cultural sensitivity, but they hit me like a slap in the face. Cultural sensitivity was something I prided myself on, but this? This was bias. I knew what was right, and I knew this candidate's potential. I dug in my heels, refusing to let prejudice guide our decisions.

In my efforts to secure her position, I began with a quest for understanding. I immersed myself in the intricacies of the local culture and business environment. I held countless conversations with local stakeholders, sought insights from industry experts, and consulted peers who had navigated similar challenges. This provided a holistic view, offering me nuances and intricacies that couldn't be gleaned from afar. With this knowledge, I had frank and sincere conversations with the naysayers, sharing undeniable facts about the candidate's qualifications and potential, and the innovative perspective she could bring to the company. My arguments were precise, backed by evidence and aligned with the core values of our organisation. It was an exercise in bridging worlds—blending the innovative spirit of our organisation with the unique challenges and potential of this third-world country.

What followed was a delicate dance of diplomacy, a challenge to biases, and a belief in what was right. I secured her position, defying doubts and proving that her gender was not an obstacle but an asset.

The candidate I hired was more than a fresh perspective; she was a force of change, leading our country's supply chain operations through triple-digit growth year after year. She was welcomed by her in-country peers, embraced for her skills, and celebrated for her uniqueness. It was her belonging that allowed her to thrive. She went on to earn an MBA, became a mother, and crafted a career that broke barriers and exceeded expectations.

The decision to hire a woman was not just a recruitment decision; it was about taking a stand for what's right, empowering others, and fostering an environment of respect and belonging. I recognised that inclusivity wasn't just about ticking boxes; it was about seizing opportunities and acknowledging the immense value diverse perspectives bring. In essence, the region's importance in our strategic narrative was undeniable. The prosperity and innovative strides we made there became integral to our global endeavours. Without embracing this particular region and integrating its unique capabilities into our strategy, the transformation we sought for our company would have remained elusive.

As I look back on that decision, I recognise it as one of the proudest moments of my career. This story is a reminder that we must look beyond the conventional, beyond our biases, and seek the potential in others. In doing so, we not only uplift others but ourselves and our organisations. Because, in the end, our greatest strengths lie in our differences, and our ability to see beyond them is the hallmark of truly disruptive leadership.

The importance of diversity in disruptive leadership

In disruptive leadership, diversity expands beyond conventional characteristics like race, gender and ethnicity. Diversity represents a wealth of differences encompassing experiences, skills, perspectives and ideas. Every individual, equipped with unique experiences and insights, contributes valuable inputs. In disruptive leadership, diversity serves as a critical element that spurs innovation and change.

Managing a team with uniform characteristics may seem comfortable, but diversity is the catalyst for groundbreaking solutions. Diverse teams, rich with various experiences and insights, stimulate creativity. They challenge the status quo, which can lead to innovative solutions, thus making diversity indispensable in a disruptive landscape.

When we analyse issues with diverse perspectives and experiences, we uncover solutions that might have remained unnoticed in a homogeneous setting. With a variety of viewpoints, the collective vision of a team is wider, its approach more comprehensive, and its problem solving more innovative.

Decision making, a significant aspect of leadership, greatly benefits from diversity. Leaders at the forefront of disruption often face complex decisions that bear far-reaching impacts. A diverse team provides a spectrum of viewpoints, enriching the decision-making process and thus making it more holistic. This helps avoid the pitfalls of groupthink, encourages critical thinking, promotes healthy debate and fosters informed decision making.

Adaptability, another asset of diversity, is important in a rapidly changing environment. Adaptability is essentially the capability to evolve in the face of change. A diverse team, with its vast array of experiences and perspectives, is better prepared to handle changes, navigate challenges and convert potential disruptions into growth opportunities. When you have a team that's already in the habit of re-evaluating narratives, challenging the status quo based on diverse inputs and reconstructing strategies, it's inherently positioned to adapt. They've built the muscle memory for it. They don't get rigidly attached to a single viewpoint because they're conditioned to consider multiple angles.

A profound advantage of diversity within teams is the way it counteracts individual biases. We all have biases, which are shaped by our personal stories. These biases can sometimes act as blinders, limiting our vision and making us resistant to alternative approaches or solutions. But in a diverse setting, one individual's bias is likely to be challenged by another's contrasting viewpoint. This continuous challenging acts as a self-correcting mechanism, making the team more receptive and malleable to change.

A leader embracing diversity also enhances credibility and influence. Such a leader not only earns respect, but inspires. By promoting diversity, leaders demonstrate their commitment to fairness, inclusivity and respect for individuality. They create an environment where everyone feels valued. An exemplar in this context is Gail Kelly, who stood as a beacon of transformative leadership in the Australian banking sector. Born in South Africa, Kelly moved to Australia and rose to become one of the leading figures in the banking industry, heading Westpac from 2008 to 2015. A fervent advocate for diversity, Kelly set ambitious targets for women in leadership roles at Westpac, and under her helm the bank realised its goal of having women occupy fifty per cent of leadership positions. Globally recognised for her leadership mettle, Kelly not only set the bar for promoting diversity in a predominantly male-dominated sector, but also showcased how diversity, when championed by leadership, can bring about monumental shifts in corporate culture and vision.

The value of misfits

There is a certain type of individual who often emerges as the catalyst for radical change. They may be somewhat unconventional or not quite fit within the established norms. We often label them misfits. Misfits are like unique puzzle pieces. At first glance, they might seem like they don't fit. But when placed in the right spot, they complete the picture.

The power of misfits lies in their divergence from the norm. They bring to the table a rare combination of creativity, curiosity, and the courage to question existing systems and processes. These are individuals who aren't afraid to voice their distinctive viewpoints, even if they swim against the tide. The depth and breadth of their thought processes can add a whole new dimension to decision making and problem solving that can influence the whole culture of an organisation.

These individuals bring fresh, diverse perspectives, challenge the status quo and drive innovative problem solving—factors that form the foundation of disruptive leadership and business. While they may seem like outliers, their potential to inject creativity and innovative thinking into a team is unparalleled. And for any disruptor, the ability to harness this potential becomes a formidable weapon in their leadership arsenal.

One might argue that misfits could disrupt the harmony of a team. But disruptive leadership isn't about maintaining harmony; it's about encouraging a creative dissonance. This dissonance, this 'creative chaos', is what fuels disruptive thinking and breeds innovation. It's the necessary 'friction' that leads to the spark of groundbreaking ideas.

Embracing misfits also sends out a powerful message about the kind of leader you are. It shows that you value diversity, not just in words but in action. It demonstrates your commitment to fostering an inclusive culture, a culture that appreciates unique perspectives and sees them as a strength rather than a liability.

Steve Jobs, co-founder of Apple Inc., knew the value of the misfit. He was known for his unconventional approach to business and design, famously recruiting people who were not just talented but who thought differently. Jobs himself said, 'It's more fun to be a pirate than to join the navy,' encapsulating his philosophy of cherishing the nonconformist spirit. Under his leadership, Apple's success was propelled by individuals who were not typical corporate personalities, but were rather the square pegs in the round holes; the ones who saw things differently. This culture of embracing the mavericks contributed to a series of innovations that revolutionised multiple industries, from personal computing and animated movies to music, phones, tablet computing and digital publishing.

Leading and integrating misfits into a team, however, requires a careful and conscious approach. Misfits aren't defined by their inability to fit into the team; they're defined by their different thinking style. Thus, the leadership challenge isn't about making them conform; it's about creating an environment where their differences are celebrated, not merely tolerated.

Cultivating inclusivity: the bridge from diversity to belonging

Inclusivity is a deliberate action to cultivate an environment where all individuals, regardless of their varied characteristics, receive fair treatment, equal access to opportunities, and are fully able to contribute to the organisation's objectives. It involves the proactive dismantling of barriers to full participation and the assurance that every voice can be acknowledged. Disruptive leaders must design and implement policies and practices that embrace a multitude of thought processes and operational styles—maximising the collective capabilities of their team members.

The path to inclusivity starts with acknowledgement—recognising the distinct experiences, abilities and insights each team member contributes. This acknowledgment must evolve into appreciation, viewing these diverse attributes not as complications but as enriching the team's collective wisdom. Such appreciation promotes an environment where enquiry is welcomed and conventional norms are examined, paving the way to more resourceful and inventive solutions.

Inclusivity goes beyond merely accepting diversity; it involves proactive encouragement for individuals to participate and share their distinct viewpoints. This encompasses creating opportunities for conversation, guaranteeing fair involvement in decision-making processes, and acknowledging everyone's contributions. Leaders adept in inclusivity not only gather a diverse group but also make certain that each person is listened to, and their ideas effectively influence decisions.

Empowerment is the essence of inclusivity. It's about providing every team member with the necessary tools, support and assurance to thrive. Empowerment unleashes the hidden potential within a diverse team. When individuals are empowered, they are more inclined to initiate, provoke change, and drive a culture of persistent innovation. Leaders who give precedence to inclusivity do not merely assemble teams capable of facing current challenges; they cultivate future visionaries.

From inclusion to belonging

Diversity without inclusivity is not sufficient. Inclusivity ensures everyone feels valued and empowered to contribute. But beyond inclusivity is something even more powerful—a sense of belonging. Promoting a culture of belonging exceeds basic inclusion steps and reaches into individuals' psychological core. This strategy cultivates an environment that celebrates, not merely tolerates, differences. As a fundamental human instinct, belonging is pivotal to emotional security and personal identity.

A deep sense of belonging transforms professional settings into welcoming spaces, assuring individuals that their voices, perspectives and contributions matter. Belonging boosts self-esteem and self-worth. Valued group members develop heightened self-confidence, promoting active participation and deeper engagement. Secure in their belonging, they are more inclined to take calculated risks and challenge norms, thus becoming catalysts for disruptive innovation.

Belonging is intertwined with emotional wellbeing. When accepted within their circle, individuals experience reduced loneliness, anxiety and stress. Their satisfaction, happiness and overall positive disposition surge. Emotionally healthy individuals exhibit resilience, productivity and motivation, effectively facing challenges, adapting to changes and persisting against adversity.

Belonging instils a sense of purpose and significance. When individuals see themselves as part of a bigger picture, their work gains new meaning, boosting motivation, commitment and ownership. This understanding compels employees to walk the extra mile, strive for excellence and display proactive behaviour.

Fostering a culture of belonging builds trust and loyalty. Employees who feel understood and supported enjoy emotional and professional security, leading to unwavering loyalty, reduced attrition and enhanced team resilience.

Belonging also nurtures mutual respect, empathy and understanding within the team. Individuals who are valued appreciate their peers' perspectives and experiences more. This helps to create an inclusive and respectful work environment, which primes the ground for innovative thinking and collaborative problem solving.

The INCLUSIVE LEADER Maturity Model

Diversity and inclusion have emerged as pivotal traits, holding the power to transform organisational cultures and outcomes. Chapter 3 introduces a model that brings these two vital facets into focus. The combination of diversity and inclusion holds transformative potential for leadership. Diversity brings a rich connection of perspectives, experiences and ideas, while inclusion ensures these different voices are heard, valued and integrated into the decision-making process. Together, they breed a culture of creativity, innovation and mutual respect, fuelling not just employee satisfaction but also business success. A leadership model that harnesses this dynamic duo can unlock significant advantages, fostering an environment that thrives on collective intelligence and collaborative decision making.

The INCLUSIVE LEADER

DIVERSITY

The TOKEN LEADER

The INCLUSIVE LEADER

INCLUSION

The IGNORANT LEADER

The NARROW LEADER

Let's take a look at our third Maturity Model and determine where your leadership style falls on the twin axes of diversity and inclusion.

The Ignorant Leader: These leaders place a low value on diversity and inclusion, which often leads to a lack of differing ideas and experiences in their teams. This absence of diversity could stifle innovation and problem-solving capabilities. Further, the low level of inclusion could undermine team cohesiveness and engagement, as team members may feel undervalued or unheard. To bolster their leadership, leaders in this quadrant should START valuing diversity and initiating an inclusive environment where every team member feels acknowledged and heard. A key action could be to consciously diversify their recruitment and promotion processes. They should STOP the inclination towards homogeneity and welcome varied perspectives and ideas.

The Token Leader: These leaders showcase high diversity but low inclusion. They may have diverse teams, but their failure to promote an inclusive culture may lead to unutilised potential and lower team morale. While they bring in diversity, they may treat it superficially, just to tick a box, instead of harnessing its full potential. Leaders in this quadrant should START fully appreciating the worth of diversity, ensuring every team member is actively engaged and their unique perspectives are integrated into team decisions. They should also START nurturing an inclusive culture where everyone's voice is respected and valued. They should STOP their surface-level approach to diversity and begin to dig deeper.

The Narrow Leader: Leaders in this quadrant are marked by high inclusion but low diversity. While they promote an inclusive environment where everyone feels heard and valued, their teams may lack diversity, which could limit the range of ideas and perspectives. Leaders in this quadrant should START actively pursuing diversity in their teams, ensuring a broad range of voices, and acknowledging its value in providing fresh perspectives and innovative ideas. They should STOP overlooking the importance of diversity in their pursuit of inclusion.

The Inclusive Leader: These leaders, ideally, embody high diversity and high inclusion. They not only appreciate the importance of diversity but also champion an inclusive environment where all voices are heard, and contributions are valued. Their leadership style is inspiring and inclusive, contributing to a highly innovative and engaged team culture. Leaders in this quadrant should START sharing their successful strategies and insights to inspire others to build a culture of diversity and inclusion within their organisations.

Inclusive leadership in action

Diversity and inclusion in the workplace is about more than simply employing people from diverse backgrounds. Creating a truly diverse workplace means creating a culture in which everybody is welcomed, all personality types are embraced, and team members experience a sense of belonging. Here are five action steps you can take now to move you towards that goal.

Create a comprehensive diversity and inclusion strategy: Understand that diversity extends beyond race, gender and background to encompass experiences, skills and ideas. Develop a company-wide strategy that emphasises the recruitment, promotion and retention of a diverse workforce. Cultivate an environment where team members are encouraged to voice their unique insights, where collaborative workshops and team brainstorming sessions are the norm, and where each perspective is acknowledged through active listening and constructive feedback.

Implement inclusion training and encourage the empowerment of misfits: Develop training programs that teach leaders and team members how to cultivate an inclusive environment. Focus on the celebration of differences, recognising that misfits or outliers can infuse creativity and innovation within a team. Hold inclusive communication workshops and equip leaders with the tools they need, such as diversity dashboard analytics, to nurture an atmosphere that recognises and validates distinctive contributions.

Foster a culture of belonging and emotional wellbeing: Prioritise creating a culture where inclusion evolves into a sense of belonging. Recognise that a celebration of differences not only enhances emotional wellbeing but also boosts innovation. Encourage leaders to model inclusive behaviour by instituting regular feedback sessions with diverse employee groups, implementing transparent hiring and promotion practices that eliminate bias, and setting clear metrics to measure and reward inclusivity outcomes.

Regularly monitor and evaluate diversity and inclusion initiatives: Implement consistent monitoring of diversity and inclusion initiatives to ensure they align with the organisation's goals and values. Encourage leaders to keep track of progress, making necessary adjustments to maintain alignment with the broader organisational culture, architecture, people and routines. Share successes and learnings across the organisation, turning insights into continuous improvements.

Utilise the Inclusive Leader Maturity Model to develop leaders: Integrate the quadrant model into leadership development, focusing on the transformation from Ignorant Leaders to Inclusive Disruptors. Identify where leaders fall within the quadrants, and provide specific actions tailored to their needs. For example, Ignorant Leaders can start diversifying their recruitment and promotion processes, while Inclusive Leaders can share their successful strategies to inspire others.

As we end our discussion on diversity and inclusion, we recognise its importance in enhancing decision making and sparking disruptive ideas. In doing so, we've laid the essential foundation of disruptive leadership—embracing disruption, harnessing personal accountability and resilience, and valuing diversity and inclusion. Moving from this foundation, Part 2 of the book will examine how trust and influence underpin the Disruptive Leadership Framework. This next part will delve deeper into building trust, negotiating change, and using storytelling as a means of influence in disruptive times.

CHAPTER INSIGHTS

- Disruptive leadership leverages diversity beyond conventional traits, incorporating a blend of experiences, skills and ideas that stimulate innovation.

- Diverse teams enhance creativity, encourage innovative solutions, and offer a broader range of perspectives that enrich decision making.

- By fostering adaptability and flexibility, diverse teams turn potential disruptions into growth opportunities.

- Leaders endorsing diversity improve their credibility, showcasing their commitment to fairness, inclusivity and respect for individuality.

- An inclusive environment ensures everyone feels valued and empowered, which is essential for the effectiveness of diversity.

- Misfits or outliers can infuse creativity and innovation within a team, necessitating an environment that celebrates these differences.

- The empowerment of misfits encourages disruptive ideas and inspires others, validating their distinctive contributions.

- Inclusion evolves into a culture of belonging, a celebration of differences that enhances emotional wellbeing and boosts innovation.

THE PRIZES OF CONTEMPORARY LEADERSHIP

In **Part 1: Contemporary Leadership**, we have explored the transformative shift from traditional to disruptive leadership, and emphasised the importance of readiness, accountability, resilience, diversity and inclusion. As we conclude this part of the book, let's look at the prizes that await the leader who embraces these concepts.

Transformational Growth

By embracing disruptive leadership, you will experience transformational personal growth. This personal growth not only enhances your leadership effectiveness, but also primes you to excel in an ever-evolving business landscape. You'll transition from conventional methodologies to innovative approaches, stimulating an evolution that expands your strategic horizons.

Enhanced Decision Making and Creativity

As you cultivate the principles of diversity and inclusion, you'll find your decision-making abilities are greatly enriched. By valuing varied perspectives, you will uncover creative solutions and strategies that might otherwise remain hidden. This appreciation for diversity fuels your creativity, enabling you to navigate challenges more effectively and identify unique opportunities.

Resilience and Adaptability

Mastering the principles of disruptive leadership enhances your resilience and adaptability. You'll learn to see setbacks as stepping stones to success, building your capability to withstand adversity and bounce back stronger. This resilience, paired with an ability to adapt to new scenarios quickly, will be your key to thriving in a turbulent business environment.

Cultivation of a Growth Mindset

Adopting disruptive leadership will foster a growth mindset within you, redefining your relationship with failure and risk. You'll see challenges as opportunities for growth and continuous learning. This shift in perspective fuels your personal and professional development, enhancing your agility and your team's responsiveness to change.

Elevated Influence and Trust

As you embody accountability and empowerment, you'll notice a significant enhancement in your influence and the trust you inspire. Taking responsibility for your actions and empowering others will earn you respect and loyalty from your team. This elevated trust not only strengthens your team's cohesion but also amplifies your influence as a leader, driving overall organisational success.

INFLUENTIAL LEADERSHIP

CONTEMPORARY

TRANSFORMATIONAL

THE DISRUPTIVE LEADER

INFLUENTIAL

LEGACY ORIENTED

FUTURE-READY

Part2: Influential Leadership moves forward by analysing essential aspects of leadership that contribute to creating and sustaining influence in an era of disruption. These include fostering trust within teams and organisations, negotiating and effecting change, and leveraging the power of storytelling as a persuasive leadership tool.

The hallmark of disruptive leadership lies in its ability to build and maintain trust within an organisation. Trust, in this context, is not merely a peripheral quality, but a foundational element that significantly impacts team dynamics, collaboration and overall productivity. Disruptive leaders not only earn trust from their teams, but they also foster an environment of trust, which is critical for encouraging risk taking, innovation and a sense of shared purpose. **Chapter 4: The Power of Trust in Disruptive Leadership** explores the importance of trust in leading teams and organisations through disruptive times. It discusses the ways to build, maintain and restore trust, and how trust can propel a team's ability to innovate and adapt to change.

In disruptive environments, the ability to negotiate change and wield influence becomes an integral part of a leader's toolbox. Disruptive leaders must be adept at negotiating changes, big and small, while maintaining team cohesion and productivity. They must also possess the skills to influence others both within and outside the organisation, to rally support for their vision and drive effective action. **Chapter 5: Negotiating and Influencing Change** details the techniques disruptive leaders can use to effectively negotiate changes within their organisations. It also delves into the art of influence in leading teams towards achieving shared objectives amidst disruption.

Storytelling is a powerful tool that disruptive leaders use to inspire, motivate and influence. It's a way to make abstract concepts tangible, to share vision, and to create a sense of shared purpose. It is through storytelling that leaders can effectively communicate their strategies for disruption and inspire their teams to engage in the journey towards innovation and growth. **Chapter 6: Harnessing the Power of Storytelling** provides an understanding of the use of storytelling as a leadership tool. It outlines the ways leaders can leverage storytelling to share their vision, inspire their teams and build a shared narrative.

Part 2 of this book equips you with the tools and understanding you need to foster trust, negotiate and influence change and leverage storytelling. These components are key to building and sustaining influence as a leader in a disruptive era.

4

THE POWER OF TRUST IN DISRUPTIVE LEADERSHIP

A team is not a group of people who work together. A team is a group of people who trust each other.

SIMON SINEK

HIS CHAPTER PRESENTS an exploration of the importance of trust in an environment fraught with uncertainty. In a volatile landscape where the traditional rules of engagement are constantly being challenged, trust forms the core of effective leadership. We will also delve into the role of self-trust and confidence in disruptive leadership, revealing how faith in oneself forms the basis of the trust that others place in us.

Conor O'Malley's office was always an intimidating place. Towering shelves, filled with books and framed pictures, overlooked a grand wooden desk. I loved going there, though, because I loved to learn from Conor—the spark of wisdom, tempered with kindness and understanding.

I was still green, a young Senior Management Accountant for Australia's largest dairy and juice producer. Those days were a hustle, full of numbers, planning, and navigating the maze of corporate life. Conor was the Senior Executive of Logistics and Planning, and I was his finance business partner. I could feel his expectations weighing on me as I prepared the management reports.

That day, it was monthly reporting cycle time. I walked into Conor's office, armed with stacks of paper covered in graphs and numbers. My heart raced as I started to explain the financials of his division. I stumbled, fumbled and stuttered. I could feel Conor's eyes on me, studying, probing.

He stopped me mid-sentence. 'Matthew are you okay?' he asked, his voice gentle but firm.

I looked up, confusion and fear in my eyes. Deep inside, I recognised some familiar trepidation. I had always struggled with presenting to senior leaders, whom I held on a pedestal. In my eyes, they were almost god-like. The immense pressure I put on myself not to fail, coupled with my lack of self-confidence, always surfaced during these moments.

Then Conor began to speak about trust. Trust within a team, trust in our bosses, peers, leaders, and how vital it was for change-impact and achieving what we set out to do. He spoke of trust in society, but he didn't stop there.

Conor's voice softened, 'But it all begins and ends with self, Matthew. Every time you second guess yourself, or let uncertainty cloud your judgements, it's evident to those around you. I've seen it, Matthew. The times you hold back, questioning your own insights and decisions. Trust yourself. Believe in your competence, the value you bring. Without trusting yourself, others can't see what you're truly capable of. You have the knowledge, the talent and the drive. Now, it's time to fully embrace and believe in those abilities, letting go of the chains of self-doubt.'

His words were not a criticism but a lesson, a revelation. He was showing me the essence of trust, not just as a concept but as a living, breathing force. A force that could move mountains, drive innovation, build connections and make real, impactful changes.

Conor became more than a boss. He became a mentor, a friend. We shared meals, beers, and endless discussions about trust. He even penned a bestselling book titled *Trust: Begins and Ends with Self*. I had the privilege to review the book before it was published and provide my input. I was the MC at his book events, and I witnessed his philosophy spread far and wide.

I learned to trust myself, to foster trust in my teams, to build a culture of openness and collaboration. I realised how trust could drive collective action during disruption, how it encouraged innovation, resilience and empathy.

Early in 2023, at the time of writing this book, Conor passed away unexpectedly. The loss was profound, not just for me but for everyone he touched. His legacy, though, lives on. The kindness, the wisdom in his words, the trust he instilled in me—it's all there, still guiding me as I am sure it does others.

In the end, it's not just about the numbers, the planning, or even the success. It's about the trust we build, the connections we nurture, and the lives we touch. That's Conor's legacy, and it's a legacy that continues to inspire and guide me every single day.

Be a trustworthy leader

Leadership in the modern era stands as a testament to the profound role of trust. But what is it that transforms an individual into a figure worthy of that trust? How does one become a beacon of credibility and reliability?

At the foundation of trustworthiness is the delicate equilibrium of what a leader says and what they do. When these align, it sends a powerful message of reliability. There's a reassurance in the predictability that if a leader commits, they will deliver. Over time, this builds a reputation—an intangible quality that speaks louder than any marketing campaign or PR exercise.

But trust goes deeper than just meeting obligations; it's intricately tied to open and clear communication. In an age where information travels faster than light, leaders are no longer the sole gatekeepers of knowledge. Yet, the role they play in interpreting, contextualising and communicating this knowledge is paramount. By choosing transparency, even when the news isn't all rosy, leaders show that they respect their team's intelligence and autonomy. This respect becomes the cornerstone of a culture where ideas flow freely, questions are encouraged and innovation thrives.

Another facet of trust is often overlooked: empathy. In a world where technology often outpaces humanity, leaders who take the time to understand, acknowledge and respond to their team's individual aspirations and challenges stand out. This isn't about being personable; it's about recognising that every team member is a unique individual with hopes, dreams and fears. By making this effort, leaders not only earn loyalty for themselves, but also create a nurturing environment where team members feel seen and valued.

Consistency emerges as a non-negotiable trait in the trust equation. Even as markets change and industries evolve, a leader's steadfastness in values, principles and approach offers a touchstone of stability. This isn't about being inflexible but about offering a reliable leadership compass, especially in times of ambiguity.

Mistakes are inevitable. The hallmark of a trustworthy leader is not the absence of errors, but the manner in which they handle them. Admitting shortcomings, taking responsibility, and actively seeking solutions not only humanises a leader but also establishes an organisational culture where learning is prioritised over blame.

Credibility often finds its roots in inclusivity. When leaders actively seek input, valuing insights from all ranks, it not only enriches decision-making but also engenders a sense of collective ownership. It sends a clear signal: every perspective is valuable, and every voice counts.

In a landscape saturated with information, a leader's ethical stance becomes their defining signature. Beyond just doing the right thing, it's about understanding the broader impact of decisions, considering long-term consequences over short-term gains, and continuously upholding the values that the organisation stands for. This goes beyond policy compliance; it's about building a legacy of integrity.

In essence, trust isn't an accolade that's bestowed; it's earned through consistent, ethical and genuine leadership actions. And as leaders embark on this continuous journey of earning trust, they not only uplift their teams but set the stage for a future where leadership isn't just about authority, but about authenticity, integrity and genuine connection.

Trust isn't about the leader at all. It's about the individuals they lead, the collective memory they tap into, and the societal voids they strive to fill. The most profound trust emerges when leaders understand and act upon the unspoken, address what has previously been taboo, and dare to walk the unexplored corridors of the human psyche, translating latent needs into tangible actions. This isn't leadership from the front but from within, which turns the traditional leadership paradigm on its head. When they lead from within, leaders don't just earn trust; they redefine it for a new era.

Trust your team

In the arena of leadership, there's often an unstated tension: the tug-of-war between control and delegation. Leaders, tasked with the monumental duty of guiding teams and ensuring outcomes, can sometimes believe that success lies in their hands alone. But the modern era tells a different story, one where leadership is less about holding the reins and more about letting go. Trusting your team might seem counterintuitive, especially when stakes are high and margins are thin. However, that's precisely where transformative leadership begins.

Trusting your team is more than just a leadership tactic; it's a strategic masterstroke. When leaders place genuine trust in their teams, they are not just delegating tasks; they are decentralising innovation. They're making room for diverse thoughts, alternative strategies and unconventional solutions to arise. It is within this space that creativity thrives, problems are viewed through multiple lenses, and solutions are not just effective but also provide benefits beyond solving the immediate problem.

Take the story of Sir Richard Branson, founder of the Virgin Group and known for his unique leadership style that heavily relies on trust. Branson once said, '*I have always believed that the way you treat your employees is the way they will treat your customers, and that people flourish when they have control over their lives.*' At

Virgin, employees are entrusted with the autonomy to innovate and take risks, which has helped propel the company to success. This philosophy has not only contributed to a global empire, but also fostered a culture that celebrates the entrepreneurial spirit. Branson encourages his team to take ownership of their projects, which in turn has spurred growth and innovation across his diverse ventures.

Placing trust in your team is a direct investment in their potential. It sends an unmistakable message: 'I believe in your capabilities.' This kind of affirmation can do wonders for team morale. When individuals feel trusted, they are more likely to take ownership of their work, drive initiatives, and display a higher degree of commitment. This sense of ownership can be the bridge between the ordinary and the extraordinary. Trusted team members don't just complete tasks; they optimise, innovate and elevate them.

And what does this openness yield? Cohesion. When trust is extended, the walls of formality crumble. Teams transition from mere groups of individuals working in tandem to cohesive units, functioning almost organically. They're not just working for a leader or an organisation; they're working for each other. This cohesion fosters a unique form of resilience, where teams can weather challenges, not just because of their skills or resources, but because of their shared trust and purpose.

True leadership trust isn't about having an unfettered belief that your team will always succeed. It's about believing that, even in failure, the team will learn, adapt and emerge stronger. It's a trust in the process and in the journey rather than just the outcomes. And it's this kind of trust that empowers teams to take risks, break moulds and redefine limits.

Trust isn't about directing from a position of power, but instead from a place of genuine connection. Leadership is evolving. We're transitioning from a time when leaders dictated the path to a moment where the most impactful leaders are those who listen, understand and empathise. Here's the profound revelation: trusting your team goes beyond expecting them to execute tasks; it's about knowing they'll uphold and advance a shared ethos. The most transformative leaders today are not those who speak the most, but those who truly hear.

Trust yourself

In the demanding realm of leadership, internal battles often pose the greatest challenges. Leaders frequently question their decisions and actions. 'Is this the right path for my team?' 'Have I made the best choice?' These questions, though deeply personal, resonate across boardrooms and teams, highlighting the critical role of self-trust in leadership.

In times of rapid change and uncertainty, self-trust becomes even more important. It strengthens decision making, allowing leaders to rely on their own knowledge, experience and intuition rather than being swayed by external factors. This clarity and conviction in one's decisions, even when faced with adversity, helps create a stable environment for teams to thrive.

More than just enhancing decision making, self-trust is also the fuel that powers a leader's resilience. Disruptions bring with them a unique set of challenges—unforeseen hurdles, unexpected setbacks, and the occasional failure. It is the leader's trust in their own ability to learn from these challenges, to adapt and to bounce back, that sets the tone for the entire organisation. This self-assurance becomes the safety net, encouraging calculated risks and fostering an atmosphere of innovation.

At its core, self-trust also paves the way for authenticity in leadership. In a world where authenticity is highly prized, people look up to leaders who are genuine, who act with sincerity and integrity. Trusting oneself and one's values means that leaders don't mimic others, but showcase the best version of themselves. This authenticity not only earns respect but also inspires those around them.

Moreover, the confidence a leader has in their own abilities has a ripple effect. It inspires similar confidence in others. When a team observes its leader standing firm in their beliefs and decisions, even during challenging times, it instils a deeper trust in that leader. Its members rally behind the vision, support the strategies laid out, and traverse the path of disruption with a unified spirit.

Leaders with high self-trust are often the trailblazers, the innovators. Their trust in their own creative abilities encourages them to think differently, to question the status quo, and to drive change. They view disruption not as a threat but as a canvas of opportunity, ripe for reimagining and reshaping.

Diving deeper, there's an aspect of self-trust that isn't often discussed: its role in shaping perception. While leaders trust in their knowledge and decisions, there's a subconscious formation of how they wish to be perceived by their teams. Here's the novel insight: it's not about projecting an image of infallibility. In fact, leaders who openly acknowledge their uncertainties, who share their process of decision making, flaws and all, are perceived as more relatable and genuine. In a world obsessed with perfection, the next evolution of leadership might hinge on embracing imperfection. Leaders who intertwine their vulnerabilities with their strengths, who merge their uncertainties with their convictions, present a holistic, human aspect of leadership. They signal that leadership isn't about having all the answers, but about navigating the journey of discovery—together. This realisation doesn't just redefine self-trust; it revolutionises leadership for the modern age.

Self-trust is fundamentally about having faith in your abilities and judgement. It's about trusting in your capability to navigate uncertainties, make difficult decisions and lead others effectively. This self-trust is the foundation upon which you build your confidence, the solid platform from which you lead. When you trust yourself, you exude an authentic confidence that resonates with your team, your peers and your stakeholders.

The TRUSTFUL LEADER Maturity Model

When leaders trust in their own abilities and judgements, they can lead with confidence and authenticity. When they extend this trust to their teams, they cultivate an environment of mutual respect, open communication and collaboration. This empowers their teams to excel. The Trustful Leader Maturity Model explores the synergistic relationship between these two aspects of trust and how they contribute to the development of resilient, inclusive and accountable leadership.

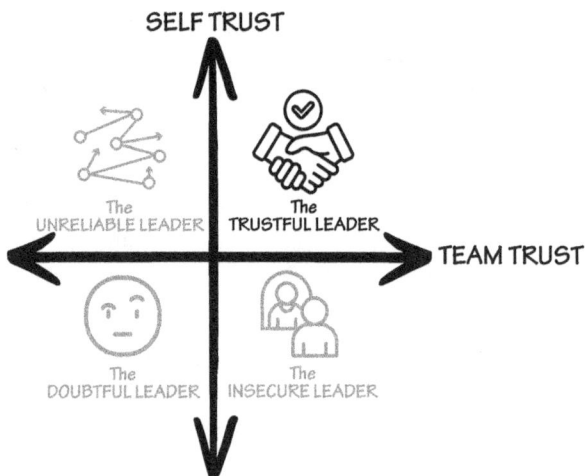

The TRUSTFUL LEADER

SELF TRUST

The UNRELIABLE LEADER

The TRUSTFUL LEADER

TEAM TRUST

The DOUBTFUL LEADER

The INSECURE LEADER

Do you trust yourself? Does your team trust you? Are your trust levels affecting your ability to lead through disruptive times? Let's find out.

The Doubtful Leader: Leaders here show low self-trust and low team trust. They may doubt their own abilities, leading to hesitation in decision making, which can create a sense of instability among their teams. Their lack of trust in their teams may hinder open communication and collaboration, leading to less-effective teamwork. To overcome these hurdles, these leaders should START building self-confidence and appreciating their team's potential. They need to STOP projecting their insecurities onto their teams and START treating every team member with fairness and respect, acknowledging their contributions.

The Unreliable Leader: Leaders in this quadrant display high self-trust but low team trust. They possess confidence in their abilities and decision making but may struggle with building trust among their team members due to inconsistent actions or lack of transparency. This mismatch can lead to a discordant team environment where trust is lacking. These leaders should START being consistent with their actions and transparent with their intentions. They should STOP breaking promises and START fostering an atmosphere of openness to build trust.

The Insecure Leader: Leaders in this quadrant show high team trust but low self-trust. Despite their ability to build a trusting team environment, they may lack confidence in their own abilities. Their insecurities can undermine their leadership effectiveness and may make it difficult for them to lead with authority and conviction. To inspire greater confidence within their teams, leaders in this quadrant should START trusting their abilities and decisions and STOP second guessing themselves.

The Trustful Leader: This quadrant, the ideal state, represents leaders with high self-trust and high team trust. They have faith in their abilities and decisions and excel at building a trusting team environment. Their leadership style creates a harmonious balance between trust in self and trust in team, fostering a supportive, effective and inclusive team culture. Leaders in this quadrant should START sharing their successful strategies and insights to inspire others to foster a culture of trust within their organisations.

Trustful leadership in action

Begin today. Begin to trust yourself and your team. Trust is earned, and the following actions will begin the process of building trust where it is lacking.

Build and foster transparency and consistency in communication: Leaders must ensure they are transparent and consistent in their communication, particularly during disruptive times. By openly acknowledging uncertainties and setting clear visions, trust is nurtured within the team.

Regular updates, aligning actions with words, and being candid about challenges and decisions enhance credibility and foster a culture of trust.

Empower teams through mutual respect and open feedback channels: Trust is reciprocated when leaders have faith in their teams. Leaders can build this trust by empowering their teams. For instance, holding regular feedback sessions where team members can voice opinions and concerns, implementing an open-door policy for spontaneous discussions, and using tools or platforms where team members can anonymously share feedback are instrumental in seeking and valuing input. Leaders can host recognition events, tailor rewards to individual preferences, or even initiate peer recognition programs to celebrate individual strengths and contributions.

Cultivate a safe environment that encourages risk taking and innovation: Leaders must create a culture where team members feel safe to take risks, express their thoughts and learn from their mistakes. Practical steps can be introduced, such as implementing a feedback system where team members can voice ideas without fear of backlash. Consider setting up regular 'innovation hours' where employees can brainstorm freely, or create a platform where new ideas can be pitched anonymously. When mistakes occur, instead of assigning blame, host constructive review sessions to understand the root cause and learn for the future. Reward risk taking by acknowledging and celebrating those who showcase out-of-the-box thinking, even if their projects don't always succeed.

Implement continuous monitoring and reinforcement of trust-building efforts: Ongoing efforts are required to build, maintain and restore trust. Leaders must ensure consistent evaluations of trust-building initiatives, making necessary adjustments to align with organisational goals. Regularly sharing successes, insights and learnings across the organisation can be done through diverse forums such as monthly team meetings, quarterly town halls, dedicated newsletters, or digital dashboards accessible to all. Additionally, consider hosting periodic 'Trust Talks' where teams share their trust-building achievements and challenges.

Utilise the Trustful Leader Maturity Model to develop resilient leaders: Integrate the Maturity Model into leadership development, focusing on the transformation from Doubtful Leaders to Trustful Leaders. Identify where leaders fall within the quadrants, and provide specific actions tailored to their needs. For example, Doubtful Leaders can start building self-confidence and appreciating their team's potential, while Trustful Leaders can share their successful strategies to inspire others.

In this chapter we've delved into the basis of effective leadership in disruptive times—trust. It's in trusting ourselves and others, and building others' trust in us, that we can navigate uncertainty with confidence. As we move forward, we'll look at how leaders can employ negotiation and influence as powerful tools to facilitate change and foster an environment of trust, even amidst the constant flux of disruptive conditions.

CHAPTER INSIGHTS

- Trust, serving as the unifying force in organisations, drives collective action during disruption, and enables leaders to undertake risky tasks with transparency and resilience.

- Building and maintaining trust in disruptive times involves acknowledging uncertainty, ensuring security, providing a clear vision and acting consistently, thus fostering a culture of empowerment.

- Leaders further cultivate trust by empowering teams, seeking feedback, learning from setbacks, and demonstrating consistent trust-building efforts.

- Rebuilding trust during disruption requires creating a safe, connected space with clear communication, demonstrated humility and a commitment to change.

- Trust plays a critical role in disruption management, encouraging open communication, fostering risk taking, hastening response to change, boosting morale and preserving customer relationships.

- Self-trust in leaders bolsters decision-making abilities, resilience, authenticity and innovative capacity during disruptive periods.

- Trust is reciprocal, with leaders' faith in their team's capabilities motivating individuals to excel, thus contributing to a culture of shared ownership.

- Beyond reliability, trust fosters safety and connection, enabling individuals to be authentic, express their thoughts, take risks and learn from mistakes.

5

NEGOTIATING AND INFLUENCING CHANGE

It is so easy to break down and destroy. The
heroes are those who make peace and build.

NELSON MANDELA

AFTER ESTABLISHING the basis of trust in leadership in Chapter 4, Chapter 5 emphasises the importance of negotiation and influence in navigating disruptive times. In this chapter, we'll explore how negotiation skills facilitate change and how leaders can leverage their influence to drive transformation. We'll also delve into understanding the dynamics of power and politics within organisations, equipping you with the tools to navigate these complex landscapes.

The subtle aroma of freshly brewed coffee wafted through the open plan workspace as I approached David's desk, a report clutched in my hand. Over the past few months, we'd had countless impromptu chats about various facets of the company. Our conversations often veered into areas beyond my primary domain of Finance and Supply Chain. I found myself commenting on the broader business operations, including store operations, even though it wasn't my core area of expertise. But I believed in the potential of these operational changes. In every conversation, not just with David but with anyone who'd listen, I shared my perspective, not in a preaching manner, I hope, but with genuine enthusiasm.

With every step, I remembered the countless hours I'd spent researching new Target Operating Models, searching for that blueprint that could rejuvenate our business. My understanding deepened when I came across an article emphasising the importance of the 'last fifty metres' in a store's operations. It was the crucial space, the distance between the back door and the shelf, that determined if a customer left content or disgruntled.

I left the report on David's desk and retreated to my workspace, my heart racing from stepping beyond my usual boundaries. Days turned into weeks, and that daring move slowly faded from memory. Until the day when David, the Chief Operations Officer, reached out: 'I need to speak with you.'

The expansive boardroom felt overwhelming, its long table shining under the ambient lights. David's familiar face offered some relief, but his expression was inscrutable. 'Congratulations,' he began, a hint of a smile playing on his lips, 'you're now overseeing the Last 50 Metres program.'

Surprise clouded my thoughts. I didn't even know that there was such a role, let alone applied for it. I was a finance person; this was out of my depth! The Last 50 Metres wasn't even a thing in our organisation. But David's ensuing words cleared the haze, 'Your vision influenced me, so much so that the executive team could visualise it. They believe in your dedication. We need that fresh view, and you're the one to provide it.'

The compliment ignited a fire in me. Eager to make a difference, I jumped into action. But I was too eager. My enthusiasm was seen as antagonistic, not engaging, and rumbles of discontent could be heard.

Another meeting with David followed. This time the atmosphere was tense.

'Remember the way you persuaded me?' he asked me. 'With respect, patience, and knowledge? You painted the bigger picture. Articulated the 'why' with clarity. You put people at the forefront, prioritising safety, opportunities, a happier workplace, and a sense of belonging even before profits. You spoke of a more team-oriented, inclusive environment, reducing frustrations and making our workplace more meaningful. You emphasised a standard process, underpinned by training and development, that not only would uplift our team but also open up opportunities to align with and deliver our broader company strategy. That's the vision I want you to share with everyone. Influence them with the same passion and clarity. That's the essence of true influence. You don't force; you guide.'

David's words provided a lesson in influence, humility and strategy. I rechannelled my energy, integrating my pace with the principles of influence. Instead of dictating, I began to listen, learn and lead.

The Last 50 Metres program wasn't just a project; it was a transformative journey for the entire company. With every hurdle, we grew stronger, more unified and more determined. The result? A legacy that, alongside some other key strategic initiatives, marked one of the most astounding turnarounds in Australian retail history.

The path to true leadership isn't about bulldozing your way forward; it's about knowing when to push, when to pull and, most importantly, when to walk side by side. It's about understanding that influence isn't a solo endeavour; it's a dance of passion, patience and partnership.

Humanity: the essence of influential leadership

In the rapidly changing landscape of the modern world, where disruption is the only constant, the age-old art of influence emerges as a cornerstone of genuine leadership. At its core, influence isn't just about the power to persuade. It's about the profound human desire for connectivity, understanding and a shared journey.

Let's reconsider our understanding of leadership. Strip away titles and tactics, and we find that leadership is about people. It's about mutual guidance and understanding, and the symbiotic relationship of shared goals and individual insights.

Influence stands out as the beacon. It's not merely about aligning people to a leader's perspective but, more critically, it's the ability of leaders to adapt and evolve based on the collective intelligence of their teams. This reciprocal exchange of insights and perspectives is the hallmark of influential leadership.

Contrast this with the command-and-control model, a relic from a time when rigidity was revered. In a disruptive era, where the pace of change is staggering, this model falls short.

Today's shift in how individuals view leadership is profound. The digital age, combined with a generational shift towards millennials and Gen Z in the workforce, has fostered a culture that values individuality, purpose and authenticity. With unprecedented access to information and a heightened awareness of global issues, these generations are driven by purpose and meaning. They aren't satisfied with just fulfilling a role; they seek to align their work with their values, aspirations and passions. This drive is further amplified by societal shifts that emphasise personal fulfillment and self-actualisation over mere job stability.

In times gone by, leadership was often equated with dominance—the strongest, most aggressive or most authoritative leading the way. But as societies evolved, so did our understanding of leadership. The digital revolution brought about a democratisation of information. No longer were people just receivers; they became contributors, shaping narratives and redefining norms. This transformational change underscored an irrefutable fact: the old model of command and control isn't just outdated, it's counterproductive.

The magic lies in understanding the 'why'. In a world where any individual can be a broadcaster, an influencer or a disruptor, the desire for recognition goes beyond a pay cheque or a title. It's about making a mark, influencing change, and feeling a sense of purpose. Command and control suppresses this innate human desire. It's like trying to contain the vastness of the ocean in a jar. The energy, passion and potential of individuals can't be harnessed by mere directives; it thrives on empowerment, respect and mutual growth. This isn't just a contemporary trend. It's the trajectory of human evolution converging with technological advancements, beckoning us to redefine leadership for a new era.

Today's individual seeks not just to be directed but to be recognised, appreciated and inspired. Their need is not only to perform a task but to be part of a larger narrative, one that resonates with their personal and professional aspirations.

The potency of influence becomes clear when we understand its lasting impact. Command might yield immediate action, but influence secures enduring commitment. A commanded individual might follow a directive, but an influenced individual is driven by belief and purpose, often going above and beyond.

From a standpoint rooted in humanity, influence understands our intrinsic need for recognition and value. In a world marked by disruption, where every individual's input can lead to groundbreaking change, the role of influence becomes pivotal. It crafts a vibrant, collaborative atmosphere where each individual feels intrinsically tied to the collective goal.

Understanding and leveraging power and politics

Power and politics exist in every organisation. While the terms may carry negative connotations, they are not inherently evil concepts. They are simply mechanisms by which individuals and groups influence each other and manage relationships. In fact, understanding power dynamics is like understanding the currents in the ocean; if you don't, you can easily find yourself swimming against the tide, wasting your energy and getting nowhere.

Power in organisations can stem from multiple sources—hierarchical position, expertise, access to information and personal influence, among others. Recognising these sources is the first step in the dance of organisational politics. This knowledge allows us to predict the possible reactions to change initiatives and manage resistance effectively, ensuring a smoother implementation and greater success.

Understanding power dynamics helps in fostering a healthy political climate. Yes, politics can be healthy when it facilitates robust debate, encourages diversity of thought, and ensures the inclusion of multiple perspectives in decision making. When organisational politics is based on fairness, transparency and the pursuit of common goals, it becomes a tool for efficient conflict resolution and for strengthening organisational culture.

Embracing transparency can help dispel the secrecy often associated with politics and cultivate trust among team members. It also provides a platform for open communication, encouraging individuals to voice their opinions, fears and ideas, which fosters an environment conducive to successful change implementation.

Leveraging power dynamics begins with building relationships. Building rapport with key stakeholders, understanding their motivations and involving them in the change process can attract strong allies. This also aids in comprehending the informal power structures that often influence organisational dynamics more than formal hierarchies.

Demonstrating your own expertise and reliability will naturally attract followers, increasing your power base. This is particularly relevant in the disruptive era, when technological changes often outpace traditional power structures, allowing leaders with specific skills and knowledge to wield considerable influence.

However, a word of caution: power is a double-edged sword. While it's necessary for effective leadership, it must be wielded responsibly. Power used recklessly or selfishly can quickly erode trust and cohesion, ultimately undermining the change process. The key is to use power not as a means of control, but as a tool to empower others, facilitate decision making and drive constructive change.

The power of 'and': expanding possibilities in disruptive leadership

In a world frequently caught between binaries—yes or no, this or that, success or failure—the power of 'AND' presents an avenue for reconciling apparent opposites, allowing perspectives to be integrated and therefore propel forward momentum. It reflects a mindset that transcends dichotomies, advocating for holistic, inclusive decision making that amplifies the potency of leadership, especially in an era marked by disruption.

In the world of influence and negotiation, this 'AND' perspective represents a transformative shift. Traditionally, negotiations were often framed around compromise—giving something up to gain something else. However, in disruptive leadership, the narrative evolves from compromise to mutual enhancement. It's not about what you're willing to forgo, but how both parties can integrate their goals AND aspirations to co-create value. It's the ethos of seeing solutions where others see conflict.

Let's explore this within the context of leadership. Say, for instance, a company wants to incorporate sustainable practices but is wary of potential financial setbacks. The old mindset might approach this as an 'either-or' situation: either embrace sustainability and risk financial strain or prioritise profits and continue traditional methods. The power of 'AND' suggests a different approach: how can the company embrace sustainability AND continue to be financially robust? This isn't merely wishful thinking but invites innovative solutions like adopting cost-effective green technologies, collaborating with eco-conscious partners, or tapping into the burgeoning market of environmentally aware consumers.

Similarly, in the face of organisational change, leaders often confront resistance. The underlying sentiment behind opposition isn't always just resistance to the new, but also an attachment to the old. The power of 'AND' in this scenario would prompt leaders to integrate the strengths of the old system AND the advantages of the new. It's not about discarding the past, but synergising it with the future.

This perspective also significantly impacts the way leaders negotiate. Instead of viewing negotiations as a battleground where each party tries to secure the most while sacrificing the least, the 'AND' mindset sees it as a collaborative space. Here, parties seek to understand each other's core values and aspirations, finding ways to ensure both can thrive. It shifts the narrative from 'What can I get out of this?' to 'How can we both grow from this?' This pivot might seem subtle, but its implications are profound. Negotiations cease to be mere transactions and evolve into partnerships.

Tim Cook, the CEO of Apple Inc., exemplifies the 'AND' philosophy in leadership. He succeeded Steve Jobs with the tremendous challenge of continuing Apple's legacy of innovation while ensuring its commercial success. Cook has managed to uphold Apple's commitment to design AND sustainability by investing in renewable energy and implementing greener materials in products without compromising their iconic aesthetic and performance. Moreover, he has embraced the potential of Apple to create technologically advanced products AND maintain strong ethical standards within the supply chain. This balance of priorities reflects Cook's ability to navigate through complexities with a mindset that views multiple objectives not as competing but as complementary, thereby expanding Apple's brand and ethical footprint simultaneously.

The 'AND' perspective actively challenges the scarcity mindset—the idea that resources are limited and one's gain is another's loss. Instead, it propagates abundance, championing the belief that with creativity, collaboration and shared vision we can unlock previously untapped resources and possibilities.

Leading leaders: navigating influence and legacy

While hierarchies within an organisation serve a purpose in terms of structure and order, it's crucial to remember one foundational truth: leaders, no matter their title or position, are people first. This human element is the cornerstone of effective influence and negotiation, especially when it comes to leading those perceived as above us in the organisational chain.

Being a leader doesn't endow someone with all the answers. It's a common fallacy to assume that those at the top echelons of power possess superior insight or wisdom. In many scenarios, leaders, whether they're executives, CEOs, or other high-ranking individuals, are as much in need of guidance as anyone else. They may have a broader perspective or more responsibility, but they don't have a monopoly on vision or insight. And this is where the concept of leading leaders comes into play.

Every individual has the capacity to be a leader because leadership is not defined by a title, but by actions and behaviour. When we view leadership in this light, the hierarchical barriers diminish, and we begin to see opportunities to lead and influence at all levels. For instance, a department head might possess critical insights into a specific operational issue that a CEO might overlook. In such situations, the department head, even though hierarchically lower, can effectively lead the CEO towards a better decision.

The very act of a subordinate leading or guiding a superior challenges the traditional paradigms of leadership. This disruption is not just in terms of challenging hierarchy, but also in the flow of knowledge and influence. It's evidence of a dynamic environment where adaptability trumps rigid structures. This disruption underscores the idea that leadership is not just top-down, but also lateral and bottom-up. Leaders can be influenced, guided, and even led by those hierarchically below them. In the modern world, it's not just about leading but also about being open to being led.

Traditionally, knowledge and power cascaded from the top, but the digital age has democratised access to information, levelling the playing field. The realisation here is profound: in a world overflowing with information, being at the top doesn't necessarily mean having the best or most relevant insights. Sometimes, the most groundbreaking perspectives emerge from where they're least expected. This shift illuminates the necessity of adaptability, suggesting that the future of leadership lies not in holding on to power, but in distributing and sharing it. In this light, the most visionary leaders aren't those who command from an ivory tower, but those who understand the strength in vulnerability, in admitting they don't have all the answers, and in being receptive to guidance from any quarter.

The INFLUENTIAL LEADER Maturity Model

Negotiation skills and influence stand as pivotal within Influential leadership. This matrix refines our understanding of leadership by putting a spotlight on the interaction between negotiation skills and influence, two critical elements that define a transformative leader. In this model, we see the vitality of negotiation and influence for leaders to be accountable, resilient and inclusive, effectively guiding their teams amidst disruptive change.

The INFLUENTIAL LEADER

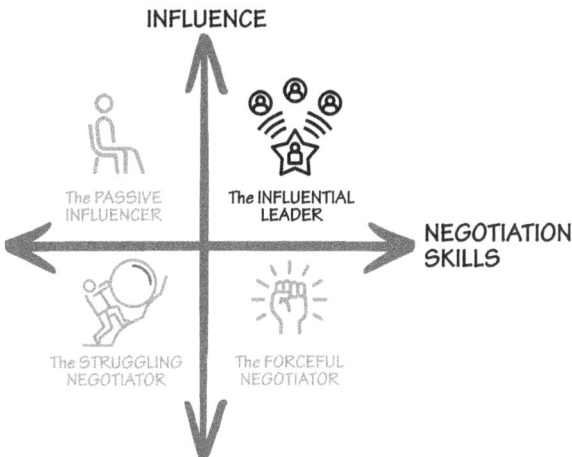

INFLUENCE

The PASSIVE INFLUENCER

The INFLUENTIAL LEADER

NEGOTIATION SKILLS

The STRUGGLING NEGOTIATOR

The FORCEFUL NEGOTIATOR

Let's look closer at the four quadrants to determine your current level of influence.

The Struggling Negotiator: Leaders in this quadrant display low negotiation skills and low influence. Their decision making may often be unilateral, disregarding the input of others. Additionally, their lack of empathy may hinder relationship building and erode trust within their teams, affecting both their influence and negotiation outcomes. These leaders need to START employing negotiation skills to foster collective decision making and STOP acting unilaterally. They should START demonstrating empathy, which can enhance trust and lead to better negotiation outcomes.

The Passive Influencer: This quadrant is characterised by leaders with high influence but low negotiation skills. They are successful at inspiring their teams and aligning them towards a shared vision. However, their ability to manage power dynamics in negotiations or find win-win solutions might be limited, affecting the sustainability of their agreements. Leaders here should START understanding and leveraging power dynamics in negotiations, and STOP avoiding conflict or difficult conversations. They should also START striving for win-win solutions to ensure that agreements are beneficial for all parties.

The Forceful Negotiator: Leaders here show high negotiation skills but low influence. They excel at understanding stakeholder needs and creating win-win solutions, yet they might struggle to persuade or build trust among stakeholders due to a lack of influence. Leaders in this quadrant should START developing persuasive communication styles and STOP relying solely on negotiation skills. To build trust, they should also START being more transparent and consistent in their communication.

The Influential Leader: This is the ideal state, with leaders exhibiting both high negotiation skills and high influence. They're proficient at understanding and addressing stakeholder needs and at driving transformation through their influence. Their balanced negotiation style and influential leadership enable them to navigate complex power dynamics and achieve sustainable outcomes. Leaders in this quadrant should START sharing their successful strategies and insights to inspire a culture of negotiation and influence within their organisations.

Influential leadership in action

The best time to begin wielding a positive influence on the world is now. Begin your career as an influential leader today and see results sooner rather than later. Here are five ways to get the ball rolling.

Implement specific empathetic negotiation techniques for building consensus: Leaders must engage in active listening, ask probing questions, and utilise mediation strategies to align diverse perspectives. This practice requires creating structured negotiation processes, employing well-defined roles and providing regular training. Emphasising empathy in negotiations fosters a culture of collaboration and understanding, critical for achieving shared visions during disruptive changes.

Establish influence through structured relationship-building programs and regular trust-building exercises: To build influence, leaders must implement formal mentorship and networking programs, fostering genuine connections among team members. Regular trust-building exercises, such as open forums and team retreats, can enhance relationships and create a balance between influence and empathy, which are vital for leading teams towards unified goals in disruptive environments.

Develop a collaborative framework with defined roles and responsibilities and employ collaboration tools: Implementing collaboration requires clear definition of roles and responsibilities, and usage of collaborative tools like shared platforms and regular workshops. Leaders must create forums for robust debate, allocate resources for team-building activities, and institute policies that encourage both collective and independent decision making. This strategic approach strengthens leadership, ensuring resilience during disruptive times.

Craft a persuasive communication strategy with clear messaging guidelines and regular stakeholder engagement: Leaders must formulate a precise communication strategy, with clear guidelines on messaging, tone and frequency. Regular stakeholder engagement through town halls, feedback sessions and transparent sharing of company goals ensures alignment of visions and motivations. This targeted approach builds trust and reduces resistance, cultivating an environment receptive to change and innovation.

Utilise the Influential Leader Maturity Model to understand and enhance negotiation and influence skills: Integrate the Influential Leader Maturity Model into leadership development, focusing on transformation across the four quadrants. Identify where leaders fall within the model and provide specific actions tailored to their needs. For example, Struggling Negotiators can enhance their collective decision making and empathy, while Influential Leaders can share their successful strategies to inspire others.

Having discovered the transformative power of negotiation and influence, we see how these tools can be utilised to navigate disruptive landscapes. Yet, a leader's toolbox isn't complete without the ability to inspire, connect and resonate with others. The next chapter takes us into the world of storytelling, a skill that plays an essential role in disruptive leadership by forging a sense of shared purpose and vision.

CHAPTER INSIGHTS

- Influence, a key aspect of transformative leadership, guides others' thoughts and actions towards shared objectives. Built on trust, respect and genuine relationships, it turns apprehension into anticipation and garners allies.

- Power and politics influence organisational relationships and resistance to change. Understanding these dynamics helps leverage individual attributes for common goals, facilitating robust debate, encouraging diversity and ensuring inclusive decision making.

- Healthy politics is about transparency, fairness and pursuit of common goals, making it a tool for conflict resolution and culture strengthening.

- Effective negotiation is critical in disruptive times, requiring understanding, empathy and communication. It aligns perspectives, alleviates fears and builds consensus around a shared vision, fostering a shared belief in the value of disruptive change.

- Persuasive communication aligns motivations with vision and builds narratives that incite action. It enhances credibility and trust and reduces resistance to change.

- Authentic persuasion fosters an understanding of change benefits. In disruptive times, it demands efficient messaging, preparation, and a deep grasp of stakeholders' motivations.

- Collaborative environments encourage collective decision making, harness diverse perspectives and foster shared responsibility. They build trust, strengthen relationships, and enhance the effectiveness of change initiatives.

- Balancing between collective and independent decision making is essential. While collaboration may initially take longer, it results in well-rounded and resilient decisions, facilitating, enabling and empowering leadership.

6

HARNESSING THE POWER
OF STORYTELLING

*Your story is the greatest legacy that
you will leave to your friends. It's the longest-
lasting legacy you will leave to your heirs.*

OPRAH WINFREY

UILDING ON our exploration of negotiation and influence, Chapter 6 presents a key aspect of communication in disruptive leadership. In this chapter, we'll delve into the role of storytelling in influencing and inspiring in disruptive times, exploring how compelling narratives can embody your leadership vision. We'll look at how storytelling helps navigate change, fosters a sense of community, and plays a role in personal brand building for disruptive leaders.

I found myself stepping into a new role, leading a prominent global company with an expansive supply chain. Located in an industrial operational setting, the sheer scale of this role, spanning several continents and countless products, was nothing short of monumental. Yet the daunting reality I faced bore little resemblance to my initial expectations.

Within days of my arrival, I was overwhelmed by a chaotic storm, evidence of a system that had lost its way. The most glaring flaw? A blatant disregard for safety. This pervasive culture of negligence posed a dual threat, endangering not just our dedicated employees but the very reputation of the multinational brand we were entrusted with. In our expansive operation, even a single oversight could easily escalate into an international debacle.

It was clear that piecemeal changes wouldn't suffice. As I met with the leadership team to strategise our way forward, I realised that the true linchpin to fostering responsibility was an emotional connection.

With this in mind, I unveiled a deeply personal chapter from my past—the story of my father's debilitating accident.

Gathering the team against the vast backdrop of our primary operational centre, I began ...

Let me tell you about someone important to me. My father, a hardworking entrepreneur, ran a transport business. He was the heart and soul of his venture, ensuring the wheels never stopped turning.

However, one fateful day, in an operational setting just like this, a momentary oversight changed everything. An unexpected accident (not in his truck but in the Distribution Centre where he was receiving goods to deliver) left him with a severe spinal injury. The after-math was a heartbreaking journey—countless surgeries, a life chained to painkillers, and the anguish of con-fronting his own limitations every day.

Our family bore witness, a silent audience to a heartbreaking performance. Here was a man who had once been the bedrock of our family, a paragon of strength, both in character and physique. His con-fidence had been infectious, inspiring us all. He walked with a stride that commanded respect and spoke with a voice that drew people in. But after the accident, that vibrant force of nature began to fade. Day by day, we watched him grapple with an unfamiliar and painful reality, seeing glimpses of the father and husband we knew, but also confronting the undeniable changes that had taken hold.

Sharing this narrative became an integral part of my reformative agenda. I repeated it in boardrooms, during casual interactions, and at large-scale gath-erings. My aim was not to evoke sympathy but to underscore the tangible, devastating ramifications of carelessness.

The impact of this story was profound. It be-came a touchstone, reminding everyone, from the newest employee to the seasoned executive, of the immense responsibility on their shoulders. By fore-grounding safety, we didn't merely elevate our operational standards; we crafted a renewed, col-lective ethos.

Reflecting on that pivotal period, our former Chief People Officer once remarked that while we made many innovative changes, it was my father's story that resonated the most with the company and is why change was accelerated. Through this powerful narrative, safety was transformed from a mere guideline to a deeply personal and collective commitment.

Stories have a unique power to bridge divides and foster deep connections. While safety presentations filled with statistics and procedures serve a purpose, they often lack the human element that truly resonates with an audience. Sharing a real, raw account—like the heart-wrenching journey of a loved one—strips away the facade and taps into the core of our shared human experience. Such stories become more than just narratives; they are emotional anchors, grounding abstract concepts in palpable realities. It's this authentic vulnerability that forms the bedrock of genuine connections, making them infinitely more impactful than any rehearsed presentation. For, in authenticity, we see reflections of ourselves, our fears and our hopes, and it's through these shared reflections that true change is birthed.

Stories don't always have to stem from profound tragedies or life-altering events. Often, the most relatable tales are born from everyday moments— simple interactions, fleeting thoughts or commonplace challenges. Whether it's a memory of a shared laugh during a break, the pride of a job well done, or the frustration of a minor mishap, these narratives resonate because they reflect the workings of our daily lives. Their strength lies not in their drama, but in their authenticity. By sharing these moments, we highlight our shared human experience, building bridges of understanding and fostering genuine connections.

The narrative: a point of stability in disruptive times

In an era where disruptions rattle the very core of our existence, narratives emerge as anchors of stability. These are not just tales whispered from one generation to the next, but are the threads that weave the very fabric of human civilisation. They guide, inspire and, most crucially, connect us on profound levels, transcending the barriers of time, space and circumstance.

Long before the advent of written language, humanity found its voice in stories. Through tales, we navigated the complexity of life, finding meaning in chaos and deriving purpose amidst ambiguity. These stories, told around ancient campfires or painted on cave walls, did more than just chronicle events—they shaped cultures, birthed traditions and fostered communal bonds. In essence, our propensity for storytelling made us innately human. It gave rise to shared wisdom, communal understanding and a collective consciousness that transcended the individual.

In the realm of disruptive leadership, the narrative emerges not as a mere accessory but as a foundational pillar. Disruptions, by their very nature, are disorienting. They challenge the status quo, pushing both leaders and followers into uncharted territories. Here, amidst uncertainties, stories serve as beacons of light. They offer clarity amidst confusion and provide a sense of continuity in times of change. When a leader articulates their vision through a compelling narrative, it resonates. It becomes more than just a strategic direction; it evolves into a shared journey, a collective aspiration.

But the true genius of narratives lies not just in their ability to guide but in their capacity to humanise. Disruptions, for all their transformative potential, can be dehumanising. They often manifest as abstract forces, overwhelming in their scope and impact. In such scenarios, stories serve as bridges, connecting the abstract with the tangible, the strategic with the personal. When a leader shares a tale of overcoming a challenge or realising a dream, it's no longer just their journey—it becomes everyone's. The leader's story morphs into a shared narrative, fostering a sense of belonging and unity.

Consider the example of Sheryl Sandberg, the former Chief Operating Officer of Meta, who navigated the company through its transition from a social media platform to a global leader in digital innovation. Sandberg's narrative strength lies in her ability to foster resilience and inclusivity, themes she masterfully weaves into her leadership. Her book *Lean In* is not just a memoir; it is a manifesto that calls for women to embrace leadership roles, told through a compelling narrative that interlaces personal anecdotes with hard-earned business lessons. By sharing her own story of overcoming adversity and challenging societal norms, Sandberg created a shared narrative that resonates with a broad audience, empowering others to join in the movement towards equality in the workplace. Her adept storytelling has become a pivotal part of Meta's culture, helping to steer the company through controversy and innovation alike by fostering a shared identity and purpose.

The influence of storytelling in disruptive leadership

We are often inundated with bursts of information; the timeless art of storytelling stands for clarity in the digital fog. While the modes of communication have exponentially grown, the essence of connecting through tales remains undiminished. For leaders navigating this intricate landscape, storytelling emerges not just as a tool but as an imperative.

The world doesn't run on data alone. At its core, every decision, every pivot, every leap is fuelled by a deeper human emotion, an underlying story. Leadership, in this age, isn't about who shouts the loudest, but about who resonates the most profoundly. It's about understanding that every individual, whether in a boardroom or a breakout room, seeks a connection, an anchor to something greater than themselves. And it is here that storytelling in leadership plays its pivotal role.

Consider for a moment the dynamics of the modern workplace. Employees today, especially the younger generations, are no longer swayed by mere job titles or hefty salaries. They seek purpose, a sense of belonging, a narrative that aligns with their own. This is also true for other key stakeholders such as suppliers, investors or customers. When a leader crafts and shares stories that encapsulate the essence of that purpose, they're not just communicating; they're forging bonds. They're building bridges of understanding and avenues of inspiration.

Yet, for all its potency, storytelling in leadership is not about crafting the most extravagant tales. It's about authenticity. It's about sharing moments of vulnerability, instances of uncertainty and episodes of learning. In a world saturated with curated perfection, genuine stories shine the brightest. They remind teams that the person at the wheel is not an infallible figure but a human, with dreams, doubts and determination. Such stories break down barriers, fostering environments where openness thrives and innovation flourishes.

Moreover, as leaders narrate, they also listen. They absorb the stories of those they lead, understanding aspirations, apprehensions and ambitions. This two-way street of narrative exchange fosters empathy, a trait indispensable in modern leadership. By understanding and integrating diverse stories, leaders can make better-informed decisions—ones that reflect collective aspirations.

Embracing change through storytelling: crafting legacies in influential leadership

Change. It's an evocative word. A word that, in most people, incites a spectrum of emotions—from apprehension to anticipation. The arc of human history is a testament to our relationship with change. We resist it, welcome it, dread it and chase it, often all at once.

So, how does an influential leader harness this intricate dance with change and steer it towards creating a legacy?

The key is storytelling.

Storytelling, as a mode of communication, stands out for its unparalleled efficacy and resonance. Unlike mere data or directives, stories weave information into a context, making it more digestible and memorable. Humans are hardwired to relate to narratives, which offer a structure that our brains instinctively follow and engage with. When information is presented in the form of a story, it becomes clearer, more understandable and more relatable.

Stories make the abstract tangible. They offer a way in which theoretical concepts of change transform into relatable anecdotes. When a leader shares a story of adaptability, of evolution, it's no longer just a directive—it's a shared vision. The story becomes a space in which every individual can see themself, leading to a collective understanding.

Yet, storytelling in the context of change management is not just about painting pictures of a rosy future. It's about embracing the vulnerabilities, the uncertainties and the challenges that come with change. By integrating these elements into their narrative, leaders foster an environment of trust. It's an acknowledgment that says, 'I see the challenges, but here's how we can navigate them together.'

What further elevates this approach is when leaders encourage stories from the ground up. When every individual, regardless of their role or position, is empowered to share their narrative of change, it creates a ripple effect. The organisation or community becomes a repository of diverse tales, each echoing a different facet of the change journey. This mosaic of narratives fosters a rich culture of inclusivity and mutual respect.

Elevating communication: the strategic essence of story in leadership

In the domain of leadership, communication isn't merely about the exchange of information; it's about making a meaningful connection with the audience. While traditional corporate communication might focus on the dissemination of data and directives, incorporating storytelling elevates this exchange, making it more engaging and impactful. Storytelling in leadership transforms routine announcements into compelling narratives, fostering an environment where messages are not just heard but felt and remembered.

When leaders embrace storytelling, they bypass the typical one-way traffic of corporate announcements and create a dialogue that invites participation and reflection. This narrative approach abandons the complexity of corporate jargon for the clarity and relatability of stories. It's not about presenting listeners with a complex puzzle, but rather guiding them through a clear path of understanding. Stories resonate with us because they are grounded in shared human experiences. Instead of abstract concepts, they provide concrete, relatable scenarios.

Within the hierarchy of an organisation, effective storytelling democratises communication. Leaders who share stories can bridge gaps between different levels of the company, making messages accessible to all, not just those versed in the nuances of business language. They create a sphere of inclusivity in which every employee feels valued and understood.

The art of storytelling avoids dry, impersonal presentations and replaces them with vibrant, engaging narratives that capture the listener's imagination. By embracing storytelling, leaders ensure that their messages are not just a list of instructions but a memorable and motivating experience. This approach moves away from a one-way flow of commands, and creates a more interactive and engaging form of communication that encourages feedback and discussion.

Leaders who understand the power of storytelling navigate through the complexities of corporate communication with ease. They know that an engaging narrative can turn the ordinary into the extraordinary. It means moving beyond simply sharing information to sharing meaning, transforming the corporate environment into a place where every voice can contribute to a collective, compelling narrative.

By integrating storytelling into their communication strategy, leaders forge a deeper connection with their audience, one that is rooted in empathy and shared values. They replace the complex structure of corporate communication with a clear, engaging, and memorable path. This ensures that the message not only reaches all corners of the organisation but also resonates on a personal level, encouraging a culture of unity and shared purpose.

The MASTER STORYTELLER Maturity Model

Chapter 6 unfolds another critical dimension of leadership—the art of storytelling and effective communication. When leaders become skilled narrators and articulate communicators, they can inspire action, engender trust and align their teams towards shared objectives with clarity and conviction. This chapter introduces us to the Master Storyteller Maturity Model, which investigates the intersection between storytelling skills and communication abilities. This model, highlighting their mutual relationship, plays an essential role in cultivating leaders who are resilient, inclusive and accountable.

How effective are your storytelling skills? Do you tell stories at all? Let's take a closer look at the four quadrants to determine where your current skills land.

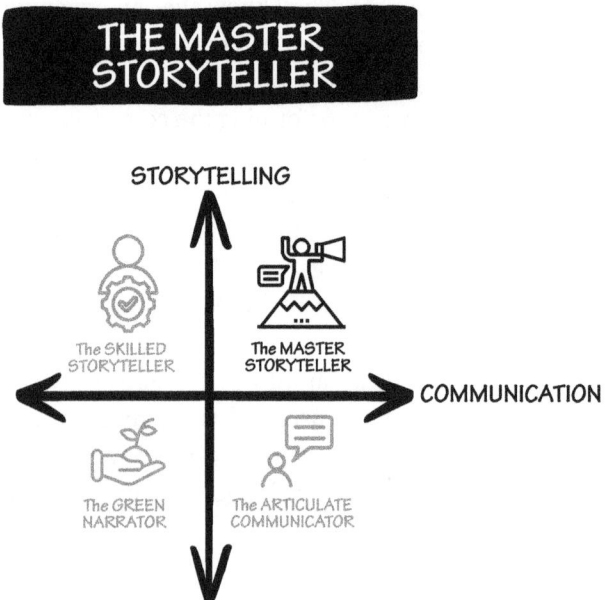

THE MASTER STORYTELLER

STORYTELLING

The SKILLED STORYTELLER

The MASTER STORYTELLER

COMMUNICATION

The GREEN NARRATOR

The ARTICULATE COMMUNICATOR

The Green Narrator: Leaders in this quadrant are characterised by a fundamental deficiency in both storytelling and general communication skills. They may fail to engage their team effectively, limiting their ability to inspire action or build strong team relationships. Their messages might come across as disengaging and may lack the necessary influence to drive change. To address these challenges, these leaders need to START developing their storytelling techniques by learning from skilled narrators and practising the creation of engaging narratives. Simultaneously, they should START bolstering their general communication skills through workshops, active listening exercises and public speaking opportunities. They need to STOP disseminating dry, uninspiring information and ignoring the crucial role of effective communication in leadership.

The Skilled Storyteller: These leaders have honed their storytelling abilities, but struggle with overall communication. While their narratives may captivate, their overall message might get lost due to poor delivery, ineffective listening, or a lack of clarity in written communication. To overcome these limitations, they should START focusing on enhancing their communication skills through active listening exercises, improving written communication, and adapting communication styles to different situations. They need to STOP over-relying on their storytelling abilities and neglecting the critical role of comprehensive communication skills in leadership.

The Articulate Communicator: This quadrant comprises leaders with strong communication skills but underdeveloped storytelling abilities. While these leaders excel at conveying information clearly and effectively, they may lack the ability to fully engage their teams due to the absence of compelling narratives. This could potentially diminish the emotional resonance and impact of their messages. To improve, these leaders should START developing their storytelling skills by learning the art of narrative creation, practising these techniques, and seeking constructive feedback. They must STOP neglecting the influence of powerful narratives in leadership and relying solely on their communication skills.

The Master Storyteller: Leaders in this quadrant embody a fine balance of high storytelling skills and advanced communication abilities. Their compelling narratives, paired with clear, effective communication, inspire and engage their teams, making them highly influential in driving change and creating a lasting impact. These leaders don't need to stop anything, given their balanced blend of the two vital leadership attributes this quadrant focuses on. However, they should START sharing their strategies and insights with others to nurture a culture that values both storytelling and effective communication.

Master Storyteller leadership in action

Not everyone is a natural storyteller, but anyone can tell a great story if they have the right education and training. Here are five actions you can take right now to make storytelling part of the communication strategies in your organisation.

Develop an organisation-wide storytelling framework to align vision and culture: Leaders must create structured storytelling guidelines, conduct regular training sessions with professional storytellers, and set up storytelling circles within the organisation. This approach, emphasising authentic narratives that align with organisational values, fosters a shared vision and culture, thereby strengthening resilience during disruptive changes.

Implement personalised storytelling development plans based on individual needs and roles: Identifying specific storytelling needs for different roles within the organisation, leaders must craft personalised development plans. This includes targeted coaching, sharing successful and failed examples, and consistent feedback to enhance narrative skills. By tailoring storytelling techniques to individual needs, leaders enable their teams to connect with and inspire others, which is vital for driving alignment in disruptive environments.

Craft a cohesive storytelling strategy that integrates values, experiences and organisational goals: Leaders must formulate a cohesive storytelling strategy, aligned with personal experiences, organisational values and strategic objectives. Regular sharing of success stories and alignment with cultural attributes turns the organisational mission into a compelling narrative. This unified approach builds trust, engages employees, and ensures readiness for disruptive changes.

Establish regular storytelling sessions to enhance collaboration and mutual understanding: Implementing regular storytelling sessions within the organisation requires clear guidelines, collaboration platforms and cross-departmental interaction. Leaders can create forums for engaging narratives, allocate resources for storytelling collaborations and encourage shared successes. This strategic approach strengthens leadership, enhances collaboration, and builds a resilient culture ready to navigate disruptive times.

Utilise the Master Storyteller Maturity Model to understand and enhance storytelling and communication skills: Integrate the Master Storyteller Maturity Model into leadership development, focusing on transformation across the four quadrants. Identify where leaders fall within the model and provide specific actions tailored to their needs. For example, Green Narrators can enhance their narrative creation skills, while Master Storytellers can share their successful strategies to inspire others. This targeted approach aligns storytelling skills with leadership needs, fostering growth and innovation.

In concluding our exploration of storytelling, we've learned how it serves to inspire and build shared purpose in the face of disruption. This brings us to the end of Part 2, where we've learned how trust, negotiation and storytelling form the scaffold for impactful leadership. As we transition to Part 3, we will focus on developing 'Leadership of the Future' competencies. This will involve understanding remote leadership, acknowledging the need for a global perspective, and appreciating the significance of intrapreneurship and entrepreneurship in disruptive leadership.

CHAPTER INSIGHTS

- Storytelling emerges as a potent leadership tool, inspiring teams through human connections, and appealing to emotions, values and dreams, especially during disruptive times.

- A well-constructed narrative expands perspectives— enabling teams to grasp their role in the face of disruption, countering fear and encouraging action towards common goals.

- Storytelling cultivates unity, creating a shared vision that transcends individual differences, thereby aligning all towards a mutual goal.

- Authentic storytelling, rooted in personal experiences and values, builds trust and credibility, augmenting the leaders' ability to influence and inspire.

- By painting a vivid picture of the vision, compelling narratives provide more than a list of objectives; they inspire by making the vision tangible.

- Storytelling aids leaders to steer through disruptive changes, making unfamiliar situations relatable, and spotlighting the benefits of change.

- Disruption-induced challenges like confusion and resistance can be mitigated by captivating narratives that foster resilience and stimulate proactive engagement.

- The art of storytelling plays a vital role in personal brand building for leaders, crafting impactful narratives that echo their growth trajectory, values and impact.

THE PRIZES OF INFLUENTIAL LEADERSHIP

Reflecting on **Part 2: Influential Leadership,** we can observe that the mastery of influential leadership requires a deep understanding of trust, negotiation, influence and storytelling.

These insights enhance a leader's ability to steer through the complex landscape of disruption, equipping them with tools to build and sustain influence, and setting the stage for further exploration in subsequent parts of this book.

Enhanced Trust-Building Skills

Navigating through influential leadership principles, you'll uncover new ways to foster and restore trust within your organisation. This skill is fundamental to creating an environment that encourages risk taking and innovation. As you learn to instil a sense of shared purpose in your team, you'll solidify your position as a reliable leader.

Elevated Negotiation and Influence

The knowledge of how to effectively negotiate change, coupled with the ability to persuade others to your vision, enhances your competence in leading through disruptive times. As you grow proficient in influencing decisions and rallying your team towards shared goals, your leadership's overall effectiveness and recognition will be significantly amplified.

Mastery in Inspirational Storytelling

By harnessing the power of storytelling, you'll gain the ability to connect with your team on a profound level. Your skills in turning complex ideas into engaging narratives will make you a source of inspiration and motivation for your team, ultimately boosting their commitment and productivity.

Improved Change Management

The mastery of influential leadership principles grants you an upper hand in managing change within your organisation. You'll be equipped with the skills to navigate change smoothly, turning potential disruptions into opportunities for growth. As a result, you'll become a resilient leader, adaptable and ready to steer your team through any challenge.

Advanced Personal Leadership Brand

The journey through empathetic leadership will significantly shape your personal leadership brand. Your ability to craft and share impactful narratives reflecting your values and experiences will enhance your credibility and influence. Consequently, this refined personal brand will cement your position as an inspiring leader, fostering a stronger connection with your team.

PART 3

FUTURE-READY LEADERSHIP

CONTEMPORARY

TRANSFORMATIONAL

THE DISRUPTIVE LEADER

INFLUENTIAL

LEGACY ORIENTED

FUTURE-READY

Future-Ready Leadership delves into the unique leadership competencies that are needed in a contemporary business landscape marked by disruptive change. The next three chapters discuss leading remotely, a skill that has become crucial; the global skills needed to navigate leadership in this disruptive era; and the role of intrapreneurship and entrepreneurship in powering disruptive leadership.

The advent of digital technologies and globalisation has significantly altered the way organisations operate and how leaders lead. In this context, disruptive leadership calls for the development of unique competencies that resonate with these shifts and the resulting new ways of working.

One such competency is leading teams remotely. In our increasingly digital and interconnected world, the ability to lead remote teams effectively is paramount. Disruptive leaders must be adept at using digital tools and communication strategies to engage with their teams, ensuring cohesion, productivity, and a shared sense of purpose despite geographical distance. **Chapter 7: Leading Remotely in the Disruptive Era** discusses how disruptive leaders can effectively lead remote teams, maintain team dynamics and drive productivity in the digital age.

Another crucial competency is the ability to navigate and lead within the global context. Disruptive leaders need to understand and appreciate the cultural, economic and political complexities that accompany global business operations. The ability to adapt and lead effectively across different cultural and geographic contexts is essential for driving innovation and success on a global scale. **Chapter 8: Global Disruption Leadership—Skills for the Future** explores the unique set of skills that disruptive leaders need to operate and lead successfully in the global business environment.

Lastly, intrapreneurship and entrepreneurship are key drivers of disruptive leadership. Intrapreneurship fosters a culture of innovation within an organisation, whereas entrepreneurship propels disruptive leadership beyond the organisation's boundaries, creating new ventures that drive industry-wide change. **Chapter 9: Intrapreneurship and Entrepreneurship—Powering Disruptive Leadership** provides insights into the roles of intrapreneurship and entrepreneurship in driving disruptive leadership, discussing how these two elements can foster a culture of innovation and propel the organisation towards success.

The principles shared in Part 3 provide another crucial piece in solving our central puzzle of how to create a powerful legacy in a rapidly changing world. Leaders who can effectively guide remote teams, navigate global landscapes and drive innovation lay the groundwork for a leadership style that is responsive, inclusive and adaptable—all vital traits in our disruptive era. As you read through, you'll also acquire practical strategies for honing these competencies and leveraging them to lead successfully in this disruptive era.

7

LEADING REMOTELY IN THE DISRUPTIVE ERA

The success of remote leadership is
defined not by the distance that separates
us, but by the connections that unite us.
ANNE SWEENEY

N CHAPTER 7 we will delve into a particularly
important topic: Leading Remotely in the Disruptive
Era. Now that workplaces are no longer confined to
the traditional office, we have the ability to work from
anywhere and we have teams scattered across continents: mastering the art of remote leadership is vital.

In this chapter we'll examine the nuances of managing remote teams, focusing on the essential components for success in the digital era. We will uncover
the dynamics of digital competency, emphasising the
importance of understanding and leveraging digital
tools for innovation and problem solving.

The year 2020, a time like no other, had its grip firmly around the world. I found myself on the brink of a massive undertaking with a global giant, facing the daunting task of resurrecting a sinking business-critical project amidst the chaos of the pandemic. The challenge was monumental, akin to navigating a storm without a compass.

Picture this: 300 new recruits, initially poised to converge at a state-of-the-art office, now scattered across the vast stretches of an emerging economy due to the sudden onslaught of the pandemic. Their pivotal role? To meticulously coordinate, plan and manage the intricate global supply chain of a major international brand. Every product and every ship-ment, from countless factories dotted around the globe, were converging towards diverse worldwide markets. The scale was immense, the complexity unparalleled, and the stakes? Monumentally high.

These recruits, caught off guard as the project commenced in tandem with the emerging pan-demic, found themselves in a whirlwind of challenge and adaptation. Overnight, their homes morphed into vital hubs of international logistics. Amidst the familiar sounds of children's laughter and the occa-sional clucking of chickens, the recruits grappled with the mammoth task at hand, striving to ensure a seamless flow in a project that simply could not afford any delay or misstep.

For such a globally recognised company, this chaos was out of place and deeply unsettling. But the stakes of this project, running into billions, meant that turning back was not an option. The real concern, however, wasn't just the monetary value. It was the dwindling trust, the plummeting morale, and the sense of unease that seemed to permeate every virtual meeting.

In this whirlwind, a profound revelation dawned upon me. The core of the struggle wasn't simply the switch to remote work caused by the pandemic. It was something more insidious, something the workers weren't immediately willing to confront: the glaring absence of genuine leadership.

Many were quick to pin blame on the physical disconnect that remote work supposedly brought. They argued that the lack of face-to-face interactions, the inability to physically gather in one room, and the sheer geographical spread of our team were the main culprits of our woes. But that couldn't be further from the truth. In fact, even if the teams had been working side by side in the same office space, the outcome would have likely remained unchanged. The primary issue wasn't the distance; it was the widening gap between the leadership and their teams.

True leadership isn't merely about managing tasks, assigning responsibilities or orchestrating meetings. It's about understanding the very heart and soul of your team—recognising their fears, acknowledging their aspirations and tuning into their needs. It's about fostering an environment where every team member feels seen, heard and valued. It's about facilitating open dialogue, cultivating trust and establishing a unified vision. At the most basic level it is also about empowering them with the most basic of training and tools required to get the job done.

The challenge in the leadership wasn't merely a product of the remote setting. Yes, the physical separation between employees was an issue to be dealt with. But it could be dealt with. Effective remote leadership is possible when the leaders are fully committed. In this case, the challenge was indicative of a deeper, systemic flaw in the approach to leadership. The leaders had become so engrossed in the operational aspect of the business that they overlooked the fundamental human element. Sure, there were moments when being physically together would've facilitated better training sessions, team-building activities or strategic brainstorms. But at the core, the vast majority of the operations and interactions could be effectively managed remotely. It was the leadership style, devoid of genuine human connection and empathy, that was the real bottleneck.

Remote work merely shone a spotlight on the pre-existing cracks in the leadership framework. The pandemic didn't create these problems; it merely magnified them. It became evident that to truly thrive, regardless of the work setting, we needed to rebuild our leadership foundation, focusing on genuine connection, trust and a shared purpose.

Grasping this, I began a journey of transformation. We chose empowerment over directives, understanding over commands, collaboration over isolation. The shouting was replaced with listening, confusion gave way to clarity, and doubt was replaced with renewed trust.

Step by step, the pieces started coming together. With the attitude of the leaders re-tuned, they leaned into making the remote-working model work. The right tools found their way to eager hands, training was provided, skills were sharpened, and a culture of respect and collaboration began to flourish. The transformation was tangible. A once disjointed team now worked in unison, efficiently and effectively.

Reflecting on this tumultuous time, I understand that this was more than just rescuing a project from the depths. It was about redefining leadership in a time of profound change. In today's world, it's the core values of trust, empathy and clear communication that stand tall. To lead in these trying times, one must do so with heart, determination and grace—whether remotely or in person.

Omnichannel Leadership: navigating the future of work in a disruptive age

In the flux of the 21st century, with technology at its helm, a quiet revolution is transpiring, radically transforming the fabric of work and leadership. This revolution, often referred to as the 'future of work', is not just about remote work or artificial intelligence taking over mundane tasks. It is about the reinvention of work structures, styles and substance. This metamorphosis poses a pertinent question: what does leadership look like in this brave new world?

Traditionally, leadership was tethered to physical spaces. Corner offices, boardrooms and face-to-face meetings were the arenas where leadership qualities were displayed, observed and judged. A leader's presence was often associated with their physical visibility, the assertiveness of their voice in a crowded room, or their ability to command attention at in-person gatherings. However, as we transition from this conventional paradigm to an omnichannel model, leadership is no longer about presence; it's about impact.

The omni approach, inspired by the retail world, implies seamless integration and consistency across multiple channels. Translated into the workspace, it means that leaders now need to maintain cohesion, culture and communication across various platforms and environments, be it in office, remote or hybrid setups. It's no longer just about managing people but about orchestrating experiences and ensuring consistency in ethos and values, irrespective of where the team operates.

Such a shift demands that leaders wear many hats: they need to be tech savvy, understanding the best tools to bring their teams together to ensure seamless communication and collaboration; they need to be visionaries, anticipating the challenges of a dispersed team and proactively addressing them; and most importantly, they need to be empathetic, recognising the diverse challenges faced by individuals in different settings and offering support tailored to each unique situation.

As the boundary between work and home blurs, leaders in this omnichannel era also bear the responsibility of ensuring the wellbeing of their teams. It's no longer sufficient to ensure project deliverables; leaders need to ensure that their teams are not burning out, that they are mentally and emotionally well, and that they feel a sense of belonging even in virtual spaces. It's about recognising that while work is omnipresent, so are the challenges associated with it.

Another important facet of this omnichannel leadership model is inclusivity. With geographical constraints minimised, organisations have the potential to tap into a global talent pool. Leaders are now at the forefront of fostering a culture of diversity and inclusion, bringing together individuals from varied backgrounds, cultures and perspectives. The richness of these diverse teams can only be harnessed if leaders are trained to navigate the nuances of cross-cultural communication, and to understand, appreciate and celebrate differences.

The interplay between the future of work and leadership is profound. As we stand at the cusp of this transformative era, it's pivotal to recognise that leadership is the anchor on which the balance of organisational success and employee wellbeing is stabilised. The journey from in-person to omnichannel is not just about new tools or strategies; it's about a renewed vision of leadership, one that is holistic, humane, and heralds the dawn of a new age in the world of work.

Embracing virtual proximity:
leadership without physical boundaries

The challenge is not merely to find ways to replicate the old ways of doing things in a new setting, but to invent entirely new ways of engaging, collaborating and creating meaning. Embracing virtual proximity and leading without physical boundaries is a concept that may be surprising and inspiring in its innovative approach to leadership.

One of the profound transformations brought about by the rise of remote work is the rendering of physical distance as obsolete in human connection. Previously, proximity and presence in the same room were seen as prerequisites for building trust, rapport and cama-raderie. Direct eye contact, handshakes, and the subtle nuances of in-person communication were viewed as irreplaceable. However, the digital era, with its array of advanced communication tools and platforms, has brought us to the threshold of a revolutionary way to connect. Virtual meetings, digital collaborations and real-time video calls allow for immediate and intimate connections, often bridging vast geographical divides. In many instances, this mode of interaction can be even more powerful than traditional face-to-face interaction, as it emphasises focused communication, shared digital experiences, and the ability to connect with individuals from diverse locations and cultures simultaneously. The evolution of technology has, in essence, expanded our ability to form meaningful connections without the barriers of physical distance.

At the heart of this new model is the psychology of virtual presence. It's not just about seeing someone's face on a screen or hearing their voice over a headset. It's about the intentional act of creating space where minds and hearts meet. It's recognising that although distance may separate bodies, nothing needs to separate intention, focus and the ability to understand and support one another. This is not just a functional shift in the way we conduct meetings or manage projects; it's a reimagining of how we connect as human beings.

Consider the challenge of building trust in a virtual environment. The traditional tools—handshakes, eye contact, shared lunches—aren't available. Yet, leaders across the globe are discovering that trust can be not only maintained, but deepened through virtual interactions. They're finding ways to share, listen and empathise that transcend geography. These methods include setting clear communication norms, celebrating team achievements virtually, and having regular check-ins that focus on wellbeing rather than just work.

The very act of adapting to virtual media is an exercise in building trust, as it communicates a sense of flexibility and willingness to evolve. For example, utilising unique virtual tools like collaborative whiteboards in real-time can enhance team brainstorming and creativity. Virtual reality meetings, where participants feel as though they are sitting next to one another, add a layer of immersion that physical meetings can't replicate.

Leaders are also leveraging synchronous communication methods, such as video messages that team members can view in their own time, allowing for more thoughtful responses and deeper reflection. The adaptability required in adjusting one's communication style to the preferences and needs of remote team members also demonstrates a higher level of empathy and consideration. This transcending of traditional relationship-building is not just an adaptation to current circumstances, but represents a paradigm shift. It signifies that we are moving towards a world where virtual interactions become an integral part of how we establish and nurture connections, even with those who were previously inaccessible due to geographical barriers or technological limitations.

Embracing virtual proximity is not a set of tactics; it's a mindset, a philosophy. It's about recognising that even as the world changes, the fundamental need for connection, trust, innovation and ethical leadership remains.

The human-centric digital ecosystem: empathy, culture and wellbeing in remote leadership

The world of remote leadership is more than a technological evolution; it's a profound shift in understanding human interaction, community and empathy. Today's leaders find themselves not just managing projects and deadlines, but forging connections and nurturing wellbeing across digital platforms. This requires reimagining leadership as more than just a series of tasks and seeing it as a human-centric digital ecosystem where empathy and connection evolve from being mere goals to become the very fabric of organisational culture.

In this new landscape, digital rituals become a fundamental pillar, not merely as ceremonial practices, but as transformative vehicles to shape, cultivate and reinforce the shared values and connections within a virtual team. This might manifest as weekly team sync-ups via video calls, spontaneous 'virtual coffee chats' for casual conversations, or structured brainstorming sessions using collaborative tools. Additionally, teams often adopt systematic routines like designated 'focus hours' or specific collaboration sessions, emphasising both productivity and camaraderie. These rituals and routines strike a balance between nurturing team relationships and ensuring that the primary goal—effective collaboration in a digital workspace—is met seamlessly.

In organisational dynamics, a ritual can be understood as a repeated pattern of behaviour or a set of activities that hold symbolic meaning for a group or community. Unlike formal processes, which are typically documented and strictly followed, rituals often operate in the background as unwritten ground-rules or norms. They might include starting each meeting with a personal check-in, holding monthly virtual team-building activities, or even sharing daily gratitude moments in chat channels.

Integrating empathy, building community, maintaining work-life balance and redefining connection in the virtual age aren't merely concepts to ponder, but living realities shaped and reinforced through these rituals. They are tangible practices that turn ideas into action, values into lived experiences, and individuals into a cohesive, thriving community.

The human-centric digital ecosystem, with rituals at its core, represents a powerful legacy in the making. It's about recognising that remote leadership isn't about managing people across screens but connecting hearts and minds despite them. It's about nurturing a culture where empathy is encoded into every interaction, where wellbeing is not just a goal but a defining feature, where success is not just about output but about human flourishing, creativity and shared purpose.

Bridging the digital divide: humanity in the virtual workspace

The concept of a 'human-centric digital ecosystem' may indeed sound abstract at first, particularly when we consider the inherently impersonal nature of technology. However, this ecosystem is precisely what counters the impersonality of the digital realm. When we speak of a human-centric approach in remote leadership, we are referring to a leadership style that goes beyond mere transactional interactions and delves deeply into creating genuine human connections, even in a space dominated by pixels and data.

Let's take a moment to unpack this: the traditional work environment was a tangible, physical space where interactions, both formal and informal, happened spontaneously. Colleagues could read body language, hear voice intonations and sense emotions, thus fostering an environment of mutual understanding and shared experiences. The shift to remote work disrupted this dynamic, and suddenly leaders found themselves managing individuals separated by screens, devoid of these in-person cues. Yet humans, by nature, are social creatures, yearning for connection and understanding, regardless of the medium.

This is where the essence of the human-centric digital ecosystem comes into play. In such an ecosystem, technology serves as an enabler, not a barrier. It becomes a tool to foster and facilitate those same genuine interactions we had in physical spaces. Leaders, therefore, are not just overseeing tasks, but are actively ensuring that team members, despite being physically apart, feel emotionally and psychologically connected. They strive to maintain an environment where every individual feels valued, heard and understood, replicating the camaraderie of a traditional office in a virtual space.

Let's address the question, 'How is the human factor so prominent in remote working?' It is prominent precisely because it is challenging. The ease of in-person interaction is absent, making it all the more crucial to intentionally incorporate human elements into the digital workspace. The rituals and practices outlined earlier are not just routines; they are conscious strategies to ensure that the 'human factor' remains at the forefront, reminding everyone involved that behind every email, chat or video call is a real person with emotions, aspirations and a need for connection. The true success of remote leadership lies in its ability to seamlessly blend technology with humanity, ensuring that while we may work in a digital realm, the human spirit remains undiminished and ever-present.

Redefining value creation in the remote era

The advent of remote work has not only altered the way we conduct our daily professional activities but has called into question the very essence of what work means. For centuries, the concept of work was tethered to a location—a place where tasks were performed, value was created and professional identities were shaped. In this new era, the transformation is profound: work has evolved from being a place where you go, to something you do. This shift calls for deep exploration, and it holds the potential to redefine not just the mechanics of work, but the core of value creation itself.

This evolution is far from trivial; it reaches to the heart of our understanding of productivity, collaboration and professional fulfilment. It's not just about technological tools that allow us to work from different locations, but a fundamental rethinking of how value is created, how talent is nurtured and how work integrates into our broader lives. Value is now being created through diverse teams brainstorming in virtual war rooms: researchers sharing insights on cloud platforms in real-time, and cross-functional teams collaboratively solving complex problems using shared digital tools. It's about employees tapping into global

knowledge pools, and companies harnessing special-
ised skills from any corner of the world. This paradigm
shift means that value is no longer confined to physical
office spaces, but is generated wherever talent meets
opportunity, innovation and collaboration.

For leaders, this shift demands boldness. It requires
letting go of the entrenched beliefs, biases and narratives that have defined work for generations. Traditional notions that tie productivity to presence, value
to visibility, or innovation to a physical location must
be challenged and reassessed. In cases where physical
presence isn't a necessity, unlike a chef in a kitchen
or a surgeon in an operating room, the real question
becomes: how do we create value? It's not about where
someone works, but about how they work, how they
innovate, how they contribute to the broader mission.

In the remote paradigm, capturing value creation
may involve digital feedback mechanisms, analysis
of virtual collaboration outcomes, and tracking the
speed of project deliveries irrespective of time zones.
Measuring it could integrate data analytics tools that
gauge online engagement and effectiveness, sentiment analysis from virtual meetings, or even the
adaptability rate of teams in shifting timeframes. Innovative methods might entail AI-driven insights into
workflow efficiencies, real-time dashboards capturing
remote team synergies, or quantifying the innovation
birthed from diverse, global team interactions. This
era challenges us to redefine and capture value beyond
traditional confines, leveraging technology and new

metrics to understand the profound effects of remote collaboration.

One prominent figure who stands out for her innovative approach in a traditionally conservative industry is Mary Barra, CEO of General Motors (GM). Under her leadership, GM took a bold step in early 2020 to introduce 'Work Appropriately', a flexible work initiative breaking the century-old paradigm of in-office presence in the automotive industry. Barra's vision went beyond the reactive measures of the pandemic, by aiming to institutionalise flexibility in where and how employees work as a permanent fixture of GM's culture. This policy not only acknowledged the changing landscape of work, but also the diverse needs of their workforce. By trusting employees to accomplish their tasks without micromanagement, Barra's initiative reflected a commitment to measuring performance by output, rather than hours at the desk, thus contributing to a more dynamic, inclusive and productive work environment.

The liberation from location-centric thinking opens the door to a world of possibilities where the focus shifts from location to contribution, from hours logged to impact made, from office dynamics to human connection. It allows leaders to tap into talent pools without geographical boundaries, to foster a culture that values output over input, and to create work environments that are tailored to individual needs and global opportunities.

Sustainable remote leadership recognises that work's true power lies in freeing up mental space and time, allowing individuals to invest in family, community, personal development and philanthropy. By nurturing this aspect, leaders not only drive organisational success but contribute to shaping a world where work becomes a catalyst for personal fulfilment and broader societal impact.

Leveraging remote work is not just about achieving business goals, but empowering team members to live richer lives. It enhances work-life harmony, enriching lives beyond professional achievements. It fosters an environment where team members can pursue philanthropy, community engagement and family connection. It emphasises mental wellbeing and capacity, going beyond traditional work metrics to nurture holistic growth.

The OMNI LEADER Maturity Model

Chapter 7 brings to light another vital aspect of modern leadership—balancing remote and in-office leadership skills. As work environments become increasingly diverse and flexible, leaders who can effectively lead in both remote and traditional office settings are uniquely equipped to inspire their teams and drive productivity. This chapter presents the Omni Leader Maturity Model, offering a nuanced understanding of the interplay between remote and in-office leadership skills. Such a model plays an instrumental role in developing leaders who are adaptable, inclusive and resilient.

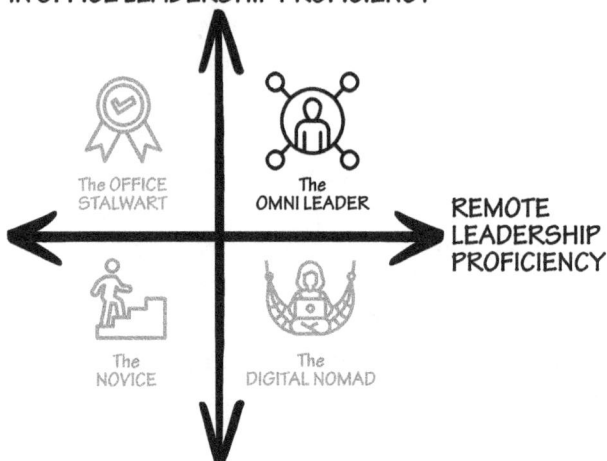

The OMNI LEADER

IN OFFICE LEADERSHIP PROFICIENCY

The OFFICE
STALWART

The
OMNI LEADER

REMOTE
LEADERSHIP
PROFICIENCY

The
NOVICE

The
DIGITAL NOMAD

Let's examine each quadrant in detail to discover where you are on the twin axes of in-office leadership and remote leadership skills.

The Novice: Leaders in this quadrant are at the beginner's stage, characterised by low proficiency in both remote and in-office leadership skills. Their struggle to manage and inspire teams effectively, regardless of the work setting, may lead to poor team dynamics, reduced productivity and decreased employee satisfaction. To address these shortcomings, these leaders need to START learning about effective leadership strategies that apply to both omni and in-office environments. They should STOP assuming that one-size-fits-all leadership approaches work and start recognising the unique demands of different work environments.

The Office Stalwart: Leaders in this quadrant are proficient in traditional in-office leadership but are novices in remote leadership. While they successfully lead their teams in face-to-face settings, their effectiveness diminishes in virtual settings, which may lead to disconnection and diminished performance in remote teams. To grow, they need to START embracing the technology and communication techniques essential for remote work, STOP relying solely on their traditional in-office leadership skills, and STOP resisting the shift to remote work, which is rapidly becoming a norm in today's world.

The Digital Nomad: This quadrant houses leaders who have a high level of competence in remote leadership but fall short in in-office leadership skills. Although adept at managing and inspiring remote teams, they struggle to replicate this success in traditional office settings, leading to reduced efficiency and potential conflicts. To improve, these leaders should START focusing on developing their in-office leadership skills (including face-to-face communication) and managing dynamics in a physical team environment. They need to STOP relying only on their remote leadership skills and acknowledge the importance of traditional in-office leadership.

The Omni Leader: Leaders in this quadrant epitomise the balance between high remote and in-office leadership skills. They excel at leading teams irrespective of the work environment, making them highly adaptable and effective in managing change. These leaders don't need to stop anything, given their holistic blend of the two leadership attributes focused on in this quadrant. However, they should START sharing their strategies and insights with others, fostering a culture that values adaptability and flexibility in leadership.

Omni leadership in action

Diving into the world of remote work and powering your organisation with digital advancements goes beyond just having the newest tech or the fastest internet connection. These tools are designed to cultivate a fresh, forward-thinking work style that prioritises people and delivers value that transcends traditional office boundaries. Here are five ways to kick start your journey into the future.

Design and implement a people-first organisational culture to enhance virtual engagement: Leaders must create a people-first organisational culture by developing a remote working policy that focuses on flexibility, inclusivity and productivity. By providing access to necessary digital tools, establishing guidelines for virtual collaboration and promoting wellbeing, leaders foster a seamless transition to remote work and enhance overall organisational resilience.

Develop adaptive communication strategies tailored to remote teams: Leaders must craft a communication strategy that is specifically tailored to remote work, taking into consideration different time zones, virtual meeting etiquette and asynchronous communication. By leveraging technology for clear and consistent communication, ensuring team members are heard, and fostering a sense of community, leaders can maintain robust relationships in a virtual environment.

Promote digital upskilling and continuous learning for innovation and problem solving: Leaders must foster a culture of continuous digital learning by implementing regular training sessions, workshops and self-paced online courses. Emphasising the application of digital tools and platforms, these initiatives promote innovation and problem solving, preparing teams to effectively navigate the disruptive digital landscape.

Establish remote trust-building mechanisms to enhance autonomy and foster inclusivity: Trust-building in remote teams requires a strategic approach that respects autonomy and promotes inclusivity. Leaders must set clear expectations, offer regular feedback, and encourage virtual social interactions. For instance, leaders might establish weekly check-ins to review tasks, utilise platforms for instant feedback on project updates, and arrange monthly virtual team-building events or casual virtual coffee breaks.

Integrate the Omni Leadership Maturity Model to balance remote and in-office leadership skills: The Omni Leadership Maturity Model helps leaders navigate the balance between remote and traditional office leadership skills. Leaders can identify where they fall within the model's four quadrants (Novice, Office Stalwart, Digital Nomad, Omni Leader) and implement specific actions to achieve adaptability and resilience. For example, Novice Leaders can seek targeted training to enhance both remote and in-office capabilities, while Omni Leaders can mentor others in finding the equilibrium between remote and physical leadership.

Mastering remote leadership is a critical competency in this disruptive era, allowing us to harness the potential of our digital age. However, to lead effectively, our perspectives need to transcend our immediate environments. This transitions us to the next chapter, where we explore global disruption leadership and the critical skills it necessitates. We'll uncover how a global mindset enhances our ability to adapt and lead amid widespread disruptions.

CHAPTER INSIGHTS

- Digital competency, crucial for effective remote leadership, covers the understanding and application of digital tools and communication platforms, promoting a continuous learning environment.

- These digital tools, when used efficiently, not only aid in seamless interaction, but also open avenues for innovation and problem solving.

- Digital competency also helps leaders navigate digital challenges, including privacy concerns, information overload and cyber threats, thereby creating a secure and healthy digital culture.

- A leader's digital proficiency sets a learning benchmark for the team, fostering an adaptive digital environment.

- Leaders need to consciously create a sense of community, shared purpose and trust in remote teams, enhancing productivity and engagement.

- Trust-building in remote teams involves respecting team members' autonomy and personal boundaries while fostering an environment of inclusivity.

- Effective communication in a remote context requires building robust relationships, ensuring every team member is heard, and promoting team spirit.

- Creating an inclusive and collaborative culture in remote settings involves valuing team members' contributions, fostering shared understanding, and leveraging technology for collaborative spaces.

8

GLOBAL DISRUPTION LEADERSHIP—SKILLS FOR THE FUTURE

The illiterate of the 21st century will not
be those who cannot read and write, but those
who cannot learn, unlearn, and relearn.

ALVIN TOFFLER

OLLOWING OUR discussion on remote leadership, we broaden our perspective in Chapter 8. This chapter highlights the importance of a global perspective in disruptive leadership, helping leaders cultivate cultural intelligence to lead across borders. We'll delve into the importance of cultivating a global perspective as leaders, comprehend the profound impact of global trends on our strategies and decisions, underscore the essence of cultural intelligence in leading amidst diverse and disruptive scenarios and, finally, embrace the 'think globally, act locally' mantra as a pivotal strategy for impactful leadership in an interconnected world.

The setting sun cast a warm glow over the back verandah, a place of sanctuary I held dear throughout my life. This was more than just a porch; it was the backdrop to countless childhood memories and profound conversations. And as the world outside raced into modernity, this spot remained an inviting cocoon of the past, where time seemed to stand still.

I settled into the familiar wooden chair beside my grandfather, who was an embodiment of resilience and gentleness, and whose entire professional life was anchored to a single job: selling furniture in the Myer department store in Adelaide, the capital of South Australia. He worked there at a time when Adelaide, though a state capital, was still a small, quaint town where my grandfather passed cows on his way to work. Such was the stark contrast between his life's experiences and mine.

'Why are you always overseas?' he asked, a hint of wonder in his voice. In his time, travel was a luxury, not the routine it had become for me. His passport, I recall, bore the marks of a few trips—New Zealand, perhaps Fiji—memories now faded with time. My frequent travels and regular shifts between companies puzzled him. 'Is it common these days to change roles so frequently?' he enquired, trying to grasp the dynamics of my professional world.

It was a puzzle for him. How did the world evolve from his linear, stable career trajectory to my multifaceted professional journey? How did his grandson, whom he remembered playing in this very yard, switch from accounting to project management to overseeing expansive operations, and then ascending to executive management in what seemed like the blink of an eye?

That evening, as crickets serenaded our conversation, I dived into the realm of modern-day commerce. I described how the boundaries between countries had dissolved and given birth to intertwined supply chains, and how a single click could summon products from continents away. How technology, especially the internet, was no longer just a tool, but a bridge connecting billions.

He listened intently, each word painting for him a picture of a world beyond his imagination. Yet, amidst these tales of global interconnection and rapid change, a single thread remained constant: the essence of leadership. Even in a world of unceasing disruption, the core values, the very skills that rendered one a successful leader, remained immutable. They were the bridge between his era and mine, between selling furniture in Adelaide and orchestrating global supply chains.

As darkness encroached and our conversation ebbed, a profound realisation settled. While the contexts of our careers were galaxies apart, the foundational lessons were intertwined. Both of us, in our unique eras, were navigating our own versions of global disruptions, wielding the timeless tools of leadership.

Not long after that evening, my grandfather passed away. It wasn't until some years later, with the unfolding of my daughter Abbey's story, that I found myself revisiting that conversation. The world had evolved even further, and global challenges had amplified. Abbey, ever since she was a young girl, showed an entrepreneurial spirit. In her late teens, she founded Ohana & Co., a venture that sourced products from around the world, and sold them into global markets.

I marvelled at how, at such a young age, Abbey's global perspective was far deeper than mine ever was. While I was amazed at the merging of borders, she was envisioning a venture that transcended them. Ohana & Co., although in its infancy, was a testament to the boundless spirit of the new generation. Abbey was not only embracing, but leading the change in a world more connected, more dynamic, and more challenging than the one I had known. It made me reflect on the circle of life—from my grandfather's tales to my stories and now to Abbey's journey—each of us building on the legacies of the past while forging our own paths in the expansive tapestry of time.

A global view

Reflect on this: you're focused on the specific details of your immediate environment, concentrating only on the aspects directly in front of you. Or, you could decide to broaden your viewpoint, taking in a larger context that encapsulates the interaction of various elements and dynamics.

Similarly, leadership can adopt one of two perspectives. You can have a narrow, localised viewpoint, which concentrates solely on the factors immediately impacting your domain. Or you can adopt a comprehensive view, understanding and appreciating the broader, interrelated scope of business, society and the world.

Now, why is this perspective critical for disruptive leadership? We live in an interconnected and interdependent world, thanks to advancements in technology, communication and transportation. An economic tremor in one part of the world can create ripple effects globally. An innovation in a remote corner of the globe can disrupt industries worldwide. The world isn't just a collection of independent entities but a complex, dynamic web of interactions and relationships.

The disruptive leaders of tomorrow are not those who merely manage their local operations efficiently. They are those who appreciate the interconnected nature of our world, who understand how global trends and forces can impact their industry, their organisation and their leadership. They are those who can look beyond their immediate environment and consider the broader, global context in their decisions and actions.

Disruptive trends, be they technological, socio-economic or environmental, don't respect geographical boundaries. As a leader, your ability to anticipate, respond to, and perhaps even shape these global disruptions will largely determine your effectiveness.

A global perspective also equips leaders with a broader and more diverse outlook. It invites us to appreciate diversity, not just in terms of nationality or ethnicity, but also in terms of thoughts, ideas and approaches.

In addition, the global perspective goes hand in hand with a sense of global responsibility. Today's challenges, be they climate change, economic inequality or societal polarisation, are global in nature. They require solutions that transcend local interests and national boundaries. Disruptive leaders with a global perspective are those who realise their role and responsibility in addressing these global challenges, who appreciate that modern leadership is as much about creating value for the world as it is about creating value for the organisation.

The interconnectedness of our world is not a mere fad; it is the defining framework of our times. With every advancement in technology and communication, the barriers that once separated markets and ideologies are rapidly eroding. For leaders, this dynamic environment poses a twofold challenge: first, to understand the vast connectivity of global systems and secondly, to position oneself within this matrix in a way that is both innovative and impactful.

The prowess of a disruptive leader does not merely rest on their capability to introduce breakthrough innovations, but on their ability to foresee the global impacts of those innovations. In an era where a start-up in Nairobi can redefine banking for someone in New York, or where a technological breakthrough in Stockholm can transform agricultural practices in Santiago, the leader's vision must transcend local triumphs. To truly disrupt, to genuinely reshape industries and craft legacies, leaders must conceptualise their strategies not as localised solutions, but as global game changers.

Understanding and leveraging global trends

It is critical for disruptive leaders to develop a robust understanding of global trends. Not merely as an academic exercise, but as a compass guiding the strategy, vision and decisions they make. The need for leaders to grasp and leverage global trends comes down to a simple yet profound concept: change. As leaders, we often focus on the change we can effect within our organisations, but equally important is the change happening outside our immediate sphere.

Global trends, whether they are economic, social, technological or environmental, are powerful forces of change that shape industries and markets. They create new opportunities, but also present challenges. They redefine customer expectations, redraw competitive landscapes and disrupt business models. For disruptive leaders, these trends aren't just phenomena to observe but dynamics to leverage.

Let's say you lead a tech start-up. You've developed an innovative solution, and you're confident about its potential. But are you aware of the global trends in technology adoption, data privacy regulations, or cyber threats? Or suppose you're steering an NGO.

Are you attuned to trends in social activism, donor behaviour or impact measurement?

Global trends have real, tangible impacts on your organisation and your role as a leader. Understanding these trends allows you to align your vision, strategy and actions with the larger global context. It equips you to anticipate challenges, seize opportunities and stay ahead of the curve.

Consider, for instance, the trend towards sustainability and climate consciousness. This global shift is transforming industries and consumer behaviour. As a disruptive leader, understanding this trend isn't just about being 'in the know'; it's about questioning how this trend influences your organisation, your stakeholders and your leadership approach.

Recognising global trends isn't merely about spotting the next significant wave to ride; it's about synthesising a spectrum of dynamic forces into a coherent strategy, creating a formidable competitive advantage. In the present landscape, where the boundary between local and global is becoming increasingly blurred, understanding these trends can be the determining factor between leading the market or playing catch-up.

Take marketing, for instance. A deep understanding of global trends is imperative for creating resonant messages. What resonates in one part of the world might entirely miss the mark in another. Disruptive leaders harness insights from these global trends to craft campaigns that transcend borders, establishing brand universality while acknowledging local nuances. Similarly, in supply chain management, recognising shifts in manufacturing hubs, workforce dynamics, or even geopolitical stability can make the difference in ensuring timely delivery and optimising costs.

Innovation isn't just about inventing something new; it's also about understanding where the world is heading and what problems will emerge. By leveraging global trends, leaders can anticipate needs and preferences, positioning their organisations at the forefront of delivering solutions. These trends are goldmines of insights, from evolving consumer tastes to the rise of emerging economies, which, when leveraged correctly, offer untapped opportunities.

The business models of yesterday were often insular, focused on a specific market or region. Today's disruptive leaders, equipped with an understanding of global trends, create models that are malleable, scalable and can quickly pivot based on global shifts. They understand that a trend starting in an emerging economy today could redefine industry standards tomorrow.

Grasping global trends isn't a mere exercise in intellectual curiosity; it's an imperative for survival and success in today's business landscape. Whether its adjusting supply chains based on emerging economies, recalibrating marketing strategies to new consumer tastes, or reshaping business models in light of technological advancements, the decisions leaders make today will directly affect their organisation's standing tomorrow. Leaders must move from simply observing trends to actively harnessing them, ensuring their strategies are not just reactive, but proactive. It's not enough to understand the game: leaders must continually be several moves ahead.

Cultivating cultural intelligence to lead across borders and amid global disruptions

Cultural intelligence is not just about acknowledging that cultural differences exist, but understanding the values, beliefs and behaviours that underpin these differences. It's about being able to adapt your thinking and behaviour to navigate various cultural contexts effectively.

Remember, disruption is not confined to your local market or industry. It can emerge from any corner of the world. Your competitor is no longer just the company across the street, but could be an innovative start-up on the other side of the globe. In such a scenario, cultural intelligence becomes an essential competency. It can enable you to anticipate and understand global disruptions, giving you a competitive edge.

The ways people perceive and react to disruptions can vary dramatically across different cultures. As a leader, you're not just managing disruption, but you're also dealing with the varied cultural reactions to it. A strategy that works in one cultural context may completely fail in another. Your ability to lead effectively through disruption in a global, diverse setting will largely depend on your cultural intelligence.

When you're culturally intelligent, you're better equipped to leverage the diversity of your team or organisation. You can facilitate the sharing and integration of diverse ideas, thereby fostering innovation.

You can also help your team or organisation develop a global mindset, a critical asset in the era of disruption.

Cultural intelligence is closely tied to trust, a key element of leadership. When you demonstrate cultural intelligence, you show respect and appreciation for other cultures. This can foster trust and collaboration in your diverse team or organisation, making it more resilient in the face of disruption.

In an era where divisions seem to grow deeper and misunderstandings can escalate into conflicts, cultural intelligence serves as an antidote to the turmoil. At its core, it is an embodiment of empathy, a beacon that illuminates the shared human experience beneath layers of difference. A disruptive leader with profound cultural intelligence doesn't just see these differences; they actively seek the universal threads that weave humanity together.

The mastery of cultural intelligence creates bridges over chasms of miscommunication. Where there could be discord, it finds harmony; where there's potential for conflict, it discovers collaboration. It's a tool not just for market expansion or strategic leverage, but for fostering global unity. When a leader leans into this understanding, they're not just driving their organisation forward; they're championing a movement of understanding and cohesion in a divided world.

Take the story of Howard Schultz and his leadership of Starbucks. When Schultz first led the company to expand internationally, he insisted that Starbucks' stores respect and reflect local customs and preferences. Recognising the cultural importance of meticulous customer service in Japan, for instance, he ensured that Starbucks' operations there adhered to these standards. Conversely, in Italy, where coffee culture is deeply ingrained and espresso is a quick, stand-up affair, Starbucks delayed its entry until it could create a format that was both respectful to Italian coffee tradition and innovative enough to appeal to local tastes. Schultz's cultural intelligence fostered an environment where local traditions were celebrated within Starbucks' global brand, allowing the company to establish a foothold in markets that were initially sceptical of an American coffee chain. His understanding that the essence of hospitality varies greatly across cultures, and his willingness to adapt and integrate these nuances into Starbucks' operations, allowed the company to be globally unified in brand yet locally distinctive in experience.

Harnessing cultural intelligence reframes the narrative. Instead of viewing diversity as a series of challenges to overcome, it's seen as a spectrum of opportunities. Differences cease to be threats and transform into enriching insights, leading to solutions that resonate on a universal scale. This mindset is not naive idealism; it's strategic optimism. For in recognising our shared aspirations, hopes and dreams, we unearth avenues for progress that are both impactful and enduring.

'Thinking globally, acting locally' — a strategy for leading in a globally disrupted world

At its core, thinking globally involves recognising, understanding and appreciating the interconnectedness of the world. It means appreciating diversity, being aware of global trends and developments, and understanding their potential implications. It's about fostering a broad and inclusive perspective, a mindset that extends beyond one's immediate environment to encompass a global stage.

On the flip side, acting locally means implementing this global awareness into concrete actions within your immediate sphere of influence. Consider a multinational corporation launching a product in a new market; while the overarching brand message might be consistent globally, the marketing strategy must resonate with the local culture, preferences and sensibilities. Or think of a tech giant introducing an app feature that addresses a global concern, but with user interfaces tailored to the language and usage patterns of each region. It's about making decisions that not only make sense in the local context, but also align with the larger global picture. Acting locally bridges the gap between broad global understanding and practical local application.

Primarily, it's about leveraging the best of both worlds to drive impactful change and innovation.

Disruption isn't limited by geographical boundaries. It's a global phenomenon that affects us all. As leaders, understanding this global context enables us to identify opportunities and threats that may not be immediately visible in our local environment. It helps us prepare for and respond to global trends and disruptions effectively.

Simultaneously, our local actions, decisions and strategies need to reflect this global understanding.

This is where acting locally comes into play. It's about tailoring our leadership approach to meet the unique needs and characteristics of our local environment while keeping the global picture in mind.

The 'thinking globally, acting locally' strategy underscores a key characteristic of successful disruptive leadership: adaptability. It's about adapting global insights to local realities. This doesn't mean merely copying what works in one context and applying it to another. Instead, it's about integrating global perspectives into a nuanced understanding of the local environment to create unique, innovative solutions.

This 'global' interplay enhances the relevance and impact of our leadership. By thinking globally, we remain connected to the larger narrative, which in turn helps us maintain relevance in our rapidly evolving world. By acting locally, we ensure that our actions have tangible impact, resonating with the specific needs, aspirations and realities of those we lead.

For many, 'thinking globally' is an exercise in economics, market trends and geopolitical strategies. However, at its most profound level, it is a journey into the heart of humanity itself. Every market trend, every economic ripple, is ultimately a reflection of collective human behaviour, driven by our shared hopes, fears, dreams and aspirations. To truly think globally is to understand these shared emotional currents that course through societies worldwide, shaping patterns of consumption, trade and innovation. It's about recognising that, amid our diversity, there are universal human truths that bind us all. By tapping into these truths, leaders can predict global shifts with uncanny accuracy, staying ahead of the curve.

Conversely, 'acting locally' goes beyond merely adapting global strategies to a regional or community context. It's about embracing the profound responsibility leaders have towards the immediate environments and communities within which they operate. This means understanding that every corporate action has social, environmental and economic repercussions. It's about fostering relationships, not just transactions. By cultivating genuine relationships based on mutual respect and understanding, businesses can thrive in symbiosis with their local communities, creating shared value that is both sustainable and expansive.

Moreover, when we dive deeply into 'acting locally', it demands of leaders an innate sensitivity to the cultural, environmental and socio-economic ecosystems with which they engage. It's about acknowledging the rich histories, values and aspirations that make each community unique. It's not about imposing a one-size-fits-all global strategy but co-creating strategies with local stakeholders, ensuring not just buy-in but shared ownership.

In essence, to lead in this globally disrupted world, one must embrace a paradox. Leaders must possess the ability to zoom out, capturing the vast panorama of global dynamics, and simultaneously zoom in, focusing on the intricate details of local ecosystems. It's this dual perspective that will define the next frontier of leadership, where success is measured, not just in quarterly returns, but in the lasting, positive impact leaders create in every community they touch.

The GLOBAL LEADER Maturity Model

Chapter 8 introduces another key dimension of modern leadership—the equilibrium between global awareness and local responsiveness. In today's interconnected world, leaders who can understand global trends while responding effectively to local contexts are in a unique position to inspire their teams and drive growth. This chapter presents the Global Leader Maturity Model, offering a detailed understanding of how global awareness and local responsiveness interplay. This model plays a critical role in shaping leaders who are inclusive, adaptable and forward-thinking.

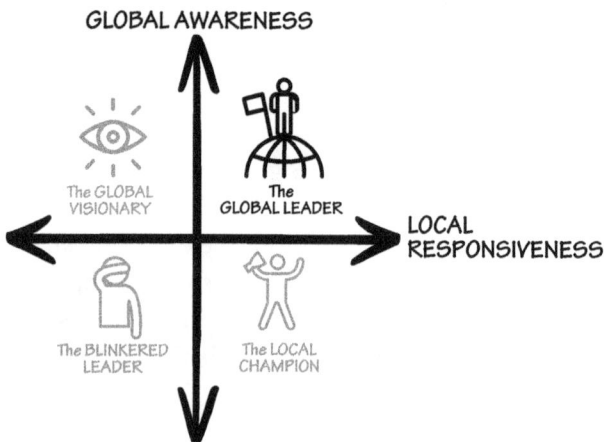

The GLOBAL LEADER

GLOBAL AWARENESS

The GLOBAL VISIONARY

The GLOBAL LEADER

LOCAL RESPONSIVENESS

The BLINKERED LEADER

The LOCAL CHAMPION

How broad is your perspective? Do you look far enough beyond your immediate circumstances? If you do, do you retain awareness of what is in front of you? Let's find out by looking at each of the four quadrants in the model.

The Blinkered Leader: Leaders in this quadrant display low global awareness and low local responsiveness. They may demonstrate a limited understanding of the world beyond their immediate environment and might struggle to respond effectively to local needs. This narrow focus can lead to missed opportunities, lower team engagement, and a lack of adaptability in the face of change. To progress, these leaders need to START investing time in understanding both the global trends and local nuances that impact their work. They should STOP focusing solely on their immediate surroundings and widen their perspective to include a more global outlook.

The Global Visionary: Leaders in this quadrant demonstrate high global awareness but low local responsiveness. They keep up with global trends and understand their broader industry context, but may fail to tailor their approach to the unique needs of their local teams or markets. This disconnection could lead to a lack of engagement or even resistance from local teams. These leaders need to START recognising and responding to local needs, cultures and market dynamics. They should STOP implementing global strategies without considering local needs and implications.

The Local Champion: Leaders in this quadrant excel in local responsiveness but lack a strong global perspective. They are highly attuned to local needs and contexts but may overlook broader trends and shifts in the global arena. This limited perspective may hinder their ability to anticipate changes and adapt effectively. To improve, these leaders need to START broadening their outlook to include global trends and changes. They should STOP operating within a local bubble and begin incorporating global insights into their strategy.

The Global Leader: Leaders in this quadrant exhibit both high global awareness and high local responsiveness. They possess a keen understanding of global trends and are also highly responsive to local needs and dynamics. Their leadership is characterised by a thoughtful balance of global strategies and local adaptations, leading to a more inclusive, adaptable and effective leadership style. These leaders should START sharing their approach with others to inspire a culture that values both global perspectives and local nuances.

Global leadership in action
Put this book down for a moment and look around you. How far do you see? Not as far as you need to. Now look down again and read on for five ways to begin broadening your perspective without losing sight of what is in front of your nose.

Cultivate a global mindset to enhance cultural intelligence and foster inclusive leadership: Leaders must consciously cultivate a global mindset within their organisation. This involves educating teams about different cultural contexts, promoting the exchange of diverse viewpoints, and leveraging global insights to drive local relevance. For instance, a company might implement a global immersion program, where employees spend time in various international offices, gaining firsthand experience of regional operations and customer behaviours. Alternatively, businesses might invest in cross-cultural training sessions, enhancing team members' ability to communicate effectively across borders and reduce misunderstandings.

Implement a 'think globally, act locally' strategy for adaptable and relevant leadership: Adopting a 'think globally, act locally' approach requires leaders to blend their awareness of global trends with locally relevant actions. By developing policies that encourage global learning while adapting to local needs, leaders foster a sense of adaptability, relevance and inclusivity, essential in managing both global and local dynamics. To discern these needs, ground level teams or designated liaisons should be assigned to engage directly with local communities, gathering insights through townhall meetings, focus groups or one on one interviews. Their findings, systematically documented, can be relayed through regular reports or digital platforms to the organisation's decision makers, ensuring strategies are based on firsthand understanding and genuine local feedback.

Leverage global trends to guide decisions, strategies and value creation: Leaders must embrace global trends to guide organisational decisions and strategies. By actively questioning the impact of these trends on their organisation and understanding how their actions can influence them, leaders can conduct scenario planning and impact assessments. These tools allow leaders to visualise potential outcomes and adjust strategies accordingly. With this foresight, leaders can leverage global trends to innovate, anticipate challenges and create value.

Promote continuous innovation by facilitating the sharing of diverse viewpoints: An enriched global perspective promotes innovation through the sharing of diverse viewpoints. Leaders must establish platforms (such as intranet forums, collaborative software tools, cross-functional workshops, global virtual town halls and international exchange programs for employees) for cross-border collaboration, encourage dialogue between various cultural backgrounds, and create an environment where different thoughts, ideas and approaches are embraced.

Integrate the Global Leader Maturity Model to balance global awareness and local responsiveness: The Global Leader Maturity Model helps leaders navigate the equilibrium between global understanding and local action. Leaders can identify where they fall within the model's four quadrants (Local Leader, Global Visionary, Local Champion, Global Leader) and implement specific actions to move towards a balanced perspective. For example, Local Leaders can invest in understanding global trends and local nuances, while Global Leaders should share their approach with others to inspire a culture that values both global perspectives and local nuances.

Global thinking is key to leading in an era characterised by global disruptions. However, the full spectrum of future leadership competencies remains incomplete without the infusion of intrapreneurship and entrepreneurship. The next chapter uncovers the critical roles these elements play in disruptive leadership and how these skills equip leaders to navigate and thrive amid disruption.

CHAPTER INSIGHTS

- A global perspective, crucial for disruptive leadership, takes account of the interconnected nature of the world and its implications for organisations, including the impact of global disruptions on local operations.

- This global outlook, enriched by cultural intelligence, allows leaders to appreciate diverse thoughts, ideas and approaches, vital for navigating and thriving in different cultural contexts.

- Global awareness extends beyond recognising trends; disruptive leaders must see their role in addressing global challenges and fostering a sense of global responsibility that transcends their organisation.

- This enriched perspective promotes innovation by facilitating the sharing of diverse viewpoints, positioning leaders to anticipate challenges and seize opportunities.

- Embracing global trends, leaders can guide decisions and strategies, questioning the impact of these trends on their organisation and how their actions could influence trends to create value.

- A vital aspect of this global perspective is the strategy of 'thinking globally, acting locally', which encourages leaders to blend their global awareness with locally relevant actions.

- This balance promotes adaptability and relevance, and fosters inclusivity and diversity, essential elements in disruptive leadership in a globally disrupted world.

- This combination of embracing global trends and fostering cultural intelligence equips leaders with the skills necessary to navigate complex global and local dynamics.

9

INTRAPRENEURSHIP AND ENTREPRENEURSHIP— POWERING DISRUPTIVE LEADERSHIP

My life didn't please me, so I created my life.

COCO CHANEL

IN THIS CHAPTER we will explore the importance of intrapreneurship and entrepreneurship in driving disruptive leadership. Drawing from our discussion on global disruption leadership, this chapter delves into key intrapreneurial and entrepreneurial skills essential for modern leaders. We'll explore how to foster an environment that encourages such thinking, and the relationship between intrapreneurship, entrepreneurship and disruptive leadership.

In the heart of Melbourne, amidst the burgeoning cityscape adorned with cranes and the shimmering facades of skyscrapers, I found myself in the office of the CEO of Australia's most innovative large-scale construction company. The firm, founded by his father, had been a modest venture, but under his leadership it had blossomed into an industry giant whose handiwork was defining the city's skyline. Skyscrapers that stood as beacons of progress were not just buildings; they were physical affirmations of a legacy that he had robustly expanded. It was here, surrounded by models of past and future projects, that he began to unfold his story—a narrative rich with ambition, innovation and an entrepreneurial spirit. This story wasn't just about scale and success; it was a testament to how he had taken the foundation his father had laid and elevated it into a towering example of Australian industry.

As he spoke, his eyes often wandered to the window, where the tangible results of his life's work stood as monolithic testaments to his vision. 'There's something satisfying about defining the skyline of this great city,' he mused, a subtle blend of pride and dreams colouring his tone.

The company's journey was marked by a relentless pursuit of excellence and an eagerness to embrace change. What began as a traditional construction firm evolved into a vertically integrated legend, which also boasted a pioneering spin-off business that created modular bathroom and kitchen pods. These high-quality, prefabricated units became instrumental in streamlining construction processes across the country, demonstrating the company's commitment to innovation and efficiency.

As I listened, he leaned in, his voice underscored by passion as he detailed the crux of his philosophy. 'To truly excel, every leader within our organisation must think and act like an entrepreneur—alert to opportunity, fervent in innovation, and unwavering in determination,' he declared. This culture of entrepreneurial leadership was not just rhetoric; it was the bedrock upon which the company stood, ensuring each project was not a mere task but a mission, imbued with the zeal and creativity of a personal venture.

Though my own experience with the company was rooted in the past, I had watched with vested interest as they ventured into new domains—most notably, data centres. During our conversation, he had shared, with animated gestures, his vision for these digital fortresses. Even after my departure, I followed their progress, watching as the leader's vision unfolded into reality, carried by the multitude of entrepreneurial spirits he had cultivated. They broke ground not just in Melbourne, but across Australia, setting the precedent for what could one day be a global digital infrastructure footprint.

While the data centres may not have transformed the skyline with towering peaks, they were etching a different kind of boundary, one delineated by the rapid streams of data crisscrossing beneath the surface. This new venture wasn't about scaling physical heights but about constructing the critical foundations of a connected, digital expanse that would stretch seamlessly from one end of Australia to the other, with the potential to span worldwide.

The leader leaned back, his gaze steady. 'We equip our leaders to be entrepreneurs because the future doesn't wait. It's crafted by those who dare to lead and dream to build the unprecedented,' he explained. His commitment to nurturing entrepreneurial leaders would be his enduring legacy, ensuring that the company's innovative spirit continued to blaze trails in the construction industry. It was no wonder that his enterprise was hailed as the most innovative in the country.

And so, as I stepped away from the towering glass of the office, the city's skyline stretched out before me—a canvas of ambition and dreams, with each structure a brushstroke of entrepreneurial spirit, each silhouette an illustration of innovation. The entrepreneurial leader had not only transformed the physical space of Melbourne, but also sowed the seeds for a digital landscape that was equally impressive and boundless—a legacy built on the foundation of developing leaders imbued with an entrepreneurial spirit.

The strategic role of intrapreneurship and entrepreneurship in future-ready leadership

Intrapreneurship and entrepreneurship, often hailed as the cornerstones of start-ups and innovators, emerge as indispensable instruments in this new age of leadership. They are no longer confined to the worlds of young enterprises or ambitious solo pioneers; they are reshaping the ethos of leadership itself.

Historically, organisations followed structured paths. Leaders took the helm, employees took directives, and the ship steered smoothly, often in predictable waters. However, the waters of the business world are no longer placid. The rapid pace of technological advancement, socio-political changes and globalisation have made the business ecosystem rocky. These unpredictable waves demand a new kind of leadership, one that is not only responsive but also proactive.

This is where the ethos of entrepreneurship comes into play. An entrepreneur is not just a business owner. They embody a mindset, a unique approach to challenges. Where others see obstacles, entrepreneurs identify opportunities. They don't merely react; they anticipate, innovate and lead the way. Now, transpose this mindset to an existing corporate structure, and you have intrapreneurship. These intrapreneurs, while operating within the confines of established organisations, think and act with the agility and innovation-centric mindset of an entrepreneur.

Even mature, established organisations stand to benefit profoundly from this approach. Incorporating entrepreneurial thinking, even in non-start-up environments, sparks proactive change. Leaders equipped with this mindset don't wait for disruption to knock on their doors. They are the disruptors, continually scanning the horizon for opportunities to innovate, improve and inspire.

Leadership, in the traditional sense, was about control, guidance and, often, maintaining the status quo. In contrast, the future-ready leadership model is dynamic. It's about fostering cultures where calculated risks are encouraged, where innovation is not just a department but an organisational-wide ethos, and where change is not feared but embraced.

Challenging conventional corporate structures with the intrapreneurial and entrepreneurial model

Traditional corporate structures, with their hierarchical models and rigid protocols, have stood the test of time. They have delivered consistency, stability and predictable results. However, as the global business landscape evolves at an unprecedented pace, the very tenets that once guaranteed stability now pose potential threats. These structures, often resistant to change and averse to risk, can unintentionally stifle innovation, agility and responsiveness—three imperatives in today's volatile market.

To understand the inherent challenges of these conventional structures, one must first grasp their foundational ethos. Historically, businesses were built on principles of control, predictability and risk mitigation. Layers of bureaucracy and stringent approval processes were implemented not to hinder progress, but to ensure that every move was measured and every risk accounted for. While effective in a more static environment, this approach becomes a liability when the external ecosystem demands rapid adaptation.

Enter the principles of entrepreneurship and intrapreneurship. At their core, these models thrive on adaptability, innovation and a proactive approach to challenges. When these principles are infused into existing corporate entities, they introduce a dynamism that directly contrasts with the limitations of traditional structures.

First, consider agility. An entrepreneurial mindset is agile by default. It seeks to quickly capitalise on opportunities and is willing to pivot when a chosen path proves less than optimal. By encouraging intrapreneurship within larger organisations, this agility can be assimilated. Instead of exhaustive review cycles and prolonged decision-making chains, empowered teams can make prompt decisions, ensuring the organisation remains in step with, or even ahead of, market fluctuations.

Next, we confront the matter of responsiveness. The digital age has condensed the feedback loop between businesses and their clientele. Customers' preferences, needs and grievances are relayed in real-time. Conventional structures, with their siloed departments and extended communication channels, often struggle to keep up. An intrapreneurial approach breaks down these barriers. It encourages cross-functional collaboration, ensuring that feedback is promptly acted upon, keeping the company attuned to its audience's pulse.

Conventional structures, in their quest for stability, often inadvertently discourage experimentation.

Traditional structures, with their rigid hierarchies, often suppress potential. Employees, no matter how visionary their ideas, are bound by layers of bureaucracy. The intrapreneurial model challenges this. It offers a more fluid organisational structure, where ideas aren't judged by the rank of the individual proposing them but by their merit. This democratisation of innovation ensures that visionary concepts aren't buried under paperwork but are nurtured and brought to fruition.

One transformative example is the leadership of Tony Hsieh, the late CEO of Zappos. Hsieh overturned conventional corporate structures by implementing a radical system of self-organisation at Zappos known as holacracy. Under his leadership, Zappos became known for its high level of employee engagement and customer service excellence, which stemmed from Hsieh's belief in the power of corporate culture and employee happiness. His approach dismantled the traditional hierarchical system in favour of empowering employees through self-managed teams, leading to enhanced innovation and agility. This new model allowed for rapid experimentation and a more responsive approach to customer service, revolutionising the way employee satisfaction can translate into customer loyalty and making Zappos a case study in successful implementation of entrepreneurial principles within an established corporation.

The unyielding power of business acumen in the era of in/entrepreneurship

This chapter is advocating for a significant shift towards in/entrepreneurial thinking. A leader fostering this mindset embraces change, boldly navigating the complexities of the modern business landscape. However, as we relate the virtues of in/entrepreneurship, it becomes imperative to emphasise the foundational role of business acumen. Without it, the most innovative of ventures can lose direction, becoming vulnerable to the rapid shifts they aim to capitalise on.

In/entrepreneurship captures the strategic role of challenging the established order. It questions, disrupts and offers fresh perspectives. At its core, this mindset seeks to transcend traditional boundaries. But true progress in this arena requires the solid grounding of business acumen. This vital knowledge, refined by understanding industry trends, financial intricacies, market dynamics and strategic planning, ensures that innovation is directed and purposeful.

Business acumen goes beyond a grasp of financial metrics, although they are essential. It involves understanding the intricate facets of the marketplace, anticipating consumer demands, and formulating strategies to meet them. This insight allows leaders to pinpoint opportunities that resonate with an organisation's core strengths and values.

In/entrepreneurship encourages questioning longstanding practices to usher in novel approaches. This attitude demands agility, adaptability, and a willingness to venture into the unknown. But it's the grounding of business acumen that dictates which areas to question and which to uphold. It helps discern between elements that have become obsolete and those that maintain enduring relevance. By making this distinction, it ensures that as we forge new paths, we retain the foundational strengths that have driven past successes.

Innovative ideas, no matter how transformative, need the backing of solid business knowledge. There are numerous instances of trailblazing start-ups that, despite their promise, couldn't sustain their momentum. More often than not, their undoing wasn't a paucity of creativity, but a lack of business acumen—challenges in scaling, prudent financial management, or a deep comprehension of their target audience.

Business acumen provides a balanced perspective. It ensures decisions, irrespective of how disruptive or revolutionary, are informed by an acute awareness of the business environment. Leaders fortified with business acumen can assess scenarios holistically, ensuring resources are deployed effectively and efficiently. They realise that every strategic initiative has ramifications, and they're adept at forecasting, preparing for and leveraging these.

Business acumen and in/entrepreneurship are not disparate concepts; they are two sides of the same coin. They complement and reinforce each other. Business acumen tempers the enthusiasm of in/entrepreneurship, providing structure and direction. In tandem, they drive organisations to achieve their objectives, ensuring adaptability and resilience in a world of incessant evolution.

Manifesting new realities: from vision to legacy
Visionary leaders recognise that while strategies and tactics may shift, the essence of leadership remains rooted in shaping the future. This is where the essence

of intrapreneurship and entrepreneurship becomes pivotal in the world of disruptive leadership.

Disruptive leadership is more than just breaking the mould. It involves perceiving the unseen, anticipating the uncharted, and forging a path where none existed. It's about creating not just products, services or solutions, but entire ecosystems that reshape industries. The roles of intrapreneurship and entrepreneurship inherently endorse this ethos. They are not merely about solving the immediate problems at hand, but envisioning what could be. They propel leaders to look beyond the horizon, challenging them to not just react to change, but to be the catalysts of it.

Look at the pillars of today's digital age. Companies like Apple, Google and Microsoft all began as fledgling start-ups, spearheaded by visionary leaders who dared to reimagine the world. These companies were founded on the principles of entrepreneurship, grounded in innovation, risk taking and a deep commitment to delivering value. Their inception, often in garages or modest spaces, might have been humble, but the dreams were anything but. The founders were not limited by their immediate environment; they envisioned a future transformed by their innovations.

Similarly, within corporate giants intrapreneurial leaders emerged, channelling the entrepreneurial spirit to drive innovation from within. These intrapreneurs, often working against the grain, managed to infuse a start-up mindset into vast organisations. They understood the need to move quickly, pivot when necessary, and continuously seek opportunities for innovation. By embracing this mindset, they could instigate change, align teams around a common purpose, and navigate the company through a rapidly evolving marketplace.

Leadership, in its highest form, is about setting a course for a future that others might not see. It's the ability to gather people around a shared vision, ignite passion, and mobilise efforts towards achieving monumental feats. When we reflect on the great leaders of the past, it's not the day-to-day decisions we recall but the enduring impact they've left on industries, communities, and society at large.

The IN/ENTREPRENEURIAL LEADER Maturity Model

Chapter 9 looks at two vital leadership traits in the face of disruption—intrapreneurship/entrepreneurship and business acumen. As the pace of change accelerates, leaders who can foster a culture of innovation while understanding the nuances of the business landscape will be best positioned to navigate the disruptions and inspire growth. This chapter presents the In/Entrepreneurial Leader Maturity Model, offering a detailed understanding of how intrapreneurship/entrepreneurship and business acumen interplay and contribute to dynamic, future-ready leadership.

THE IN/ENTREPRENEURIAL LEADER

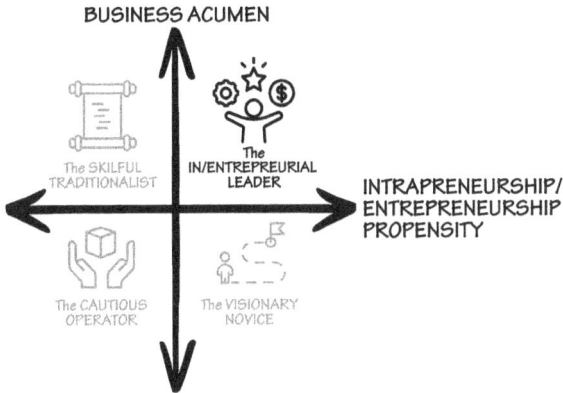

BUSINESS ACUMEN

The SKILFUL TRADITIONALIST

The IN/ENTREPREURIAL LEADER

INTRAPRENEURSHIP/ ENTREPRENEURSHIP PROPENSITY

The CAUTIOUS OPERATOR

The VISIONARY NOVICE

The Cautious Operator: Leaders in this quadrant display low levels of both intrapreneurship/entrepreneurship and business acumen. Their leadership style may be characterised by traditional, risk-averse methods, potentially inhibiting innovation and growth. They may struggle to identify opportunities and devise innovative strategies to capitalise on them. To enhance their leadership, these leaders should START cultivating a culture that encourages intrapreneurship and entrepreneurship. They should also work on developing their business acumen to effectively understand market dynamics and guide their strategic decisions. They should STOP clinging to outdated methods and practices that limit innovation and growth.

The Skilful Traditionalist: Leaders in this quadrant demonstrate high business acumen but low intrapreneurship/entrepreneurship. They possess a strong understanding of the business environment but may lack the initiative and innovation that characterise entrepreneurial leadership. Their ability to navigate market dynamics and make informed strategic decisions may be undermined by a lack of creativity and risk taking. To grow, these leaders should START promoting intrapreneurial and entrepreneurial mindsets, leveraging their business acumen to guide and support these initiatives. They should STOP suppressing innovative ideas and initiatives solely because they deviate from traditional norms.

The Visionary Novice: Leaders in this quadrant are high on intrapreneurship/entrepreneurship, but display low business acumen. These leaders are adept at fostering a culture of innovation and risk taking, but their limited business acumen may inhibit their ability to make sound strategic decisions. Their visionary ideas and initiatives might struggle to gain traction due to a lack of understanding of market dynamics and business strategy. To enhance their leadership, these leaders should START developing their business acumen to effectively guide their teams' innovative efforts and make informed business decisions. They should STOP pursuing ideas without fully analysing their viability and market relevance.

The In/Entrepreneurial Leader: Leaders in this quadrant exhibit both high intrapreneurship/entrepreneurship and high business acumen. They skilfully foster a culture of innovation and risk taking while leveraging their deep understanding of the business landscape to make strategic decisions. This blend of attributes enables them to drive their teams towards innovative solutions while ensuring alignment with broader business goals. These leaders should START sharing their strategies and insights with others to build a culture that values and balances both intrapreneurship/entrepreneurship and business acumen.

In/entrepreneurial leadership in action

If you work in an organisation with a traditional corporate structure, you may find it difficult to introduce a spirit of in/entrepreneurship, but once these mindsets have taken hold, you won't look back. Here are some ways to encourage a new way of thinking in your organisation.

Foster an organisational culture that embraces intrapreneurship and entrepreneurship: To drive disruptive leadership, leaders must actively encourage a culture that values intrapreneurship and entrepreneurship. By recognising and rewarding innovative thinking, (not just breakthrough ideas, but the exploration and engagement in the thinking), facilitating collaboration and providing resources for experimentation, leaders can stimulate creativity and risk-taking. This creates an environment where employees feel empowered to seek out new opportunities, contribute fresh ideas and drive organisational growth.

Implement a balanced approach to risk management to facilitate informed innovation: Navigating disruption requires leaders to take calculated risks. By developing and communicating a clear risk-management framework, leaders can strike a balance between fostering innovation and maintaining responsible oversight. Guiding teams in understanding acceptable risks and supporting them in pursuing opportunities ensures that creativity thrives without jeopardising overall stability and success.

Encourage collaborative innovation through cross-functional teams and knowledge sharing: Intrapreneurial and entrepreneurial mindsets thrive on collaboration. Leaders can create opportunities for cross-functional teams to work together, share knowledge and leverage diverse skills. Facilitating regular innovation labs or hackathons, encouraging cross-departmental project involvement, and promoting transparency in organisational goals and strategies can ignite creativity and build synergies across the organisation.

Invest in continuous learning and development to enhance in/ entrepreneurship skills and adaptability: Building a resilient organisation requires constant learning and growth. Leaders must invest in targeted training, mentoring, and development programs that focus on nurturing intrapreneurial and entrepreneurial skills. Offering opportunities for employees to engage with external innovation ecosystems, participate in industry events, and access resources to stay updated on market trends fosters adaptability and relevance in a disruptive environment.

Integrate the In/Entrepreneurial Leader Maturity Model to cultivate In/Entrepreneurship skills and business acumen: The **In/Entrepreneurial Leader Maturity Model** distinguishes leaders into four quadrants (Cautious Operators, Skilful Traditionalists, Visionary Novices, In/Entrepreneurial Leaders), aiding them in understanding and nurturing their intrapreneurship/entre-preneurship skills and business acumen. By identifying their position within this model, leaders can develop specific strategies to enhance their innovation and market understanding. For instance, Visionary Novices may invest in building their business acumen, while In/Entrepreneurial Leaders can mentor others to foster a culture that balances innovation with strategic alignment.

With a better understanding of how intrapreneurship and entrepreneurship empower disruptive leadership, we conclude Part 3. We've journeyed through the critical competencies of leading remotely, adopting a global mindset and leveraging entrepreneurial thinking in leadership. As we step into Part 4, our focus shifts to the legacy and impact in disruptive leadership. The upcoming chapters will delve into building a legacy, adaptability as a disruptive leader, and the importance of vulnerability and humility.

CHAPTER INSIGHTS

- Intrapreneurship and entrepreneurship are vital mindsets in disruptive leadership, driving innovation and discovering opportunities within organisations.

- These principles equip leaders with the adaptability and courage necessary to navigate dynamic organisations in disruptive environments, serving as key navigational tools.

- The inherent innovation of intrapreneurs and entrepreneurs involves challenging norms and taking informed risks for value creation: essential characteristics for leaders in times of disruption.

- Entrepreneurship extends beyond start-ups; it is a mindset that involves spotting opportunities and guiding organisations towards growth amidst disruption.

- Like entrepreneurship, intrapreneurship within an organisation propels innovative solutions, fostering adaptability and relevance during disruptions.

- The combined roles of entrepreneurs and intrapreneurs in leadership are crucial for navigating disruptive changes and preparing teams for complexities and uncertainties.

- Understanding the interconnectedness of entrepreneurship and intrapreneurship can spark transformative change within an organisation.

- Entrepreneurial leaders inspire an intrapreneurial culture, while intrapreneurs leverage an entrepreneurial mindset to identify and exploit opportunities, creating a balance within organisations.

THE PRIZES OF FUTURE-READY LEADERSHIP

In **Part 3: Future-Ready Leadership**, we've ventured into the essential leadership competencies necessitated by our contemporary, disruptive business environment. We've unveiled the significance of leading remotely, the nuanced skills essential for thriving in a globalised world, and the paramount roles of intrapreneurship and entrepreneurship in disruptive leadership.

Efficient Remote Leadership

The digital age demands an understanding and proficiency in leading teams remotely. By mastering this ability, you'll not only ensure your team's productivity but also maintain its dynamics irrespective of geographical distance. Your competence in fostering a sense of community, shared purpose and trust within your remote team will significantly enhance engagement and performance.

Global Leadership Acumen

In our interconnected world, effective leadership requires an enriched global perspective. By understanding the cultural, economic and political complexities of global business operations, you'll be able to navigate different contexts and influence decisions that drive your organisation's success. This skill is instrumental in fostering innovation and leveraging diverse viewpoints for the collective growth of your organisation.

In/Entrepreneurial Leadership

The insights into intrapreneurship and entrepreneurship will help you drive innovation within your organisation and beyond its boundaries. As you nurture this mindset, you'll become adept at spotting opportunities and leading your team through change. This ability to navigate disruptive changes and uncertainties is a vital aspect of leadership in the contemporary business landscape.

Sharpening Your Digital Competency

Leading in the disruptive era requires a robust understanding and application of digital tools and communication platforms. As you hone these skills, you'll set a benchmark for continuous learning within your team. This digital proficiency will help you create a secure and healthy digital culture, ultimately boosting the team's overall productivity.

Inclusive Global Leadership

Striking the balance between global awareness and local responsiveness is an invaluable competency you'll acquire. By integrating global trends and fostering cultural intelligence, you'll lead effectively across diverse contexts. This inclusivity and adaptability will set you apart as a leader who is able to drive growth amidst the complexities and diversity of the modern world.

LEGACY-ORIENTED LEADERSHIP

Having gleaned the importance of future-focused leadership competencies, we find ourselves ready to transition to **Part 4: Legacy-Oriented Leadership**. This portion of our journey will take us beyond the immediate challenges of leading—in the present and into the world of lasting influence and legacy.

Part 4 explores the long-term consequences of effective disruptive leadership, such as building a legacy and creating significant positive impact. This part of the book also dives into two paramount qualities of disruptive leaders: adaptability and the combination of vulnerability and humility. Legacy is built not just by achievements, but by the character imprints a leader leaves behind. Adaptability signifies a leader's commitment to evolution and growth, ensuring their teachings remain timely and actionable. On the other hand, vulnerability and humility speak to a leader's authenticity, setting an example for subsequent generations to lead with heart and sincerity, thereby perpetuating a leadership style that values both results and relationships.

Disruptive leadership is not just about influencing the present; it's also about creating a future that extends beyond one's tenure. In a world marked by rapid change, leaders are tasked with building sustainable legacies that endure and continue to create positive impact. Disruptive leaders achieve this by driving meaningful transformation, fostering a culture of innovation and empowering others to lead. **Chapter 10: Building a Legacy Through Positive Impac**t details how disruptive leaders can craft lasting legacies that continue to drive change and yield positive results beyond their tenure.

Adaptability is a key attribute of disruptive leaders. In the face of uncertainty and constant change, the ability to adapt to evolving circumstances and shift strategies accordingly is crucial. Successful disruptive leaders are not rigid in their approaches; instead, they are agile, continually learning, and flexible in their decision-making processes. **Chapter 11: Adaptability—the Imperative Skill for Disruptive Leaders** underscores the significance of adaptability in disruptive leadership, discussing strategies to enhance this essential skill for leading in the face of constant change.

In addition to adaptability, disruptive leaders also exhibit vulnerability and humility. These qualities foster transparency, promote a learning culture and build trust within teams. Leaders who demonstrate vulnerability and humility create a safe environment for risk taking and innovation, critical elements for success in disruptive times. **Chapter 12: Vulnerability and Humility in Disruptive Leadership** illuminates the role of vulnerability and humility in leading effectively and discusses key ways in which a leader can display these human qualities and leverage them to build a legacy.

By understanding and integrating the principles discussed in Part 4, leaders can significantly advance their journey towards creating a powerful legacy in a rapidly changing world. Leaders who strive to build a positive legacy, adapt swiftly to change, and lead with vulnerability and humility are well on their way to cultivating a leadership style that is resilient, empathetic and impactful. As we move towards the final part of our exploration, we'll further refine our understanding of disruptive leadership, ultimately empowering you to leave an enduring legacy.

10

BUILDING A LEGACY THROUGH POSITIVE IMPACT

The true meaning of life is to plant trees;
under whose shade you do not expect to sit.
NELSON HENDERSON

HAPTER 10 invites us to reflect on the role of the leader in shaping not only the present but the future. True leaders don't merely exist in the present; they shape the future through their vision, their actions and the impact of their leadership. We will explore how ethical leadership contributes to creating a positive impact and legacy. Then we will provide strategies to align personal and professional goals, thus ensuring that your leadership has enduring influence. Finally, we'll delve into the task of measuring your leadership's impact—an often complex but crucial aspect of understanding your role and contribution.

The park was alive with the vibrant greens of spring as Guy Russo and I looked to find a bench where we could sit and talk. The café where we bought our coffees was still humming with late breakfast-seekers, a testament to the leisurely pace of the season.

We chose a spot where the sunlight filtered through the newly leafed trees, casting a mixture of light and shadow on the path. We settled onto a bench; the wood warmed by the sun. The open space seemed to echo the expansive nature of our impending conversation.

'Sit down, take a moment, breathe,' he said, as if he knew that the world had been weighing heavily on my shoulders. I obliged, the smell of rich coffee mingling with the earthy scent of dew-soaked grass.

Guy wasn't just the architect behind one of Australia's most remarkable business revivals; he was a maestro of human potential. At Kmart Australia, he had achieved the corporate equivalent of turning water into wine, transforming a failing enterprise into a retail legend. But as I sipped the coffee he had thoughtfully brought, it was clear that his greatest pride lay not in profit margins, but in the leaders he had cultivated and the lives he had touched.

'Remember, it's not the numbers that define our legacy,' he said, echoing the thoughts that often reverberated through the halls of Kmart under his leadership. 'It's the people, the lives we lift up, that weave the stories of our true success.'

As Guy shared his tales, I saw not the corporate titan but the fifteen-year-old who once flipped burgers at McDonald's, whose every word and action were chapters of a story where resilience was the central theme. His rise to CEO of McDonalds in Australia, and then in greater China, was not just a journey through the ranks, but a testament to a relentless drive and an unwavering belief in the power of people.

His anecdotes unfolded with a certain grace; each a veiled lesson, a window into the soul of a leader whose vision extended far beyond the boardroom. He shared memories steeped in the heartfelt work at the Half the Sky Foundation, his dedication a beacon of new hope for countless orphaned and at-risk children across Asia. And as the light played upon his features, he recounted with equal passion his tenure as Director and Chairman for Ronald McDonald House Charities in Australia and Hong Kong, as well as his time as President of this global non-profit. His involvement with Ronald McDonald House was another chapter of his commitment, where his efforts were instrumental in providing a home away from home for families in the midst of medical crises. These stories were not merely past experiences retold; they were the narratives of a man whose leadership was deeply intertwined with compassion, care, and the profound impact of community support.

The vulnerability he shared was disarming; he entrusted me with a story deeply personal to him. The act of sharing it was a profound gesture of his humanity. This candid moment came about because Guy was aware of the personal challenges I was facing. His story was not about his work or his career, but a moment that reminded me of the intricate, often delicate tapestry of human experience. His willingness to be so open, to illustrate that he, too, navigated the complexities of life beyond the boardroom, was a powerful reminder of our shared humanity. It was this human connection, this genuine display of empathy and trust, that deeply impacted upon me. It reminded me that before all else we are human: full of flaws and beauty, constantly learning and growing through our interactions with one another.

Our talk lingered until the park filled with the sounds of life and the city breathed in the day's bustling rhythm. And as we parted ways, I realised that the coffee had long gone cold, but the warmth of the encounter had kindled something within me, a spark that I knew would light my way through the trying times.

To the emerging leaders reading our story, know this: authenticity and a heart for people are the cornerstones of leadership. Guy Russo's legacy is not just found in the profit margins of Kmart, or in the strategic redirection of Target. It is etched in the spirit of the people he lifted: the leaders he built, the lives he changed, and the children he gave a new sky to dream under.

The role of ethical leadership in creating positive impact and legacy

Ethical leadership is a powerful force that influences every aspect of an organisation and extends its impact beyond immediate boundaries. Leaders who act ethically become agents of profound and lasting change. Their influence isn't limited to their decisions and actions; it's also embodied in the values they uphold and project, thereby inspiring others to adopt a culture of integrity, transparency and respect.

While leaders inevitably leave a mark when they exit, those who lead ethically leave more than just financial success. Some leaders, without a solid ethical grounding, might make choices that result in mistrust or even lasting damage to the organisation and its stakeholders. On the other hand, leaders guided by ethics lay a foundation that fosters trust, promotes genuine collaboration, and establishes a legacy characterised by positive influence and integrity. Their legacy lies in their character, principles and contributions to societal betterment. Their leadership illuminates a path that transcends the boundaries of their immediate environment, inspiring followers to aim for higher goals, and giving them a sense of purpose and direction.

The importance of ethical leadership is particularly evident in the face of the complexities and challenges of our time. Rapid changes and constant disruptions require leaders to make complex decisions and face multifaceted dilemmas. A robust ethical compass serves as a guiding principle, enabling leaders to navigate through uncertainties with clarity and confidence.

Today's heightened social consciousness among consumers and employees turns ethical leadership into a competitive advantage. Leaders who act responsibly and contribute positively to society not only foster goodwill, but also create an environment that attracts exceptional talent and cultivates loyal customers. This positions their organisations favourably, attracting employees who seek meaningful work and customers who align their purchasing decisions with their values.

The resulting virtuous cycle, driven by ethical leadership, forms a powerful growth engine. Engaged and productive employees who are motivated by their company's ethical stance drive innovation. Loyal customers provide financial stability, supporting the company's growth and innovation.

At the core of every individual is a quest for authenticity. When leaders act with genuine ethical intent, it's not merely a strategy; it's an alignment with the deep-seated human desire for truth and purpose. This alignment doesn't just build organisations; it crafts legacies, touching lives in ways metrics can't capture. Ethical leadership doesn't simply guide actions within the confines of an office; it shapes the essence of human connection, trust and inspiration. For emerging leaders, understanding this is not about mastering a skill, but recognising the profound impact of their truest intentions on the world around them. It's here, in this realm of authentic intention, that leadership transcends from a role to a transformative force.

Aligning personal and professional goals for lasting influence and congruence

The harmony between personal and professional objectives isn't just about work-life balance or personal fulfilment. It heightens your leadership influence, effectiveness and authenticity, as you fulfill your internal values and aspirations alongside external success metrics.

Why is this alignment critical? It bestows clarity, a prerequisite for setting effective priorities and decision making. This clarity is navigated through your actions and maintains focus amidst disruption and change.

It also instils resilience. When your work echoes your personal values and objectives, it transcends mere professional duties and embodies your mission and your purpose. This purpose-fuelled resilience aids in weathering challenges, recovering from setbacks, and persisting when the path is difficult.

Harmonising personal and professional objectives enhances engagement—both yours and your team's. Personal investment in your work elicits increased energy, commitment and passion. This infectious enthusiasm motivates your team, fostering a dedicated, high-performing workforce.

It also triggers innovation. Personal passion and curiosity encourage questioning the status quo, exploring novel ideas and instigating change—a critical mindset for disruptive leadership in a rapidly evolving world.

Authentic, purposeful leadership inspires others to follow suit. It propagates a ripple effect that extends your influence beyond your immediate team or organisation. You become a beacon, encouraging others to harmonise their personal and professional objectives and lead with authenticity and purpose.

In navigating our leadership journey, the quest is not just about becoming effective or efficient, but becoming whole. The true power of alignment between personal and professional aspirations is that it unearths a depth of authenticity within us that's often untouched. When this authenticity emerges, it doesn't merely guide our actions or decisions, but resonates deeply with those around us and speaks directly to their own search for meaning and authenticity. This resonance is transformative. It doesn't just change how we lead, but why we lead. And in that shift lies the profound realisation: leadership is not just about influence, it's about connection. True leadership is when our most authentic selves meet the authentic needs and aspirations of others. And in that space, extraordinary things happen.

Measuring impact and legacy

Measuring the impact and legacy of your leadership enables you to assess whether you're achieving these broader leadership objectives. It gives you a more comprehensive understanding of your effectiveness as a leader, highlighting areas where you're making a significant difference and where there may be room for improvement.

In terms of measuring impact, consider both the tangible and intangible. Tangible impacts are usually easier to measure; they're represented in improved productivity, revenue growth or increased market share. The intangible impacts, though harder to measure, are equally important. These include employee morale, team cohesion, a culture of innovation, or the level of trust within your organisation.

Legacy, though more elusive, can be gauged by looking at sustained change. Ask yourself, are the values you've instilled persisting? Are the systems you've put in place continuing to drive performance? Perhaps most crucially, are the leaders you've developed carrying forward your vision and ethos?

Measuring leadership impact and legacy is not a one-off exercise. It's a continuous process that needs to be woven into your leadership practices. It's about consistently checking in with yourself and others, gathering feedback, and reflecting on your actions and their ripple effects. It's about course-correcting when needed and doubling down on the areas where you're making a real difference.

In the end, the true measure of your leadership will be in the empowered employees, the thriving corporate culture, the innovative solutions and the sustainable practices. It will be in the new leaders who were nurtured under your guidance and are now driving their teams forward with the same integrity and vision.

The journey of leadership is not a straight path, but a series of interconnected moments, choices and actions that collectively shape our influence and legacy. Often, leaders find themselves in a relentless pursuit of tangible successes, equating them to their worth or effectiveness. Yet, the profound shift happens when one realises that the true essence of leadership isn't found in mere numbers or accolades, but in the silent spaces between actions, in the unspoken words of trust, and in the unseen bonds of connection; it's these invisible threads of impact that linger long after you've left a room. Impact and legacy aren't just about the big moments, but occur in the small, everyday actions that foster growth, instil trust, and create an environment of genuine care and understanding. When leaders embrace this perspective, they don't just measure their worth in achievements, but in the profound, positive changes they inspire in others.

Nurturing future leaders

Your leadership journey should be seen as an ongoing process, where your role isn't just to excel in your duties but also to prepare the next line of leaders to perform at an equal or superior level. This entails more than just guiding them along; it necessitates strengthening each future leader's unique ability to traverse their path, surmount obstacles and anticipate potential challenges.

This preparation should concentrate on shaping a robust 'capability architecture' within your future leaders. These capabilities cut across cognitive, emotional, social, and contextual spheres, offering a comprehensive resource kit to steer through the disruptive environment. They empower future leaders to dissect intricate problems, sustain emotional stability during crises, comprehend and harness the dynamics within their teams, and modify their leadership approach to conform with the ever-changing circumstances.

Gail Kelly, who served as the CEO of Westpac from 2008 to 2015, not only spearheaded significant growth for the bank, but also became known for her commitment to developing future leaders. She implemented a range of progressive human resources policies that included support for women in leadership roles and a focus on diversity and inclusion. Kelly's mentorship programs within Westpac sought to nurture the unique talents of emerging leaders, ensuring that the legacy of the bank was not just in its financial success, but in the cultivation of a forward-thinking, adaptive leadership team capable of guiding the bank through an era of rapid change and technological disruption. Her belief in the potential of her staff to rise to leadership roles resulted in a notable increase in female representation in the bank's upper management and solidified her reputation as a leader who was truly invested in empowering the next generation.

In this context, your role transcends teaching or directing, and becomes one of inspiring and challenging, and providing constructive feedback. Establishing a safe space where future leaders can experiment, fail, learn and grow is essential. There is an opportunity to embed a culture of learning and reflection where leadership development becomes an inherent part of routine activities.

In this manner, each future leader becomes a carrier of the legacy, propelling it forward through their actions, choices and influence. Their leadership style may diverge from yours, but the foundational values, resilience, adaptability and foresight—the traits you've helped nurture—remain constant. They then become the guiding figures for the ensuing generation of leaders, thereby extending the reach of your legacy even further.

The leaders you nurture will remember less about what you achieved and more about how you made them feel: capable, resilient and prepared. Your real triumph will be when these leaders don't just replicate your steps, but dance their own dance, taking your teachings as a foundation and building upon them in ways you hadn't imagined. That's when you'll know that your leadership was never about continuing a personal legacy, but about starting countless new ones.

The LEGACY LEADER Maturity Model

Chapter 10 delves deeper into the tenth component of our comprehensive fifteen-part leadership model, focusing on two key leadership aspects—ethical leadership and personal-professional alignment. As the landscape of leadership becomes more complex, the leaders who can effectively weave an ethical fabric within their organisation, while ensuring their personal and professional goals are in alignment, will be best positioned to navigate these complexities and carve out a legacy of value. This chapter introduces the Legacy Leader Maturity Model, providing an in-depth understanding of how ethical leadership and personal-professional alignment interact and contribute to sustainable, legacy-driven leadership.

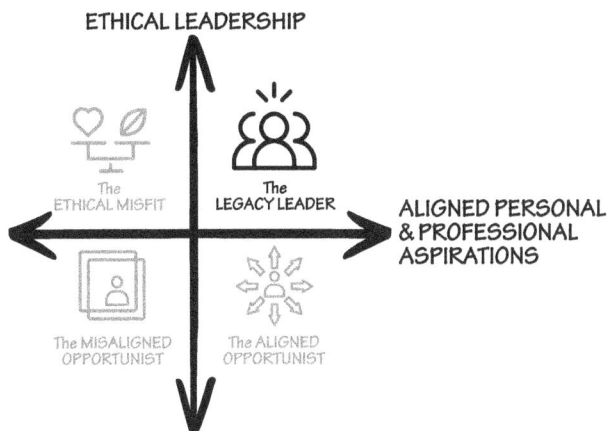

The LEGACY LEADER

How committed are you to leaving a legacy through your leadership? Let's examine each quadrant of the model to understand your position.

The Misaligned Opportunist: Leaders in this quadrant display low ethical leadership and low alignment between personal and professional goals. Their decisions may be driven primarily by opportunistic motives, with little consideration for ethical implications. The discord between their personal and professional aspirations could undermine their leadership effectiveness and impact. To improve, these leaders should START prioritising ethical considerations in their decisions and actions. They should also START striving for a harmonious alignment between their personal and professional goals, thereby enhancing the continuity and impact of their leadership. They should STOP making short-sighted decisions based solely on immediate gains while dismissing ethical implications.

The Ethical Misfit: Leaders in this quadrant demonstrate high ethical leadership but low alignment between personal and professional goals. While they adhere to robust ethical standards, they might struggle to reconcile their personal aspirations with their professional ones. This disconnect can lead to a lack of fulfilment and potential burnout, which could negatively affect their leadership effectiveness and legacy. To grow, these leaders should START identifying ways to align their personal and professional goals, thereby enhancing their overall leadership effectiveness and legacy. They should STOP compartmentalising their personal and professional lives to the point where they hinder each other.

The Aligned Opportunist: Leaders in this quadrant showcase low ethical leadership but high alignment between personal and professional goals. They have succeeded in harmonising their personal and professional objectives, but their decision making may lack ethical considerations. Their leadership impact might be undermined by a perception of them as being opportunistic and self-serving. To elevate their leadership, these leaders should START incorporating ethical considerations into their decision-making processes and daily actions. They should STOP prioritising personal gains at the expense of broader ethical considerations.

The Legacy Leader: This quadrant is the ideal state where leaders display both high ethical leadership and high alignment between personal and professional goals. These leaders not only prioritise ethical considerations in their decisions and actions, but also successfully reconcile their personal and professional aspirations. They embody a leadership style that is both ethical and authentic, which significantly enhances their influence and legacy. These leaders should START sharing their strategies and insights to inspire others and cultivate a culture that values both ethical leadership and personal-professional alignment.

Legacy leadership in action

Tomorrow will be here before we know it. The time to start impacting the future is today. Here are five ways to begin.

Embed ethical leadership in organisational culture and practices: Ethical leadership must go beyond mere compliance shaping the culture and practices of the entire organisation. Leaders can take specific actions to instil integrity, respect, fairness and social responsibility in everyday decision making. By conducting regular ethics training, promoting transparent communication, setting clear ethical guidelines and leading by example, leaders ensure that ethical considerations become integral to the organisational fabric.

Align personal and professional goals to enhance leadership influence and authenticity: The alignment of personal and professional goals is critical to building a positive legacy. Leaders can demonstrate their commitment to this alignment by clearly articulating their values, setting goals that resonate with personal passions, and ensuring that these align with organisational objectives. To put this into practice, leaders can undertake an 'alignment audit'. This involves listing their personal passions and goals alongside their professional ones and identifying areas of overlap and divergence. Additionally, they can engage in monthly reflection sessions, dedicating time to journal their experiences, assess the congruence between their actions and values, and set actionable steps for deeper alignment in the coming weeks.

Foster an organisational environment that emphasises social responsibility and positive impact: Leaders must champion a mindset that extends beyond profit by emphasising social responsibility and establishing a positive impact on people, society and the planet. By implementing policies that promote sustainability, community engagement, diversity and inclusion, leaders create an environment where employees feel part of something greater. Encouraging volunteerism, establishing partnerships with socially responsible organisations, and integrating social responsibility metrics into performance assessments solidify this commitment.

Implement robust assessment mechanisms to measure leadership impact and legacy: Assessing the impact and legacy of leadership is essential for continuous growth. Leaders can establish regular review processes that evaluate both tangible and intangible aspects of leadership influence. These might include monitoring sustained changes within the organisation, soliciting feedback from stakeholders, tracking alignment with ethical standards, and using non-monetary measures such as employee engagement and community involvement.

Integrate the Legacy Leader Maturity Model to guide ethical leadership and personal-professional alignment: The Legacy Leader Maturity Model, distinguishing leaders according to four quadrants (Misaligned Opportunists, Ethical Misfits, Aligned Opportunists, Legacy Leaders), offers a practical framework for understanding and enhancing ethical leadership. Leaders can actively assess and position themselves within this model, focusing on specific actions to improve their effectiveness. For instance, Misaligned Opportunists may emphasise ethical decision making, while Ethical Misfits might focus on reconciling personal and professional aspirations.

The aspiration of leaving a positive legacy is a notable milestone in the journey of leadership. Yet, to ensure the longevity of this legacy in the disruptive era, leaders must possess an adaptive mindset. In the next chapter, we will delve deeper into adaptability, a crucial competency for disruptive leaders, and explore how it underpins enduring leadership success.

CHAPTER INSIGHTS

- Ethical leadership, embodying integrity, respect, fairness and social responsibility, extends beyond compliance, impacting not only businesses, but also people, society and the planet, thus creating a positive and enduring legacy.

- These leaders impact the organisation broadly through their actions and the standards they uphold, by using ethics as a compass to navigate complexities, build trust and foster successful relationships in today's rapidly changing world.

- As social consciousness rises, ethical leadership becomes a competitive advantage, propelling growth and innovation by attracting top talent and customer loyalty through authentic actions.

- The alignment between personal and professional goals magnifies a leader's influence and effectiveness, promoting authenticity, resilience, engagement and innovation.

- A leader's integration of a positive impact mindset in their daily practices includes articulating impact goals, showing commitment through daily decisions, fostering teamwork, and embedding impact within routine operations.

- Assessing leadership impact and legacy includes evaluating tangible and intangible aspects—monitoring sustained change, soliciting feedback and regularly checking effectiveness beyond monetary measures.

- Preparing future leaders involves identifying and nurturing potential within teams, offering mentorship and growth opportunities, and encouraging the emergence of unique leadership styles in this disruptive era.

- Leadership's future depends on cultivating leaders resilient to disruption, whose influence outlives their tenure and contributes positively to the leadership ecosystem.

11

ADAPTABILITY: THE IMPERATIVE SKILL FOR DISRUPTIVE LEADERS

The art of life is a constant readjustment to our surroundings.
KAKUZŌ OKAKURA

RANSITIONING FROM our exploration of building a positive impact and legacy, Chapter 11 explores why adaptability is a key competency for disruptive leaders and investigates strategies for enhancing this trait to meet new challenges and opportunities. Adaptability ensures that a leader's legacy is not just a reflection of past successes, but a dynamic blueprint that evolves with the changing landscape. By continuously adapting, leaders ensure their contributions remain relevant and provide a foundation for future innovation and resilience. We'll delve into how adaptability can be cultivated at personal and team levels, setting the stage for long-term leadership success.

As the shadows lengthened, the fire's glow wove through the intimacy of the conversation I shared with my wife, Kelly. In this quiet space, framed by the clink of our wine glasses and the soft sigh of settling logs, the question emerged almost of its own accord, a natural continuation of our many shared dialogues on life's unpredictable journey: 'What's been the catalyst for your remarkable resilience?'

Sitting beside me, Kelly's response, reflective and resonant, carried the weight of her experiences. It was not a speech rehearsed for applause but a chapter from the soul, a candid revelation of an internal landscape transformed by loss, shared in the sanctuary of our mutual understanding.

Kelly's narrative was not just the culmination of a series of professional shifts; it was the embodiment of a profound, relentless tale of adaptability that was magnified with the most personal disruption of all—the loss of her mother.

Elena, her mother, had been a force of nature. Raised on the rich earth of a Western Australian farm, Kelly had inherited the sturdy, rooted spirit of the land and the fiery passion of her Italian heritage. Elena had made sacrifices that were as vast as the outback itself to ensure Kelly had the right education, always whispering to her in their native tongue, '*Crescere significa cambiare*'—to grow is to change.

As we sat there, the warmth of the fire enveloping us, Kelly shared how the disruption that shook her the most was the one that came without warning and without a project plan—the passing of her mother. It was the kind of life event that you can't pivot from with a well-placed business strategy. Her voice, usually so steady, trembled slightly as she spoke of the void her mother left behind. It was a reminder that the hardest challenges are not those we face in boardrooms, but those that touch our souls.

Kelly's journey of adaptability, the thread that I had only now fully grasped, didn't simply surge forward from her early career as an accountant, the meticulous CPA. It didn't spring from the thrill of pioneering new technology in wealth management or the grit of handling billion-dollar client-facing projects. It was deeper than negotiating contracts or mastering the art of board presentations. It was a path paved by the values and resilience instilled in her by a mother who taught her that every end has a new beginning.

As Kelly became a leader in her field, every transition she made was a lesson in adaptability, a testament to her ability to use the knowledge of yesterday to navigate the unknowns of tomorrow. Yet, in her voice was the touch of her mother's wisdom. With each leap—from finance to technology, from operations to the boardroom, from project management to innovation—Kelly wasn't just moving roles; she was exemplifying adaptability, seamlessly integrating her core skills into diverse landscapes and evolving demands.

Each transition was another step in the journey of adaptability that she led by example. Kelly never aimed to inspire; it was the byproduct of her unwavering commitment to growth. But inspire she did—mentoring young women to embrace the unknown, to be fearless in the face of change, and to lead not just with intelligence, but with courage and humanity.

Kelly's journey was punctuated not by the achievements on her résumé, but by the lives she touched through powerful human connection, the confidence she instilled, and the ripple effect of empowerment that she launched. It was a testament to the legacy of a mother who saw strength not as a birthright, but as a gift we give ourselves through relentless personal growth and adaptability.

As the night deepened and the fire dwindled to glowing embers, I understood that adaptability was indeed about mastering the art of transformation—not through a simple progression of events, but through a vibrant dance with the ebb and flow of circumstances. It was about the agility with which Kelly navigated each new chapter, the boldness of her decisions when facing unprecedented challenges, and the smooth incorporation of new ideas into time-tested frameworks.

And as Kelly's husband, a witness to the incredible journey that unfolded before me, I realised that the woman I loved was not just a leader in her field; she was a role model for the next generation, illuminating the path of adaptability that will empower them to navigate their own fires of change and forge a resilient legacy in a world that never stands still.

Why adaptability is a key competency for disruptive leaders

Adaptability is the ability to recognise, comprehend and effectively respond to changes. It is a crucial quality for disruptive leaders at the helm of change who are steering organisations into uncharted territories. Adaptability involves discarding old paradigms, embracing novel ideas, and altering your approach based on fresh data or situations. It's about staying attuned to your team's, customers' and broader business ecosystem's changing needs and aspirations. It's about being the catalyst propelling your team or organisation into the future, rather than merely reacting. And it's about dictating the pace of change rather than scrambling to keep up.

Adaptability in disruptive leadership involves actively harnessing its momentum. Disruptive leaders don't simply adjust to new information; they use it to recalibrate their strategies, ensuring their goals remain within reach even as the landscape evolves. This willingness to continuously re-evaluate and refine in the face of change is the essence of adaptability.

But adaptable leadership isn't only about responding to change; it's about actively moulding it. Actively moulding change allows a leader to imprint their unique vision onto the trajectory of their organisation or team. By shaping the course of change, they don't just address the challenges of the present, they set the tone for the future and leave an enduring impact that persists even after their tenure. This approach ensures that their leadership is not just a fleeting moment in time, but a foundational force that influences the direction for years to come. In essence, by moulding change, leaders etch their philosophies, values and strategies into the very fabric of an organisation, ensuring their legacy is woven into its future successes and innovations.

Our world today is marked by exponential technological progress, societal-attitude shifts, and a global economy more interconnected than ever. Envision leading in this world with a fixed mindset or rigid strategies. Such rigidity blinds leaders to emerging possibilities, locking them in cycles of repetitiveness even as the horizon widens.

The fallout is twofold: not only do they become obsolete, but they also stifle the potential of those they lead. In a realm where adaptability is currency, an inflexible stance drains vitality from organisations, making them susceptible to disruption rather than driving it. Consequently, leaders tethered to unyielding strategies risk not just irrelevance, but the gradual erasure of their legacy in an era that celebrates nimbleness and foresight.

Take Satya Nadella's journey at Microsoft, for example. Under his leadership, Microsoft didn't just stay in its lane. As the tech scene transformed with new innovations like cloud tech, Nadella pivoted. He expanded Microsoft's horizons to cloud, bridged gaps with previously distant tech communities, and positioned the company as a forerunner in emerging technologies. And he didn't go it alone; he rallied the entire company behind this vision. This is the essence of influential leadership: it's not about merely adapting, but about pioneering change.

While we can and should strive to shape the future, it's equally crucial to recognise our limitations in predicting it. The world is complex, and the variables are many. But it's in the face of these unpredictable challenges that true adaptability shines. Being adaptable means acknowledging that our envisioned future might not unfold exactly as we've imagined. It means understanding that our well-laid plans might need reworking or even complete overhauls. And instead of seeing these as failures or setbacks, viewing them as opportunities for growth and recalibration.

Redefining knowledge: the art of unlearning, relearning and learning in leadership adaptability

The capacity to unlearn, relearn and learn is the cornerstone of adaptability, serving as a compass for disruptive leaders navigating uncertain landscapes. This cycle is the key to unlocking agility and continuous growth, allowing leaders to remain relevant amidst evolving circumstances.

Unlearning refers to consciously letting go of old notions, outdated practices and deep-seated beliefs that no longer serve their purpose in our dynamic world. Unlearning requires leaders to confront their comfort zones, challenging them to release pre-existing knowledge that might be hindering progress. This process requires the humility to acknowledge that what once worked may no longer be applicable or effective. Leaders must critically assess their approach, strategies and beliefs, objectively identifying elements that may be out of sync with current realities. Recognising and severing emotional ties to these elements can be challenging, but it's an essential step in creating space for new, more relevant knowledge.

Relearning follows the process of unlearning. It involves reacquainting oneself with past knowledge or skills but through the lens of fresh perspectives, updated information and novel methodologies. It's about taking familiar concepts and reframing them in the light of new understanding. Relearning empowers leaders to repurpose their foundational knowledge in line with changing contexts, enabling them to maintain the relevance of their expertise. It's akin to refurbishing an old house, keeping the sturdy structure but updating the interior to meet modern standards.

Consider the journey of Shemara Wikramanayake, who became the CEO of Macquarie Group, Australia's largest investment bank. Shemara, who was born in Sri Lanka, redefined the process of unlearning, relearning and learning in her ascent to leadership. In her role, she has emphasised the importance of sustainability, steering the traditionally conservative banking institution towards investments in renewable energy. By unlearning traditional investment strategies that focused heavily on fossil fuels, Shemara has led Macquarie to divest from carbon-intensive assets, embracing the relearning process to adapt the group's portfolio to the modern demand for clean energy. Her commitment to learning is reflected in the group's continual innovation and expansion into new markets, ensuring its growth in a financial world that is increasingly conscious of environmental impact. Shemara's adaptive approach not only enhances Macquarie's competitive edge but also aligns the bank with global sustainability goals, demonstrating the profound impact of a leader adept in the art of knowledge evolution.

Learning is the continuous quest for new knowledge, skills and insights. In the context of disruptive leadership, it means relentlessly pursuing innovation, staying updated with industry advancements and embracing diversity of thought. Leaders need to cultivate a culture of curiosity, not only within themselves but also within their teams. Encourage questions, stimulate dialogue, and foster an environment where learning from mistakes is not just accepted but celebrated. Continual learning fuels intellectual agility and fosters a proactive approach to change, allowing leaders to anticipate, rather than react to, shifts in their landscape.

In our journey of disruptive leadership, it's easy to become absorbed with the idea of constant acquisition—more knowledge, more skills, more insights. Yet, the most transformative moments often come not from what we gather, but what we willingly let go. It's in the silent spaces created by unlearning that our true potential emerges. The value isn't just in the continuous cycle of unlearning, relearning and learning; it's in the courage to regularly step back and evaluate not just what we know, but how and why we know it. We should remember that growth isn't just about moving forward, but also about pausing, reflecting and, sometimes, taking a step back to leap further. This simple yet profound realisation can be the difference between leaders who merely adapt and those who truly thrive in ever-changing times.

The surprising role of emotional intelligence in adaptability

Adaptability in leadership isn't merely a function of technical prowess or strategic insight; it's deeply rooted in the emotional interplay between a leader and those they influence. Emotional intelligence acts as the unseen hand guiding leaders through complex terrains of human emotions, revealing hidden concerns, aspirations and triggers. It's about recognising that the emotional bandwidth of an organisation or group is directly proportional to its adaptability quotient—a measure of how effectively one can pivot in response to change.

Emotional intelligence is often hailed as the quiet influencer of leadership effectiveness. While adaptability allows leaders to adjust to changing environments, it is emotional intelligence that provides the nuanced understanding of people and situations that informs these necessary shifts. The essence of emotional intelligence in this context is to decipher the emotional undercurrents that underlie change, ensuring leaders can navigate the choppy waters of transformation empathetically and strategically.

At the heart of emotional intelligence is the ability to read, understand and react to the emotions of others. This competence allows leaders to decode the sentiments and motivations of their team members, particularly during times of change. By being aware of their team's emotional landscape, leaders can preempt resistance, provide targeted support and pave the way for smoother transitions.

To further enrich your understanding of others' emotions, encourage open dialogue about emotions within your team. Normalise discussions about emotional responses to changes and promote a culture of emotional literacy. This openness not only enhances your emotional understanding, but also fosters an empathetic, supportive work environment that is conducive to adaptability.

Remember to use the insights gained from understanding emotions to guide your leadership decisions. Tailor your communication style to resonate with your team's emotional state, provide support that addresses specific emotional needs, and adapt your strategies to minimise emotional resistance.

Possessing emotional intelligence is a crucial skill in leading your team through disruption. But equally, emotional intelligence allows leaders to tap into the emotional pulse of the wider organisational and market contexts. This skill enables them to gauge stakeholder reactions, predict potential roadblocks and seize opportunities in shifting circumstances, which are vital for enhancing business agility and driving strategic adaptability.

Engaging with emotional nuances allows leaders to anticipate hurdles and harness opportunities. This makes them not just reactive to change, but able to proactively shape it. By leveraging emotional intelligence, leaders create environments where vulnerabilities are addressed, aspirations are amplified, and emotions are channelled towards positive outcomes. In essence, the most adaptable leaders don't just respond to change; they resonate emotionally with it, shaping the future with insight and empathy.

The ADAPTABLE LEADER Maturity Model

Chapter 11 ventures into the eleventh component of our comprehensive fifteen-part leadership model, accentuating two pivotal leadership dimensions—individual adaptability and team adaptability. In an era of continuous disruption, the ability of a leader to adapt personally and foster a culture of adaptability within their team becomes indispensable. This chapter, thus, introduces the Adaptable Leader Maturity Model, a tool to decode the dynamics of these elements and equip leaders to build resilience in the face of change, helping them leave a powerful legacy.

The ADAPTABLE LEADER

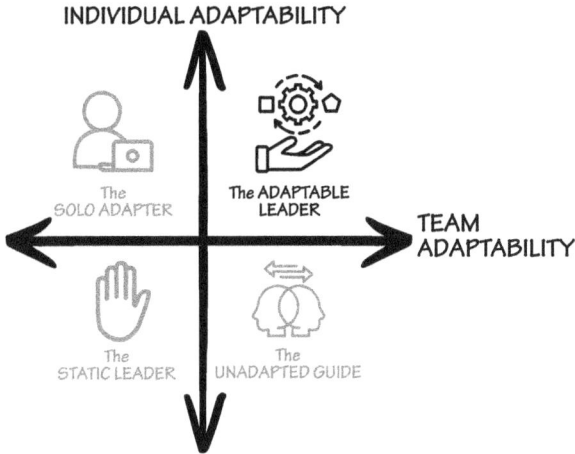

INDIVIDUAL ADAPTABILITY

The
SOLO ADAPTER

The ADAPTABLE
LEADER

TEAM
ADAPTABILITY

The
STATIC LEADER

The
UNADAPTED GUIDE

How adaptable are you as a leader? As an individual? Let's find out.

The Static Leader: Leaders in this quadrant demonstrate low individual adaptability and low team adaptability. Their rigid mindset may prevent them from effectively responding to changes and they may also struggle to foster a culture of adaptability within their team. To move towards a more adaptable leadership style, these leaders need to START recognising the value of adaptability in a rapidly changing world. They should also START creating an environment that encourages learning and change within their teams.

They should STOP resisting change and clinging to outdated methods or mindsets that hinder progress and innovation.

The Solo Adapter: Leaders in this quadrant exhibit high individual adaptability but struggle to inspire the same in their teams, indicating low team adaptability. While they personally adapt well to changes, their teams may lag, potentially due to a lack of guidance or a culture that doesn't support adaptability. To enhance their leadership effectiveness, these leaders should START instilling a culture that encourages adaptability. This involves helping their team members to develop resilience and embrace innovation in the face of change. They should STOP isolating their adaptability journey and ensure they're actively involving their teams in the change process.

The Unadapted Guide: Leaders who fall into this quadrant nurture high team adaptability, but personally struggle with adaptability and display low individual adaptability. They have successfully cultivated adaptability within their teams, but their personal struggle with change may limit their ability to guide their teams through disruptive circumstances effectively. To improve, leaders in this quadrant should START investing in their personal adaptability. They should embrace continuous learning and see change as an opportunity rather than a threat. They should STOP relying solely on their teams for adaptability and begin to embody the change they wish to see.

The Adaptable Leader: This quadrant represents the ideal state where leaders display both high individual adaptability and high team adaptability. They have not only mastered the art of adapting to changes themselves, but also succeeded in instilling an adaptable culture within their teams. These leaders should START sharing their successful strategies and experiences to inspire others. They should also continue their efforts in nurturing a culture of adaptability within their organisations.

Adaptable leadership in action

Action is at the heart of adaptability. It's dynamic, exciting, always in flux. Here are five ways to encourage your team to step out of their comfort zones and embrace a fluid, more unpredictable way of working.

Cultivate a growth mindset and encourage continuous learning: Adaptability begins with a growth mindset, where change is seen as an opportunity, not a threat. Leaders must encourage continuous learning within themselves and their teams. By embracing new methods, technologies and strategies, leaders create a culture that thrives on change. This includes providing learning resources, celebrating creative thinking, and recognising those who actively pursue growth and adaptability. To bring this into practice, consider creating a monthly learning challenge, where team members explore a new skill or topic and share their insights. Additionally, leaders can establish 'innovation hours', dedicated time each week for exploring new strategies or tools relevant to their roles.

Empower team autonomy and self-direction: To truly foster adaptability, leaders must empower their teams to operate autonomously and encourage self-direction. By giving team members the freedom to make decisions, experiment with new approaches and take calculated risks, leaders cultivate a culture where innovation is not only welcomed, but expected. This autonomy breeds responsibility, accountability and a deep sense of ownership, enabling team members to adapt swiftly to changing circumstances without waiting for top-down instructions. Practical ways to integrate this approach include implementing decentralised decision-making models, encouraging cross-functional team collaborations, and providing platforms for team members to voice innovative solutions and ideas.

Foster emotional intelligence to enhance adaptability: Leaders who possess high emotional intelligence can understand, interpret and respond to their own emotions as well as those of their team members. This allows them to navigate changes with greater ease and foresight, anticipating potential challenges and addressing them proactively. An emotionally intelligent leader is attuned to the team's morale and can adjust strategies based on the emotional climate. This can be done by promoting emotional intelligence through workshops, mentoring programs and team-building exercises.

Harness neuroplasticity and bio-adaptive strategies from nature: Drawing insights from the natural world, leaders can fuse the principles of neuroplasticity and bio-adaptive strategies to shape organisational resilience. Just as the brain's neurons reorganise for optimal function, companies can foster fluid role definitions and cross-functional collaborations. Similarly, nature's adeptness at evolving to thrive in diverse conditions serves as a blueprint for organisations to anticipate, respond to and capitalise on shifts in their ecosystems.

Integrate the Adaptable Leader to guide leadership and team adaptability: The Adaptable Leader Maturity Model, distinguishing leaders into four quadrants (Static Leaders, Solo Adapters, Unadapted Guides, Adaptable Leader), offers a practical framework for understanding and enhancing adaptability within leadership. Leaders can actively assess and position themselves within this model, focusing on specific actions to improve. For instance, Static Leaders may work on cultivating personal resilience, while Solo Adapters might concentrate on guiding their teams to embrace adaptability.

Having recognised adaptability as a cornerstone of successful leadership, especially during transformational change, we look ahead. In the following chapter, we shift our focus to two lesser-discussed but immensely powerful leadership attributes—vulnerability and humility. Join us as we delve into how these qualities can enhance leadership effectiveness, and their profound implications in disruptive leadership.

CHAPTER INSIGHTS

- Adaptability, crucial in our dynamic era, is the ability for leaders to effectively recognise and respond to change.

- Leadership mandates the leveraging of collective intelligence to navigate this changing terrain, with leaders adjusting their approach based on fresh data and circumstances.

- Not just reacting to change, adaptable leadership actively shapes it, controlling the pace of change rather than attempting to catch up.

- This form of leadership fosters a culture of ongoing learning, viewing change as an opportunity for growth rather than a threat.

- It involves cultivating a growth mindset, fostering a learning culture, promoting resilience and diversity, all while upholding a clear sense of purpose and direction.

- The concept of adaptability underlines the necessity of a cycle of unlearning, learning and relearning, placing the ability to acquire new knowledge above the knowledge already possessed.

- In a leader, personal adaptability triggers personal growth and resilience, and is reliant on an open mindset, emotional intelligence and continuous learning.

- Leaders play a key role in promoting an adaptive mindset in their teams, encouraging curiosity, acceptance of new ideas and learning from mistakes.

12

VULNERABILITY AND HUMILITY IN DISRUPTIVE LEADERSHIP

We are all apprentices in a craft
where no one ever becomes a master.

ERNEST HEMINGWAY

LEADERSHIP IN the disruptive era demands a recalibration of traditional norms, specifically the notions of vulnerability and humility. This chapter illuminates these underrated yet essential leadership traits, revealing the strength that lies in showing up authentically. We explore how expressing vulnerability—sharing mistakes, acknowledging challenges—creates connection and fosters trust within your team. Similarly, we delve into the practice of humility—admitting when we're wrong and taking lessons from these instances. This chapter initiates a shift in perspective, allowing you to embrace the power of vulnerability and humility and leverage them as instruments for building effective, human-centred leadership.

Writing a book feels like standing naked on a stage with a spotlight fixed on you, except your thoughts, ideas and fears are exposed for the world to not only see, but critique. I often liken it to a chef cooking their signature dish for a renowned food critic. The ingredients are all there, but the balance must be perfect. The creation is delicate, an essence of your soul put onto the plate or, in my case, the page.

I remember sharing my feelings of vulnerability with a fellow author. Her response was as cutting as it was wise: 'This isn't about you; this is about your message. So, get over yourself.' The sting of those words resonated deeply within me, but they were an important realisation. This book, this creation, was never about me. It was about you, the reader.

The success of my first book, *Fit for Disruption*, gave me a swagger, a sense of invincibility. It felt like conquering a mountain. Elated, I jumped straight into my next project, letting arrogance guide my pen instead of humility.

The result? A draft filled with shortcuts, missing the structure, integrity and authenticity that writing requires. Sentences left incomplete; ideas left unpolished. What was I thinking? My editor's feedback, while respectful, was brutally honest. The manuscript was nothing short of a disaster (my words, not hers).

My ego was bruised, battered and laid bare for three long years. Three years I could have spent inspiring others, guiding leaders, sharing wisdom.

Instead, I was trapped in a cycle of self-doubt and frustration.

But those three years were not a waste. They were a lesson, a challenge that shaped the very essence of my philosophy. Vulnerability and humility are not just words; they're practices. They require facing into your fears, acknowledging imperfections, learning from mistakes and growing stronger.

This book is my third attempt, shaped by the scars of previous failures. It's not a literary masterpiece, nor does it aim to be. It's honest, authentic, a reflection of my journey and growth. It's an attempt to touch lives, to inspire leaders to create a legacy.

In embracing vulnerability and humility, I've discovered an incredible reservoir of strength. It's allowed me to navigate the complexities of change, to foster trust, and to connect more deeply with you, the reader.

While imperfect, it is real, a testament to resilience and growth. My hope is that it serves you, even if it's only you and nobody else, in your journey to become a better leader, a catalyst for change, a beacon of empathy and strength.

Through writing this book, I've learned that perfection is not the goal. Growth, authenticity and perseverance are what matter. Like a well-cooked dish, it may not suit everyone's palate, but its essence and flavour are true to its core.

Remember, it's not about being perfect; it's about being real, embracing the vulnerability and humility that make us human, and using those qualities to lead, inspire, and change the world—one page, one idea, one person at a time.

Perfection, as a societal construct, often acts as a deceptive mirage, constantly shifting and always just beyond our grasp. Yet, the true essence of perfection lies not in achieving an unblemished existence, but in embracing the intricate tapestry of imperfections that make us who we are. Every stumble, every misstep and every vulnerability is a testament to our journey, a unique signature of our existence.

The pursuit of an illusory perfection can often divert our energies away from our true potential, stalling progress. Instead of masking our flaws, it's essential we recognise them as integral parts of our narrative. Celebrating our authentic self, with all its quirks and blemishes, not only frees us from the shackles of unrealistic expectations, but also propels us forward. It allows us to redirect our energy from concealment to growth, from pretence to genuine progress. By acknowledging that being imperfect is, in fact, the most genuine form of perfection, we step into a realm of self-acceptance and empowerment, where our energies are channelled into meaningful evolution rather than the endless chase of a fleeting ideal.

The paradigm shift towards vulnerability and humility

Leadership, a deeply personal journey, has undergone a transformative shift in its conceptualisation and practice. For years, leaders were depicted as invincible characters, unerring in their strategic judgements and decisions. This image of invulnerability was hailed as a sign of strength, poise and control. A leader was viewed as an impenetrable fortress of ideas, navigating the path with unflinching certainty.

Increasingly, invulnerability in leadership is being recognised as a veneer, a meticulously crafted guise that conceals the person underneath. Leaders who were once admired for their steady composure are now seen as detached and aloof, disconnected from the realities and intricacies of today's dynamic business realities.

The problems associated with invulnerability stem from its inherent rigidity and emotional distance. Invulnerable leaders, in their quest to appear unbreakable, often miss out on opportunities for learning, growth and connection. They risk fostering an environment where mistakes are feared, creativity is stifled, and employees are hesitant to express their ideas or concerns.

Furthermore, invulnerability can lead to isolation in leadership. By maintaining an image of perfection and infallibility, leaders may inadvertently build a wall that separates them from their teams. This can lead to communication gaps, lack of trust and a disengaged workforce, all of which can severely impact an organisation's performance and culture.

The move towards vulnerability and humility is not a degradation of leadership but an elevation, a necessary evolution. The understanding that the traditional armour of invulnerability often obstructs not just the leader, but their potential for growth and connection, is changing the way we comprehend leadership.

The importance of vulnerability and humility in leadership

In a world that has often idolised strength and certainty, vulnerability and humility may seem counterintuitive in the context of leadership. Yet, these qualities are essential in modern leadership and particularly relevant in disruptive times. Both vulnerability and humility are about letting go of our facades and pretences and revealing our authentic selves.

Vulnerability in leadership is about courageously accepting our imperfections and uncertainties, and not being afraid to make them visible to others. It's about embracing the reality that we don't have all the answers, and we too, like everyone else, are on a continuous journey of learning and growth. It means having the strength to say, 'I don't know,' 'I was wrong,' or 'I need help,' to those we lead.

The fact is, vulnerability sparks innovation. When we acknowledge that we don't have all the answers, we open ourselves up to new ideas, perspectives and solutions. We create space for others to contribute their expertise, and we encourage a culture of collaboration and co-creation. In disruptive times, this ability to tap into the collective intelligence of the team becomes an invaluable asset.

Humility, also, is about recognising and accepting our limitations and the fact that we don't have a monopoly on wisdom or ideas. Humble leaders are open to learning from anyone, regardless of their rank or role. They value others' contributions and see them as vital to the success of the team and the organisation. It's in the moments of uncertainty that looking beyond oneself becomes crucial. Turning to others, whose experiences are freshly aligned with present challenges, can unveil innovative approaches. It underscores the idea that in an ever-evolving landscape, humility and openness can be a leader's greatest assets, ensuring adaptability and resilience in the face of change.

Vulnerability is crucial in leadership because it is rooted in our shared human experience. Vulnerability paves the way for genuine connections and relationships because it allows others to see and connect with our human side. It helps build trust, and trust is the foundation of any successful team or organisation. When leaders exhibit vulnerability, it creates an environment where it's safe for others to do the same, leading to open, honest conversations and shared understanding.

Vulnerability and humility are not signs of weakness in leadership, but marks of strength. They are the qualities that humanise leaders, bringing them closer to their teams and facilitating deeper, more meaningful connections. They are the attributes that fuel innovation, resilience and success in disruptive times. As counterintuitive as it may seem, showing up with vulnerability and humility might just be the most courageous and impactful thing a leader can do.

Embracing one's flaws and shortcomings does not imply a deficit in self-esteem; rather, it is a testament to an individual's self-awareness and the courage to confront imperfections. Similarly, acknowledging one's limitations doesn't denote a lack of backbone; it reflects a heart that is open to growth, understanding and empathy. In a world that often rewards bravado, true power lies in the grace of humility and the authenticity of vulnerability.

Expressing vulnerability to create connection

Vulnerability in leadership, far from being a sign of weakness, is a testament to a leader's courage to embrace both triumphs and tribulations. This openness paves the way for mutual understanding and fosters an environment of trust, which is the bedrock of successful teams.

Imagine a scenario where a leader openly discusses a significant error they committed. Not only does this candidness humanise them, making them more relatable and approachable, but it also shatters the conventional image of leaders being infallible. However, vulnerability is not an open invitation for excessive personal disclosure; it's a measured revelation of experiences that underscore our collective human journey.

Leaders who embody this trait inspire a culture of resilience, adaptability and collaborative problem solving. Importantly, when a leader reveals their vulnerability, it empowers team members to voice differing opinions or even challenge the leader's perspective, especially in turbulent times. This feedback loop is crucial for innovation and growth, as it fosters a culture where ideas are weighed on merit rather than hierarchy and where calling out missteps is seen as a step forward, not a setback.

One leader who embodied the power of vulnerability is New Zealand's former Prime Minister Jacinda Ardern. Ardern demonstrated exceptional leadership following the Christchurch mosque shootings in 2019. Her response was not one of unyielding stoicism, but of compassion and vulnerability. She openly grieved with the families, sharing in their pain and not shying away from showing her emotions in public. Ardern's willingness to be vulnerable on a global stage went beyond mere political gesture; it connected her with her people and the world, setting a powerful example of how leaders can use vulnerability to create a profound connection, and lead with empathy and humanity in times of crisis. This instance starkly illustrates how a leader's open expression of vulnerability can catalyse unity and collective strength, turning a moment of despair into a beacon of shared resilience.

Embracing vulnerability means stepping into uncertainty and discomfort. It requires letting go of the illusion of control and accepting our shared human experiences. When leaders transparently share their mistakes and challenges, they form an emotional connection that's the trust cornerstone, upon which successful teams are built.

Picture a meeting where the leader reveals a major mistake they made. They delve into not only what went wrong but also how it felt, the doubts it triggered, the questions it brought up. They discuss their struggle. This clashes with traditional leadership expectations—leaders are expected to be steadfast and invincible. But this authenticity, honesty and vulnerability make a leader genuinely approachable and human.

However, expressing vulnerability isn't about over-sharing or turning the workplace into a personal therapy space. It's about disclosing pertinent experiences that highlight our shared humanity and boost our collective resilience. Leaders may say, 'I don't have all the answers,' or 'I made a mistake, and this is what I learned,' or 'This is also hard for me.' Achieving this balance requires self-awareness, discernment and emotional intelligence.

Lastly, expressing vulnerability means being open to others' vulnerability. Leaders should create a safe environment for team members to reveal their challenges and failures and respond empathetically. When leaders can say, 'I see you, I hear you, and I appreciate your courage,' they not only validate their team members' experiences but also empower them to be resilient in facing their own challenges.

Practising humility: how to accept being wrong and learn from it

Humility is often eclipsed in leadership discussions by more assertive qualities such as confidence, decisiveness and vision. However, in disruptive times, humility gains a new, profound significance.

Leadership humility begins with acceptance—acknowledging that leaders don't know everything. They can be wrong, and their ideas and paths can lead to dead ends. In leadership, where power and control often take centre stage, this is a radical concept. But in disruptive leadership, it's transformative.

When leaders accept fallibility, they depart from the pedestal of perfection and join their team in the reality of trial and error, exploration and discovery. They replace infallibility with a liberating sense of shared humanity, fostering a culture where everyone can make mistakes and learn from them.

Being wrong is not a weakness or incompetence marker; it's a learning, growth and innovation opportunity. Each mistake is a waiting question, a begging problem, a yearning lesson. Leaders, by their role, can leverage this opportunity for their and their team's learning.

The acceptance of being wrong is a potent learning act. It educates leaders about their blind spots, assumptions and biases. It compels them to question, investigate and explore; pushing them out of their comfort zones into the exciting unknown. Here, they discover new solutions, ideas, and their own leadership potential.

Leadership's real magic occurs when leaders learn from their mistakes. This is where humility transforms from a passive attribute into an active practice. Leaders don't just admit mistakes—they dissect, analyse and learn from them. They convert their failures into stepping stones to success and their missteps into guideposts for the future.

In the process, they inspire their team to do the same, creating an environment where failure is seen not as a threat, but as a learning and innovation catalyst. They foster a culture where everyone is a learner, a discoverer, an explorer. In this culture, our time's disruptive challenges become exciting puzzles to solve and thrilling journeys to embark on.

Humility in triumph: leading from a place of gratitude

While humility in accepting mistakes is pivotal, equally significant is the humility displayed in moments of success. Overconfidence, spurred by repeated successes, can make leaders blind to potential pitfalls and risks. They may fall into the trap of thinking they have all the answers, making them vulnerable to unforeseen disruptions and challenges. Such overconfidence can be a silent saboteur, subtly eroding the very foundation upon which their success was built.

A true leader recognises that success is not an individual achievement, but a collective endeavour. Every win is the result of countless contributions, often unseen and unacknowledged, from teams, mentors, peers, and even competitors, who've pushed the leader to excel. Humility in success means sharing the limelight, giving credit where it's due, and understanding that the leader is but a part of the larger effort and dedication.

Staying grounded during periods of achievement makes a leader more approachable. Leaders who remain humble are often more accessible, encouraging open communication, nurturing talent, and building future leaders from within their teams. They understand that true success isn't just about reaching the pinnacle themselves, but ensuring others can follow in their footsteps and even surpass them.

In essence, humility, both in times of challenge and triumph, isn't just an admirable trait—it's a strategic one. It ensures that leaders remain alert to changing dynamics, fosters an inclusive and empowering organisational culture, and guarantees a sustainable leadership model that can weather both storms and sunny days.

Humility in leadership, previously misinterpreted as a deficit of confidence, is now acknowledged as an indicator of strength. It involves the realisation that the essence of leadership is not about amassing authority, but in its distribution. Humble leaders value everyone's contribution, appreciating the potential for exceptional ideas from all quarters.

Integrating vulnerability and humility into leadership involves shedding the pretence of invincibility to reveal the genuine person beneath the role. It's about accepting the inherent worth of each team member's input, which fosters an atmosphere where all voices are heard, appreciated and empowered.

The VULNERABLE AND
HUMBLE LEADER Maturity Model

Chapter 12 delves into the twelfth segment of our comprehensive fifteen-part leadership model, focusing on two interconnected dimensions of leadership—vulnerability and humility. In a disruptive world, leaders who embrace their vulnerabilities and embody humility create an environment of trust and resilience. This chapter introduces the Vulnerable and Humble Leader Maturity Model, a tool that helps decode these elements and arms leaders with insights to cultivate these virtues, thereby paving the way for a strong legacy.

THE VULNERABLE &
HUMBLE LEADER

VULNERABILITY

The TRANSPARENT
EGOIST

The VULNERABLE &
HUMBLE LEADER

HUMILITY

The GUARDED
LEADER

The PROUD
EMPATH

The Guarded Leader: Leaders in this quadrant demonstrate low vulnerability and low humility. They may find it difficult to reveal their weaknesses and may put their own needs over those of their teams, indicating a lack of humility. To develop a more effective leadership style, these leaders need to START recognising vulnerability as a strength that fosters trust and connection. They should also START practising humility, acknowledging it as a strength that enhances their ability to learn and grow. They should STOP hiding behind a facade of invulnerability and putting their needs and ego above the needs of their teams.

The Transparent Egoist: Leaders in this quadrant show high vulnerability but low humility. They are open about their shortcomings and challenges, but they may struggle to prioritise their team's needs over their own, indicating a lack of humility. For personal and professional growth, these leaders should START acknowledging the importance of humility and strive to place their team's needs and contributions above their own. They should STOP overshadowing their team's efforts with their openness and learn to balance vulnerability with a genuine recognition of others.

The Proud Empath: This quadrant encapsulates leaders who demonstrate low vulnerability but high humility. These leaders place high importance on humility and prioritise their team's needs over their own, but they may struggle to display vulnerability. Leaders in this quadrant should START openly sharing their struggles and fears, realising that vulnerability fosters trust and connection within their teams. They should STOP guarding themselves too tightly, understanding that true connection arises from shared experiences and vulnerabilities.

The Vulnerable and Humble Leader: This quadrant represents the ideal state where leaders demonstrate both high vulnerability and high humility. They exhibit vulnerability by openly sharing their shortcomings and fears, and display humility by prioritising their team's needs. These leaders should START sharing their strategies and experiences to inspire others and should continue to foster a culture of vulnerability and humility within their teams.

Vulnerable and Humble leadership in action

Life is easier when you don't have to try so hard to be invulnerable; when your mistakes and flaws are catalysts for growth and change, rather than a source of deep shame. Here are five ways to start embracing these qualities now and encourage them within your organisation.

Encourage open expression of mistakes and challenges: In a rapidly changing environment, acknowledging mistakes and challenges is a sign of strength, not weakness. Leaders must actively foster a culture where team members feel safe to openly share their failures and difficulties. By doing so, leaders humanise themselves, showing that they, too, are learners in the journey, not infallible figures. This

practice not only builds trust but encourages innovative thinking, as team members feel free to explore
new paths without the fear of failure. In practice, this
can be achieved by holding regular team reflection
sessions where members discuss challenges faced and
solutions attempted, creating a constructive feedback
loop.

**Promote an environment of respect and acknowledge
others' contributions:** Humility in leadership is about
recognising that wisdom does not reside solely at the
top of the hierarchy. Leaders must value each team
member's input and create a respectful environment
where everyone's voice is heard. This encourages
open communication and collaboration, recognising
that great ideas can come from anywhere within the
organisation. By actively appreciating and utilising the
diverse perspectives of the team, leaders build a more
innovative and resilient organisation. Practically, leaders can set up regular brainstorming sessions where
everyone's ideas are equally welcomed and considered, fostering a sense of collective ownership.

**Develop learning opportunities from failures and adap-
tations:** Embracing vulnerability in leadership means
seeing failures as opportunities for learning and growth,
rather than setbacks. Leaders must implement practices that allow the organisation to learn from mistakes
and make necessary adaptations. By systematically
analysing failures and deriving lessons from them,
leaders build a culture that values continuous learning

and improvement. This approach aligns with the disruptive era's demands, where adaptation and growth from challenges are essential. In practical terms, post-project debriefs can be institutionalised, focusing on what went wrong, what went right, and the takeaways for future endeavours.

Lead by example in showcasing humility and vulnerability: Leaders must not only talk about vulnerability and humility, but must actively demonstrate these traits. By openly sharing their own mistakes, uncertainties and learning, leaders set a powerful example for their team. This authentic approach fosters deep connections and encourages team members to also show their human side. It turns leadership into a collective, human-centred journey where leaders and followers grow together, navigating the complexities of the modern business world. For instance, leaders can hold monthly 'share and learn' sessions where they discuss personal challenges and how they overcame them, inviting others to do the same and thus humanising the leadership process.

Integrate the Vulnerable and Humble Leader Maturity Model to guide authentic leadership: The Vulnerable and Humble Maturity Model, distinguishing leaders into four quadrants (Guarded Leaders, Transparent Egoists, Proud Empaths, Vulnerable-Humble Leaders), offers a practical framework for understanding and enhancing vulnerability and humility within leadership. Leaders can actively assess and position themselves within this model, focusing on specific actions to improve. For instance, Guarded Leaders may work on revealing weaknesses and prioritising team needs, while Transparent Egoists might strive to balance their openness with a greater acknowledgment of others' contributions.

In acknowledging vulnerability and humility as leadership strengths, we conclude Part 4 We've understood how positive impact, adaptability, vulnerability and humility shape our leadership legacy. As we transition into the final part of the book, we'll investigate how the integration of action and reflection contributes to disruptive leadership. We will delve into driving action, the significance of reflective leadership, and the necessity of embracing self-transformation.

CHAPTER INSIGHTS

- Leadership is undergoing a paradigm shift from displaying invulnerability to embracing vulnerability and humility. The archetype of the unassailable leader is giving way to leaders who show their human side and connect more deeply with their teams.

- The drawbacks of invulnerability in leadership, such as rigidity and potential isolation from teams, can be mitigated by embracing vulnerability and humility, which can significantly enhance the organisational culture.

- Vulnerability and humility are essential aspects of contemporary leadership, enabling leaders to be authentic, acknowledge their imperfections and accept the lack of all answers.

- Vulnerability fosters trust and opens avenues for innovation through the recognition of knowledge gaps and encouragement of new ideas. Simultaneously, humility values each team member's input and promotes an environment of open communication and respect.

- Leaders practising vulnerability should articulate their uncertainties and failures, fostering a safe environment where team members can share their challenges. In parallel, humility requires accepting mistakes, which transforms failures into opportunities for learning and growth.

- The synergy of vulnerability and humility in leadership enhances team bonds and performance, and sparks transformation within individuals and organisations.

- Practising vulnerability and humility equips leaders to address disruption, where learning from failures and adapting to changes are the norm. This approach humanises leaders and positions them within their teams.

- The move from invulnerability to vulnerability and humility signifies a profound understanding of strength and power, empowering everyone to contribute and fostering collective strength to navigate modern business complexities.

THE PRIZES OF LEGACY-ORIENTED LEADERSHIP

In **Part 4: Legacy-Oriented Leadership,** we consider the long-lasting repercussions of effective disruptive leadership. Our voyage reveals the profound art of crafting a sustainable legacy combined with the ambition of seeding profound positive impacts. Emphasising two distinct, yet intertwined attributes— adaptability and a harmonious blend of vulnerability with humility—this section is a beacon for leaders aiming to mould a legacy that not only stands the test of time but also propels future generations.

Building a Lasting Legacy

As a leader, the impact you create extends beyond immediate tasks and milestones. Through your ethical leadership practices and alignment of personal and professional goals, you'll initiate transformational changes that will resonate long after your tenure. Your ability to build and maintain this enduring legacy will serve as a beacon for future leaders, inspiring innovation and positive change.

Adaptability in Leadership

The pace of change in today's world necessitates a leader's ability to adapt effectively. Your proficiency in recognising and responding to these changes will set the stage for your team's success. As you foster a culture of continuous learning and resilience, you will better navigate the uncertainties, seizing emerging opportunities and ensuring your organisation stays ahead of the curve.

Exercising Vulnerability and Humility

In an era when authenticity and connection are highly valued, vulnerability and humility become potent leadership traits. By embracing these qualities, you'll create a supportive environment that encourages innovation and risk taking. These traits will also allow you to foster deeper relationships with your team, enhancing trust, promoting open communication and cultivating a collaborative culture.

Promoting an Agile Mindset

In the face of constant change, agility becomes a key attribute of disruptive leaders. As you foster a growth mindset within yourself and your team, you'll enable your organisation to adapt quickly and thrive in disruption. Your commitment to promoting resilience, diversity and a clear sense of purpose will guide your team through shifts and changes, fuelling their readiness to face future challenges.

Creating a Safe Environment for Innovation

By exhibiting vulnerability and humility, you'll foster an atmosphere of trust and transparency within your team. This safe environment will encourage risk taking and innovation, equipping your organisation to successfully navigate disruptive times. Your ability to humanise leadership and connect deeply with your team will serve as a solid foundation for your long-term leadership impact.

PART 5

TRANSFORMATIONAL LEADERSHIP

CONTEMPORARY

TRANSFORMATIONAL

THE DISRUPTIVE LEADER

INFLUENTIAL

LEGACY ORIENTED

FUTURE-READY

With our insights on creating a legacy firmly in place, we navigate to **Part 5: Transformational Leadership**. This part of the journey brings us to the heart of leadership in action, exploring how leaders can inspire action and influence change.

Transformational Leadership examines the critical interplay between action and reflection in effective leadership during times of disruption. It illuminates the path and shows leaders how to initiate and drive impactful actions, derive valuable learning from disruption through conscious reflection, and pursue personal transformation to foster evolution in their leadership roles.

We live in an era of relentless change, where planning and strategising form only half the equation of effective leadership. Leaders must also consolidate and steer action. Action-oriented leadership in disruptive times necessitates taking considered risks, making prompt and strategic decisions, and following through on the implementation of these decisions to instigate real change and progression. **Chapter 13: Driving Action in Disruptive Leadership** discusses the importance of leaders taking initiative, driving action, and making decisions that lead to tangible outcomes in a disruptive business environment.

While action forms the cornerstone of progress, actions devoid of reflection can potentially cause pitfalls. Reflective leadership offers a robust platform to learn from the turbulence of disruption. It promotes the habit among leaders to introspect their actions and experiences, comprehend their consequences, and extract insights that can inform and refine future strategies and decisions. The act of reflection allows leaders to constantly fine-tune their approach, tailor their strategies to emerging realities, and reduce the likelihood of repeating past mistakes. **Chapter 14: Reflective Leadership: Learning from Disruption** highlights the value of reflective practice in leadership, illustrating how leaders can learn from their experiences during disruptive times to continually improve their leadership approach and decision making.

Moving beyond action and reflection, disruptive leadership also necessitates leaders embracing personal disruption. This involves recognising and accepting the continuous journey of personal growth and transformation as a fundamental requirement for effective leadership in disruptive times. Leaders need to be agile in their personal development, matching the pace of external change with internal evolution, and building resilience for overcoming challenges that disruption invariably presents. **Chapter 15: Personal Disruption: Embracing Self-Transformation**, explores the concept of personal disruption. It emphasises the need for leaders to continually evolve and transform themselves to navigate the challenges and demands of disruptive leadership effectively.

Part 5 aims to guide leaders in balancing action with reflection, while embracing personal transformation as an integral part of successful leadership in this disruptive era. By embracing and incorporating the principles discussed here, leaders will be equipped to thrive and leave a lasting mark in a rapidly evolving world. Leaders who master the art of driving action amidst disruption, learning from their experiences, and embracing personal transformation are paving the path to a leadership style that is agile, insightful and transformative. As we progress further in our exploration, we'll continue to deepen our understanding of disruptive leadership, enabling you to forge an influential and enduring legacy that resonates well beyond your tenure.

DRIVING ACTION IN DISRUPTIVE LEADERSHIP

Done is better than perfect.

SHERYL SANDBERG

C HAPTER 13 unveils the crucial role of action in leadership. Passive observation is no longer enough; leadership demands active participation. We will discover how to inspire an action-oriented mindset within your team. We will discuss how to strike the right balance between proactive decision-making and thoughtful contemplation, ensuring that action is always purposeful and measured. We'll also address the risks associated with a high-action environment, offering strategies to avoid the trap of burnout, and the way to sustain a healthy and productive pace of change. As we delve deeper, we'll unpack the intricate relationship between decision making, action, and effective leadership amidst disruption.

I had been engaged with yet another retailer on an Operation Efficiency program. As I crossed the threshold of the sprawling retail store, a sense of déjà vu engulfed me; the scene recalled operational landscapes I'd traversed before, where systemic inefficiencies were crying out for coordinated change by leaders willing to embrace action.

I met Steve amidst the racks and registers; he was to be my partner in transforming just one store. But it was a start, and he was brimming with sharp observations and latent skills.

We started small—orchestrating the jumbled chaos of delivery schedules and providing simple equipment that turned cumbersome chores into small successes—but each minor triumph laid down a foothold. In Steve's domain, these 'quick wins' soon translated into visible improvements. A streamlined checkout process dramatically cut down waiting times, while a newly coordinated alignment of delivery schedules from distribution centres and direct suppliers reduced logistical bottlenecks. Feedback mechanisms were put in place to fine-tune inventory levels, preventing overstocking and understocking. Efforts to optimise delivery and packaging methods markedly increased the efficiency of getting products onto shelves. A critical review of existing processes led to the identification and elimination of outdated practices that were no longer serving the store's needs. Each of these steps, small in isolation, together composed a symphony of operational excellence that resonated throughout the store.

Every aisle traversed, each interaction with Steve, became puzzle pieces of possibility. Simple adjustments in inventory handling or process optimisations, though seemingly minor, cascaded into significant time and cost savings. Collectively, these quick wins ignited a spark of enthusiasm within the team. Hesitant staff members transformed into engaged contributors, keen to share innovative ideas and become champions of their own workspaces.

The storeroom, once a maze of disorder, became a model of efficiency with the introduction of a 5s program, which brought order that was both physical and symbolic, and imbued the team with a newfound sense of ownership and pride. And Steve, previously just a face among many, stepped forward as the unsung hero, leading by quiet example and inspiring his peers to do the same.

These small steps—a policy reimagined, a process polished, or a staff member uplifted—created a rich and transformative impact. Steve and I created a collection of modest victories that, together, became a grand strategy. As this lone store set off on its transformation, the swell of change engulfed more and more stores and became a benchmark for operations everywhere—from the factory floor to the realms of knowledge work.

This story was replicated across countless stores and operations, and began to sculpt a legacy where each quick win, each empowered employee like Steve, built upon the last and created a competitive yet collaborative spirit among branches vying not for rivalry, but for shared excellence.

Transitioning from the success stories within a single store to a widespread culture of excellence doesn't happen through grand gestures, but through the aggregation of many small, practical steps. The journey of Steve and his store paints a relatable picture of this process. Each individual improvement, while seemingly small, lays the groundwork for a broader transformation. A Centre of Excellence emerges from these humble beginnings, illustrating how focused efforts can evolve into a standard for others to emulate. It's about taking the tangible lessons learned on the shop floor and applying them on a larger scale, turning everyday wins into a cohesive strategy that uplifts entire operations. This is the real-world translation of ambition into action, where the dedication to continuous improvement in familiar, everyday settings paves the way for sweeping organisational progress.

A Centre of Excellence stands as a beacon of transformative leadership and operational prowess across any environment, be it a high-tech manufacturing floor, a strategic distribution hub, or a bustling logistics operation. It's within these centres that leaders practise action-oriented leadership, applying nimble strategies to secure quick wins that accumulate into substantial progress. These centres act as incubators for innovation and exemplars of efficiency, serving as reference points for all other operational facets. Here, leaders do not just direct; they embed themselves in the fabric of the work-flow, discerning opportunities for improvement and acting decisively to implement them.

Leaders in these environments champion the ethos of 'learning by doing' and 'teaching by example.' They are the harbingers of change, who understand that the creation and nurturing of a Centre of Excellence involve a hands-on approach, fostering an atmosphere where every team member is empowered to suggest and participate in the change. By leading from the front, they demonstrate what it takes to iterate towards perfection, creating a culture where excellence is the norm, not the exception.

These centres are not isolated islands of efficiency; they are interconnected with the organisation's broader strategic objectives. Leaders leverage the successes from these centres to drive organisational strategy, recognising that operational excellence is a critical pillar that upholds the larger corporate vision. The quick wins, and efficiencies gained, become the fuel that powers the engine of organisational change, demonstrating the practical execution of an often intangible strategy. In essence, the Centre of Excellence becomes both a physical and metaphorical manifestation of the organisation's dedication to continual improvement and a testament to the power of action-oriented leadership in achieving strategic ambitions.

The need for action-oriented leadership in the disruptive era

Imagine a scenario where a leader possesses extensive expertise, a profound understanding of their domain, and access to advanced tools for analysing and predicting outcomes. However, if the leader remains passive, solely comprehending the situation without taking proactive measures, their endeavours will ultimately fail. Leadership, like this example, relies not only on knowledge, strategy and vision, but also on the crucial element of decisive action.

Action-oriented leadership is not about reckless movement; it's about purposeful, strategic action. It's about understanding the change, creating a strategy, and then setting it in motion with decisiveness and agility. In the disruptive era, there's no room for indecision or procrastination. The pace at which change is happening is staggering. Opportunities, once spotted, need to be seized quickly before they disappear or are snapped up by competitors. And challenges need swift action to prevent them from snowballing into crises.

Action-oriented leadership inspires action in others. Your actions have a trickledown effect, igniting a sense of urgency, momentum and proactivity within your team. When your team sees you making decisions and taking steps swiftly and decisively, they are inspired to do the same. They learn to be more proactive, more decisive and more result oriented. This creates a culture of action within your organisation, a culture that fuels growth and success amidst disruption.

If you fail to take decisive action or have a bias towards inaction, the consequences for your personal leadership can be detrimental. Without proactive measures, your leadership effectiveness may diminish, and your ability to navigate the disruptive era may be compromised. Inaction can lead to missed opportunities, stagnation, and the inability to address emerging challenges effectively. A tendency towards inaction can erode confidence in your leadership, both within your team and among stakeholders. By not embracing action-oriented leadership, you risk falling behind, losing momentum, and ultimately hindering the growth and success of your organisation in the face of disruption.

Building momentum through quick wins and nudges

Leaders face numerous challenges in driving their teams and organisations towards success. One key strategy that can make a significant impact is the deliberate pursuit of quick wins and the effective use of nudges. These tools provide leaders with the opportunity to build momentum, boost morale and achieve tangible progress.

Quick wins can be defined as small scale victories that can be achieved relatively quickly, providing a sense of progress and accomplishment. They have a profound psychological impact on individuals and teams, influencing motivation, engagement and morale. When individuals experience these wins, they gain a heightened sense of confidence and belief in their abilities. These small victories propel further action and success. By celebrating incremental achievements, leaders can create a compounding effect that drives continuous progress and inspires the team to reach higher goals. Quick wins can take the form of achieving a short-term project goal ahead of the scheduled timeline, or introducing a small process change that results in noticeable efficiency improvements. For instance, successfully implementing a new communication tool that enhances team collaboration can be seen as a quick win, fostering immediate positive feedback and improved communication within the organisation.

In addition to quick wins, leaders can harness the power of nudges to guide behaviour and shape outcomes. Nudges are subtle interventions that influence decision making and actions without imposing restrictions or mandates. Drawing on principles from behavioural economics, leaders can design effective nudges that lead to desired behaviours. For example, strategically placing healthy snacks in the office pantry can nudge employees towards making healthier food choices. By understanding the psychology behind decision making, leaders can create a supportive environment that encourages the desired behaviours and outcomes. Nudges can be used to shape organisational culture by reinforcing positive habits and behaviours. By intentionally designing the work environment and implementing nudges that align with the desired values and goals, leaders can drive positive change and create a culture of continuous improvement and innovation.

The power of quick wins and nudges, when used in leadership, lies in their ability to empower and motivate teams. Quick wins give individuals and teams a sense of accomplishment, empowering them to act and tackle more significant challenges. When leaders create an environment that values quick wins and recognises the efforts of the team, individuals are motivated to push boundaries and strive for excellence. Nudges, on the other hand, help overcome resistance to change and drive adoption of new behaviours. By strategically implementing nudges, leaders can influence decision making and guide individuals towards embracing necessary changes. Incremental progress becomes the foundation for managing larger-scale change initiatives.

Sustaining momentum and long-term success requires leaders to integrate quick wins and nudges into their leadership practices consistently. Leaders must create a culture that celebrates small victories and embeds nudges in daily routines. By fostering an environment where progress is valued and celebrated, leaders ensure that momentum is sustained even during challenging times. Regular communication, feedback and recognition are essential for maintaining the momentum generated by quick wins. Leaders must also foster a learning mindset that encourages individuals and teams to continually improve and build upon their achievements.

Balancing action and rest—
how to avoid burnout

Burnout is an acute concern in today's demanding, fast-paced work environments. As leaders, we must balance the action bias with a focus on the wellbeing of our team members to ensure their health and sustain performance.

Failure to address burnout can lead to numerous negative repercussions. First and foremost, it diminishes productivity as fatigue-prone employees struggle to meet deadlines and maintain quality work. This loss in performance can result in missed opportunities and inferior results. Moreover, employee morale and engagement suffer as burnt-out individuals feel overwhelmed, which reduces motivation and causes them to lose sight of the organisation's goals. These morale issues can trigger higher absenteeism, increased turnover rates, and challenges in attracting and retaining top talent.

Burnout also carries significant health implications. Chronic stress and excessive workloads can result in conditions such as anxiety, depression and chronic fatigue. An environment that prioritises productivity over wellbeing is a breeding ground for illness—both physical and mental. Employees who are physically unable to work are a liability to an organisation, and those whose mental health is affected are unable to perform optimally. Moreover, a workplace culture that creates health issues, albeit inadvertently, erodes trust in leadership and leaves an organisation vulnerable to attack from within.

Preventing burnout while encouraging action requires prioritising workload management. This involves proactive workload assessment and distribution, providing support, and ensuring no individual team members are overloaded. A culture of work-life integration is essential. Leaders should encourage boundaries between work and personal life and promote regular breaks, vacations and time off, while exemplifying a healthy work-life balance.

Open communication is another preventative tool. Leaders should foster a safe space for dialogue, listening to team members and encouraging them to voice concerns, challenges and pressures. Early identification of burnout signs, such as fatigue, decreased performance, increased irritability, emotional exhaustion, physical symptoms, and disengagement, is crucial. Leaders can prevent burnout by fostering open communication, emphasising psychological safety and addressing workload management proactively. Emphasising psychological safety is key, and helps to create an environment where taking risks, making mistakes and seeking support are accepted.

Supportive team culture is critical. Leaders should foster an environment promoting collaboration, empathy and mutual support. Empowering team members to assist each other cultivates camaraderie. Appreciating individual and collective efforts, and highlighting the importance of teamwork, contributes to a positive work environment. Advocating for self-care and organisational wellbeing, and promoting regular exercise, mindfulness and stress management, are equally vital.

Leaders must also take steps to prevent becoming burnt out themselves. Arianna Huffington, co-founder and former editor in chief of *The Huffington Post*, is a compelling example of a leader who learned to balance action and rest. After collapsing from exhaustion and sleep deprivation, she became an outspoken advocate for the importance of wellbeing in the workplace. Huffington's personal transformation led her to establish Thrive Global, a company dedicated to combating burnout and promoting wellbeing among employees. Her story is a testament to the fact that even the most dedicated leaders are not immune to burnout, and that recognising one's limits can be a catalyst for creating a more sustainable work culture. Huffington's approach underscores the necessity for leaders to lead by example in setting boundaries and ensuring rest is held in equal regard to action, thereby safeguarding the team's health and preventing burnout.

As leaders, we play a pivotal role in preventing burnout while promoting action within our teams. This involves prioritising workload management, fostering work-life integration, advocating open communication, promoting psychological safety, cultivating a supportive team culture, and encouraging self-care practices. By doing so, we can maintain a healthy, productive work environment and be resilient in the face of demanding conditions.

Strategic decision making; navigating complexity with analytical rigour

In addressing the imperative of aligning decisions with vision and strategy, it's crucial to underscore that the essence of transformative leadership lies in the fusion of thoughtful deliberation, strategic alignment and dynamic action. The disruption that characterises our times does not afford the luxury of extended contemplation, yet it demands more than the haste of uninformed decisions. A leader's prowess is reflected in their ability to weave together the threads of strategic foresight, vision and timely action, creating a tapestry of progress and innovation.

Critical analytical thinking is a competency paramount for leaders navigating the complexities of our era. Leaders must hone their ability to dissect problems, evaluate options rigorously, and anticipate the potential ramifications of their decisions. This analytical rigour becomes the linchpin within which decisions are refined, strategies are validated, and alignment with the organisational vision is ensured. It ensures that choices made in the heat of the moment are not just reactions to immediate pressures, but are informed, calculated moves that align with the organisation's overarching goals and strategic direction.

Critical analytical thinking requires leaders to dig deeper, questioning assumptions and challenging the status quo. It involves a relentless pursuit of clarity, systematically breaking down complex issues to uncover underlying patterns and relationships. Leaders must develop a keen sense of discernment, separating fact from fiction and signal from noise. This level of analytical depth ensures that decisions are not just reactive but are based on a comprehensive understanding of the situation at hand, guided by the organisation's vision and strategic objectives.

Empowered by this depth of analysis and strategic alignment, leaders can navigate the ambiguity and uncertainty of disruption with a level of precision and insight that sets them apart. They are able to distinguish between fleeting trends and enduring shifts, making decisions that are both timely and timeless. By integrating this depth of critical thinking and strategic focus into the decision-making process, leaders ensure that their actions are not just expedient, but are also deeply rooted in insight, foresight, and a clear strategic direction.

Transformative leadership in disruptive times is not just about driving action; it is about ensuring that every action, every decision, is a deliberate step towards a future that is congruent with the organisation's vision, strategy and core values. It is about creating a culture where decisions, no matter how swift, are imbued with strategic intent, purposeful direction and analytical rigour.

The ACTION-ORIENTED LEADER Maturity Model

Chapter 13 delves into the thirteenth segment of our comprehensive fifteen-part leadership model, examining the critical dimensions of action-orientation and

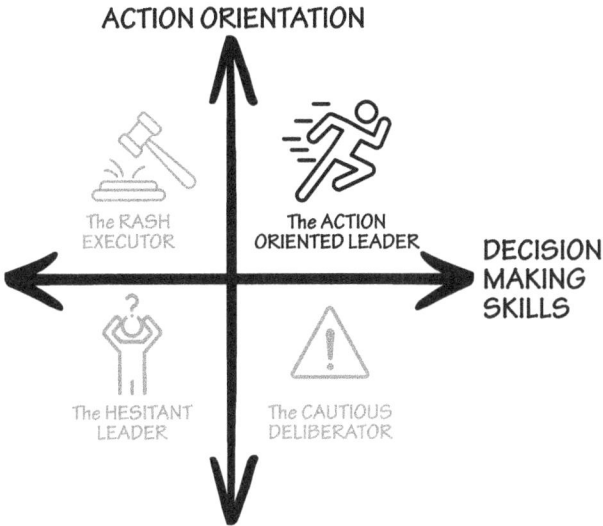

THE ACTION ORIENTED LEADER

ACTION ORIENTATION

The RASH EXECUTOR

The ACTION ORIENTED LEADER

DECISION MAKING SKILLS

The HESITANT LEADER

The CAUTIOUS DELIBERATOR

balanced decision making. Unpacking these attributes gives leaders the tools to enhance their decisiveness and cultivate an action-oriented mindset, equipping them to navigate the disruptive landscape more effectively. This chapter introduces the Action-Oriented Leader Maturity Model, a tool that aids leaders in understanding these traits and leveraging them to create a legacy.

How vigorous and confident is your leadership? Are you paralysed by decision making? Let's find out.

The Hesitant Leader: Leaders in this quadrant demonstrate low action-orientation and poor decision-making skills. They may fall prey to procrastination, delaying decisions and losing momentum. Additionally, their decisions may often be rushed or uninformed, potentially undermining their team's efforts. To enhance their effectiveness, these leaders should START embracing an action-oriented approach and ensure that their decisions are well informed and balanced. They should STOP second guessing themselves and postponing critical decisions.

The Rash Executor: Leaders in this quadrant exhibit high action-orientation but poor decision-making skills. They tend to act impulsively, without fully considering the potential consequences of their actions. As a result, their hasty decisions may lead to adverse outcomes. To improve their leadership, these leaders should START making well-informed and balanced decisions to ensure their actions lead to beneficial outcomes. They should STOP acting on impulse without sufficient forethought or consultation.

The Cautious Deliberator: This quadrant represents leaders with low action-orientation but sound decision-making skills. These leaders may overanalyse situations, causing delays in taking necessary action despite their decisions being well informed. Leaders in this quadrant should START adopting an action-first mentality, understanding that swift action, even if imperfect, often leads to better results than prolonged deliberation. They should STOP getting trapped in analysis paralysis and doubting their decision-making capabilities.

The Action-Oriented Leader: This quadrant represents the ideal state, where leaders exhibit both high action-orientation and balanced decision making. These leaders act promptly, and their decisions are well thought out and balanced, leading to effective outcomes. They should START sharing their strategies and experiences with others to instil an action-oriented and balanced decision-making mindset in their teams.

Action-oriented leadership in action

The time to act is now. Here are five ways to jump start your action-oriented leadership and build momentum in your organisation.

Cultivate an action-oriented mindset: The ability to seize opportunities and swiftly address challenges is vital in a disruptive era. Leaders must actively create a culture that promotes agility, initiative and responsibility. By consistently modelling proactivity and adaptability, leaders encourage their teams to act decisively and purposefully. For instance, a leader in a retail business, noticing a sudden shift in consumer preferences due to a cultural trend, might immediately convene a brainstorming session with their team. Instead of waiting for quarterly reviews, they adapt in real-time, rolling out a pilot product or campaign in response.

Promote alignment between actions and vision: Leaders must ensure that their decisive actions are in harmony with the organisation's vision and values. This involves constant communication, strategic planning and alignment with stakeholders' interests. By maintaining this balance, leaders prevent chaos and scattered efforts, safeguarding the wellbeing of the team and the organisation. A sustainable apparel company with a vision of environmental conservation might prioritise sourcing eco-friendly materials and investing in green technologies. By doing so, the leader's actions of selecting suppliers and allocating resources directly align with the organisation's overarching vision of sustainability, thus providing a tangible representation of their commitment to the environment.

Foster a culture of quick wins, nudges and recognition: Quick wins and nudges can build momentum, boost morale and foster confidence within the organisation. Leaders must recognise and celebrate these successes, providing continuous feedback and reinforcement. For instance, as described above, a company aiming to promote wellness might place healthy snacks in communal areas, subtly nudging employees towards healthier snack choices. Another organisation striving for transparent communication might introduce a weekly open forum, allowing team members to voice concerns and ask questions directly to management.

Balance action with prevention of burnout: While promoting a strong bias for action, leaders must also be attentive to workload management and work-life integration. Advocacy for open communication, supportive team culture and strategic decision making helps in preventing burnout and sustaining a healthy pace of change. Leaders must recognise the importance of this equilibrium and actively incorporate strategies to nurture both a vigorous action-oriented approach and the overall wellbeing of the team. For instance, a leader may introduce mandatory 'no-meeting' days once a week, allowing team members focused work time and mental rejuvenation. Additionally, implementing flexible work hours or promoting 'digital detox' weekends can help employees manage their workload while also dedicating time for personal rest and recovery.

Integrate the Action-Oriented Leader Maturity Model to guide effective leadership: The Action-Oriented Leader Maturity Model, categorising leaders into four quadrants (Hesitant Leader, Rash Executor, Cautious Deliberator, Action-Oriented Leader), provides a practical guide for understanding and improving leadership decisiveness and action-orientation. Leaders can use this model to recognise their current position, focusing on specific areas for growth. For example, Hesitant Leaders can develop an action-oriented approach, while Rash Executors may work to make more balanced and well-informed decisions.

As we end the exploration of driving action in disruptive leadership, we acknowledge the essential role of timely decision making and action-implementation in navigating disruptive times. Action-oriented leadership, we've learned, doesn't promote uncontrolled haste; it advocates a calculated approach for generating change and progress. But action alone isn't the key. In the next chapter, we will transition into understanding the other half of this leadership balance—reflective leadership. Here, we'll delve into how the introspective process of reflection complements action and provides a basis for learning and growth.

CHAPTER INSIGHTS

- Leadership in a disruptive era necessitates proactive, agile and strategic actions that seize opportunities and swiftly address challenges. It discourages indecisiveness and procrastination.

- Leaders must strike a balance between acting decisively and maintaining direction, aligning their actions with vision and values. This prevents chaos from uncontrolled action and safeguards stakeholders' interests.

- Decisive leaders instil an action-oriented culture that drives growth amidst disruption. In contrast, a leader's inaction can erode confidence within the team and stakeholders, leading to missed opportunities.

- An action-oriented mindset in a team is fostered through a leader modelling initiative, responsibility, adaptability and proactive problem solving while providing the right environment and resources.

- Quick wins and nudges help to build momentum, boost morale and build confidence for further action. Nudges are subtle interventions guiding behaviour without imposing restrictions.

- Celebrating quick wins and recognising efforts fosters a culture that motivates individuals to strive for excellence. Communication, feedback and recognition are essential in maintaining this momentum.

- A balance must be struck between promoting a bias for action and preventing burnout. Workload management, work-life integration, open communication and a supportive team culture must all be cultivated.

- A clear strategic direction prevents wasted resources, scattered efforts and negative effects on team morale, while fostering a culture of action that aligns with the organisation's vision and values.

14

REFLECTIVE LEADERSHIP: LEARNING FROM DISRUPTION

We do not learn from experience . . .
we learn from reflecting on experience.

JOHN DEWEY

N CHAPTER 13 we discovered the importance of action-oriented leadership. Chapter 14 brings to light the significant counterpart—reflection. In this chapter, we'll explore the role of reflection in learning and growing as a leader, equipping you with techniques for effective self-reflection. We'll delve into how incorporating reflection into your leadership practice can improve decision making and foresight amidst disruptive environments.

I was penning down the last words of this chapter. My study was silent, save for the muted sounds of the world outside. As I leaned back in my chair, my eyes were drawn to the framed photographs of my children displayed on my desk. They were candid shots, moments of pure innocence, frozen in time. I reached for one, feeling the cold glass under my fingertips, and a flood of memories washed over me. There they were, my reasons, my motivators, the driving forces behind each decision, each sacrifice, every late night and early morning.

To the side of the photographs, a collection of handwritten notes, scribbles and reminders lay scattered—my story bank. Each piece a memory or a lesson, collectively telling the story of my journey. They served as grounding reminders of where I started and how far I've come. The humbling moments, the wins, the losses, the days when everything seemed impossible and the days when everything fell into place.

The stillness of the room was palpable, providing a stark contrast to the chaos that often defined the outside world. In this quiet space, I felt a sense of clarity. Reflection, I realised, was more than just a pause; it was a deliberate act of looking inward, understanding one's motivations, and recognising the growth that comes from both triumphs and challenges. This moment of solitude, of introspection, sharpened my resolve and purpose as a leader. The world outside could wait. For now, this was a moment for me, a moment of understanding, acceptance and gratitude.

I then found myself pausing to absorb the magnitude of the journey I had embarked upon. This book was not merely an assembly of thoughts, theories or academic pursuits. It was my soul's deepest reflection, laid bare for the world to see.

As a leader, I recognised the transformative power of reflection. It was not just about understanding successes and failures but about forging deeper connections with those we lead. It was about nurturing empathy, balancing emotional intelligence with logic, and embracing objectivity to make decisions that resonate with our true selves.

In this moment it occurred to me that reflection exposed my vulnerabilities, which allowed me to acknowledge my achievements, and taught me the delicate art of self-compassion. It revealed the small wins that often go unnoticed, but are the very stepping stones towards aligning actions with values and building a legacy.

On my desk, a photo of my children brought a smile to my face. Their vibrant expressions reminded me of a younger version of myself, full of dreams and uncharted paths.

While it was not what I set out to do, I realised in this moment that this book had become my reflection, my contribution to the world. Through it, I sought to serve others, to become a better leader, a better human. It brought me closer to my legacy. I'm continually drawn back to the stories. Each narrative carries with it profound insights. They serve as mirrors reflecting my evolving understanding of life and leadership. Just as I had my stories of challenges, triumphs and learning, so too will you. Your reflections, your lessons, will be birthed from the stories that make up your life. They are invaluable touchstones in your leadership journey, teaching you, guiding you, and ultimately leading you to the legacy you aim to leave behind.

In the silence of my study, surrounded by the scattered stories and memories that have shaped my journey, I found I pondered the connection between reflection and leadership. It's in these quiet moments, like looking at my children's photographs, that the essence of effective leadership lies.

Reflection is not just about understanding the past; it's a strategic tool for personal growth and aligning our actions with the creation of our legacy—whether that be personal or through our organisation. It allows leaders to connect their experiences to valuable lessons, fostering a culture of empathy, innovation and adaptability. Through this practice, we balance emotional intelligence with critical thinking, enhancing decision making and communication. Acknowledging our vulnerabilities and achievements equally, we nurture resilience and gratitude. Reflection teaches us to appreciate the small wins, guiding our steps towards a meaningful legacy, just as the narratives within this book reflect my own leadership journey.

As I closed my laptop, I realised that I had not just written a chapter but captured a moment in time, a snapshot of my soul's reflection. It was my truth, and it was now time to share it with the world.

The role of reflection in learning and growing as a leader

In our action-oriented, fast-paced world, the idea of taking time out to reflect might seem counterintuitive, even indulgent. Why sit in quiet contemplation when there's so much to do, so many challenges to tackle, so much disruption to navigate?

But here's a compelling thought. What if reflection is not a pause from the race, but a crucial part of the journey? What if it is not an optional luxury, but a vital necessity for learning and growing as a leader? What if you considered this a fundamental aspect to your leadership—as you would to building trust or being a better communicator?

Amidst the ever-changing landscape, reflection enables leaders to understand the broader context and make sense of their successes and failures. It empowers them to extract valuable insights, refine their strategies and stay aligned with their organisation's vision. This introspective process fosters personal growth and development, allowing leaders to adapt, evolve, and make well-informed choices in the face of uncertainty. By incorporating regular moments of reflection into their leadership practices, leaders can effectively navigate the disruptive era and ensure sustained success for themselves and their organisations.

Reflection is where leaders connect the dots. It's where they look back at their journey, understand the patterns, the cause and effect, the interconnectedness of things. It's where they gain a deeper understanding of themselves, their decisions, their actions and their impact. It's where they not only learn from their experiences, but also transform those experiences into valuable lessons for the future.

Reflection helps leaders to become more self-aware, more in tune with their thoughts, feelings, values and beliefs. This heightened self-awareness is key to authentic leadership, to leading with integrity and congruence. It enables leaders to align their actions with their values, to lead from a place of authenticity, to inspire trust and respect in their team.

Also, reflection allows leaders to cultivate empathy and understanding, to see things from different perspectives, to appreciate the diversity and complexity of the world around them. This enhances their emotional intelligence, their ability to connect with and inspire their team, their capacity to navigate the complexities of the disruptive era with grace and wisdom.

But here's the clincher: reflection does not just enhance individual leadership; it also contributes to a learning culture within the team and organisation. When leaders model reflective practices, they encourage their team members to do the same, to learn from their experiences, to continually grow and evolve.

The role of objectivity and bias awareness in leadership reflection

Throughout your leadership journey, reflection emerges as a potent ally, illuminating insights, fostering experiential learning and refining decision making. But to maximise the benefits of reflection, you need the critical component of objectivity. This is the capability to detach oneself from personal biases, predetermined notions and emotional ties while evaluating past actions or experiences. Let's delve into how you, as a leader, can cultivate this crucial trait during reflection, thereby fostering authentic growth.

Objectivity in reflection prompts you to analyse situations and outcomes without the cloud of bias, rendering a more accurate understanding of your strengths, areas requiring improvement and growth opportunities. Casting a discerning eye on your unique leadership style, the decisions you make and your interactions with others enables you to heighten self-awareness and carve a pathway towards personal evolution.

Often operating below the level of conscious awareness, biases can bend your judgement, acting as subtle yet significant barriers to growth. It's essential to be vigilant of biases such as confirmation bias, the halo effect or availability bias, which have the potential to twist your reflective practices. Recognising these biases, interrogating them and challenging their influence guards against distortion, paving the way for a more authentic evaluation of your efficacy as a leader.

In the world of entrepreneurship, one cannot overlook the strategic vision of Elon Musk, CEO of SpaceX and Tesla. Musk's commitment to objectivity is evident in his approach to learning from the various failures he has encountered. When a SpaceX rocket exploded during testing, Musk didn't let biases towards his own technology or team cloud his analysis. Instead, he publicly dissected the failure, examining each detail without sentimentality to understand the root causes. This objective reflection allowed SpaceX to adjust its course, leading to the successful landing of the Falcon 9 rocket, marking a pivotal achievement in reusable space technology. Musk's leadership thus illustrates how bias awareness and objectivity can turn setbacks into milestones.

By inviting objectivity into your reflective practice, you empower yourself to confront your weaknesses, critically examine assumptions and unearth avenues for growth. Such a practice allows you to view experiences through multiple lenses, fostering informed decision making and nurturing the growth of practices that honour diversity. Upholding objectivity infuses your leadership with fairness, accountability and integrity, strengthening the foundations of trust and credibility among your team.

The practice of objective reflection, while requiring effort, is also an opportunity for rich learning. It's a process of uncovering your biases, understanding their impact, and working to lessen their influence. This journey towards more objective reflection is not a linear one, but rather a spiral, where each cycle of reflection reveals new layers of understanding about yourself and your leadership style.

Objectivity in reflection encourages a willingness to challenge the status quo, not just externally, but within yourself. It pushes you to question your current beliefs, assumptions and practices, paving the way for transformative growth. It urges you to examine whether your actions align with your espoused values and, if not, it provides the impetus for change.

In the arena of leadership, your decisions impact not just you, but your team, your organisation, and perhaps even beyond. Objective reflection, therefore, isn't merely a tool for personal growth, but also a mechanism to foster a more inclusive, empathetic and effective leadership style. By maintaining objectivity and mitigating biases, you empower yourself to confront your weaknesses, make enlightened decisions and cultivate practices that respect and celebrate diversity.

Navigating the reflection process: balancing hard truths and positivity to avoid self-sabotage

Engaging in reflective practices can be challenging, requiring you to confront uncomfortable truths while also upholding a positive mindset. Let's take a deep dive into how to avoid the pitfall of self-sabotage during reflection and strike a healthy balance.

Reflection has the potential to uncover areas that need improvement, exposing vulnerabilities that might be tough to face. It's during these introspective moments that you may risk self-sabotage—through negative self-talk, overly harsh self-criticism or crippling self-doubt. It's important to approach reflection with a balanced mindset, staying aware of these potential obstacles to your growth.

Unpleasant truths are an integral part of the reflective process, compelling you to honestly assess your actions, decisions and areas for growth. However, constantly dwelling on your shortcomings is counter-productive. Effective reflection acknowledges these realities, but also celebrates your achievements and strengths.

Reflection includes recognising your wins, acknowledging what went right, and rejoicing in those moments that made you feel great. Celebrating your accomplishments and savouring joyful experiences can add a positive dimension to your reflection, fostering a sense of fulfilment and contentment. By including positive factors in your reflection, you can steer clear of self-sabotaging behaviours that overly focus on negatives.

Maintaining this balance means nurturing self-compassion, and treating yourself with kindness, understanding and forgiveness. Reflection is not a tool for self-punishment; it's a pathway to growth and improvement. Seeing your failures as learning opportunities allows you to uphold positivity and display resilience in the face of challenges.

Practising gratitude can further enhance your reflective process. By focusing on lessons learned, experiences gained and progress made, you can shift your mindset from self-doubt to appreciation. Gratitude helps sustain positivity, nurturing motivation and optimism.

Realistic expectations ensure a healthy reflection practice. It's crucial to resist comparisons with others or pursue unrealistic standards. Keep in mind that reflection is a journey, and growth takes time. By setting attainable goals and appreciating small victories, you can foster a positive mindset and prevent self-sabotage from unrealistic expectations.

Having a supportive network is invaluable in preventing self-sabotage. Constructive feedback from trusted mentors, coaches or peers can provide much-needed insights and objective perspectives. These dialogues can offer a balanced view of your strengths and weaknesses, lending clarity and objectivity to your reflection.

When reflection strikes a balance between confronting hard truths and embracing positivity, it equips you as a leader to navigate disruptions. You'll be in a better position to identify areas for improvement, challenge assumptions and make courageous decisions. Reflection encourages you to welcome change, explore new possibilities, and lead with confidence and clarity. By making self-reflection a habit, you can drive innovation, promoting agility and adaptability.

Continuous self-reflection enables you as a leader to gain deeper insights into your values, purpose, and long-term vision. This awareness aligns your actions and decisions with the legacy you aspire to leave behind. Reflective practices allow you to make intentional choices that are consistent with your values and long-term goals, ensuring that you leave a lasting, positive impact on your teams, organisation, and the broader communities you serve.

Applying reflective insights
in the face of disruption

In an era characterised by relentless disruption, leaders find themselves at the crossroads of innovation and uncertainty. At this junction, one might assume that taking swift actions and making quick decisions would be the hallmark of effective leadership. Yet, the most transformative leaders today understand that to truly thrive amid turbulence, they must master the art of reflection. This isn't a passive retreat into one's thoughts but an active, deliberate quest to understand one's experiences, to anticipate challenges, and to forge a path forward with clarity and conviction.

This mastery isn't about mere nostalgia or a casual glance backward. It's a rigorous mental exercise, a forward looking mirror, where the past informs decisions of the present to shape an adaptable and resilient future. Reflection becomes the bridge, linking disruptive leadership with transformational leadership. It's not just about reacting to disruptions but transforming them into opportunities, turning challenges into catalysts for change.

Incorporating reflection into leadership is not only about understanding where one has been but also predicting where one might go. Enter the concept of pre-mortems. Unlike a post-mortem, which dissects past events to find what went wrong, a pre-mortem is an exercise in forward reflection. Before a project starts or an important decision is made, leaders anticipate what could go wrong, where the pitfalls might lie, and how they can be avoided. It's a proactive approach, ensuring that leaders aren't blindsided by unexpected challenges. By visualising potential failures before they happen, leaders can devise strategies to prevent them, ensuring smoother execution and a higher chance of success.

This isn't to suggest that leaders should dwell in the realm of pessimism. On the contrary, pre-mortems empower them with a heightened sense of realism, ensuring their strategies are not just based on hopes but are anchored in tangible realities. It's an example of how reflection can be applied to shape outcomes, not just understand them.

Every leader knows the sting of a decision gone awry or an action that didn't produce the desired outcome. In the aftermath, the most potent lesson isn't necessarily in the mistake itself but in the reflective insights derived from it. Reflective insights act as the cornerstone for transformative leadership. By periodically examining one's actions and decisions, and their outcomes, leaders can continuously adjust their strategies, ensuring that they are in tune with the changing dynamics of their environment.

In the face of disruption, it is these insights that equip leaders with the agility to pivot. Reflective insights help in understanding the underlying currents of disruption, enabling leaders to not just ride the wave but to steer the disruption in a direction that aligns with their organisational goals. This transformational approach allows them to harness disruption, turning potential threats into currents of opportunity.

But the true power of reflective insights lies in their potential to be put into operation. Knowing is only half the battle; the real challenge is in applying this knowledge in actionable ways. As leaders move from reflection to action, they create a loop of continuous learning and improvement. Today's mistake informs tomorrow's strategy, ensuring that leaders are always a step ahead, always learning, always growing.

Reflective insights foster resilience. In the unpredictable terrains of the business world, disruptions, setbacks, and failures are inevitable. By consistently engaging in reflective practices leaders develop the ability to bounce back from adversities with renewed vigour. They learn to view challenges not as insurmountable obstacles but as opportunities to learn, adapt and grow.

The REFLECTIVE LEADER Maturity Model

Chapter 14, the penultimate segment in our comprehensive fifteen-part framework, delves into the interconnected realms of depth of reflection and application of reflective insights. As leaders grapple with an ever shifting and uncertain environment, those capable of applying reflective insights deeply and effectively are poised to navigate challenges and guide their organisations to prosperity. The Reflective Leader Maturity Model illustrates the intersection of depth of reflection and application of reflective insights, underscoring their critical role in progressive, resilient leadership.

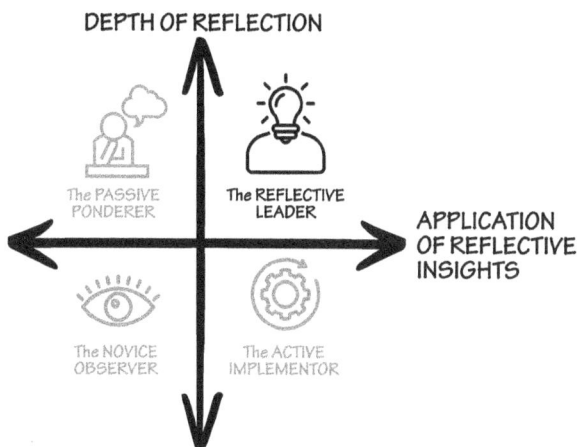

The REFLECTIVE LEADER

DEPTH OF REFLECTION

The PASSIVE PONDERER

The REFLECTIVE LEADER

APPLICATION OF REFLECTIVE INSIGHTS

The NOVICE OBSERVER

The ACTIVE IMPLEMENTOR

Please take a moment now to begin your journey of self-reflection by determining which quadrant of the model best describes your leadership style.

The Novice Observer: These leaders engage in only cursory reflection and fail to utilise insights in any significant way. Leaders in this stage often underestimate the power of reflection or find it challenging to set aside adequate time for it. This lack of deep reflection could lead to poorly informed decisions and missed opportunities for growth. Leaders in this quadrant should START dedicating time for regular, profound reflection and begin applying the insights obtained from their reflections to their decision-making processes. They should STOP neglecting the importance of reflection in their leadership practice.

The Passive Ponderer: Here, leaders engage in profound reflection but stumble when it comes to effectively applying these insights. They often grapple with recognising patterns and integrating their insights into their decision-making processes. This could result in their reflective efforts not fully translating into practical actions. To progress, leaders in this quadrant should START connecting their reflective insights to their decision-making processes actively and STOP overlooking the practical application of their insights.

The Active Implementer: Leaders in this quadrant show effectiveness in applying insights gained from surface-level reflection. They recognise patterns and make connections between reflection and decision making. However, they often miss the profound insights that could be obtained from more in-depth reflection. This can lead to a lack of comprehensive understanding and holistic decision making. Leaders here should START investing in deeper reflection techniques to enhance the quality of their insights and STOP limiting their reflective efforts to surface-level examination.

The Reflective Leader: This is the most mature quadrant, where leaders both engage in deep reflection and effectively apply their insights. They appreciate the significance of reflection, ensuring regular reflection sessions, and utilise the insights obtained for personal and team growth. This leads to more-informed decision making and more-effective leadership. Leaders in this quadrant should START sharing their reflective practices and promoting a culture of reflection within their teams and continue their established practices.

Reflective leadership in action

It sounds counterintuitive—taking action on reflection. But it's essential to avoid getting caught up in the busyness and flux of leadership in the disruptive era. Think of it as constructive rest time, not as checking out. As essential time that allows you to course-correct based on insights gained and consequently lead with renewed vigour and insight.

Encourage regular, structured reflection: In an era marked by disruption, leaders must cultivate an environment where reflection is a routine and valued practice. By implementing structured reflection sessions and encouraging team members to introspect, leaders create a learning culture that continuously adapts and grows. This nurtures personal development, builds resilience, and strengthens the organisation's capacity to face unforeseen challenges. For example, a manager might dedicate the last fifteen minutes of weekly meetings for team members to share their reflections on what went well and areas of improvement.

Integrate emotional intelligence with objective analysis: Leaders must balance emotional intelligence with logical analysis to enable holistic decision making. By acknowledging feelings and emotions while reflecting, while also maintaining an objective perspective, leaders create a nuanced understanding of situations. This dual approach aids in effective communication, empathy and well-rounded decisions, fostering a culture of trust and collaboration. A leader could facilitate a team discussion post-project, first asking how everyone felt about the outcome, then to analyse the data and feedback, ensuring both emotional and objective perspectives are considered.

Build safe spaces for dialogue and encourage diverse perspectives: Leaders must create environments where open dialogue and diverse perspectives are welcomed. By encouraging team members to share their insights and actively seeking feedback from various viewpoints, leaders enhance objectivity and reduce personal bias in reflection. This openness cultivates innovative thinking and ensures that decisions are well rounded and inclusive, reinforcing an adaptable and growth-oriented organisational culture. For instance, a CEO might initiate a monthly open forum where employees from all departments share their perspectives on company-wide decisions, ensuring varied voices are heard.

Acknowledge achievements and cultivate gratitude while reflecting: Reflection may expose vulnerabilities or highlight failures. Leaders must balance this by recognising successes, expressing gratitude and practising self-compassion. By celebrating achievements, however small, leaders foster a positive perspective that motivates and sustains team morale. This balance ensures that reflection is an empowering process rather than one that leads to self-sabotage. After analysing a failed product launch, a team leader might also highlight the innovative features the team developed and express gratitude for the hard work and dedication, ensuring the reflection process remains balanced and constructive.

Utilise the Reflective Leader Maturity Model to enhance reflection practices: The Reflective Leader Maturity Model, categorising leaders into four quadrants (Novice Observers, Passive Ponderers, Active Implementers, Reflective Leader), offers an essential tool for developing reflective leadership. Leaders can identify their current stage and focus on specific areas for growth. For instance, Novice Observers might work on deeper reflection practices, while Passive Ponderers may strive to translate their profound insights into actionable steps.

Concluding our exploration of reflective leadership, we recognise the power of learning from disruption. We've learned how this practice allows leaders to assess their experiences, derive insights and evolve their strategies, creating a constant cycle of improvement. This introspection and understanding aren't limited to professional experiences. In our final chapter, we'll venture into the concept of personal disruption, understanding how leaders must embrace personal transformation to effectively navigate the challenges of disruptive leadership.

CHAPTER INSIGHTS

- Reflection, a crucial leadership aspect, aids in understanding successes and failures, and refines strategies to align with the organisation's vision. This practice fosters personal growth, enhances decision making and boosts self-awareness.

- Regular reflection allows leaders to connect the dots and transform experiences into valuable lessons. This habit is especially crucial when navigating the disruptive era.

- Cultivating empathy, understanding and emotional intelligence are additional benefits of reflection, enabling leaders to lead with grace and wisdom and forge deeper connections with their teams.

- By modelling reflective practices, leaders can foster an innovative, adaptable and growth-oriented culture within their team and the larger organisation.

- Balancing emotional intelligence with logical analysis during reflection cultivates effective communication, empathy and holistic decision making.

- Objectivity and personal bias awareness during reflection are vital for accurate self-assessment and effective decision making. Leaders should also cultivate safe spaces, seek feedback, and engage with diverse viewpoints.

- Reflection may expose hard truths and vulnerabilities, potentially leading to self-sabotage. Leaders should maintain a balance by acknowledging achievements, practising self-compassion and cultivating gratitude.

- Approaching reflection with realistic expectations and appreciating small wins can help leaders align actions and decisions with their values and long-term objectives.

15

PERSONAL DISRUPTION: EMBRACING SELF-TRANSFORMATION

Remembering that you are going to die is
the best way I know to avoid the trap of thinking
you have something to lose. You are already naked.
There is no reason not to follow your heart.

STEVE JOBS

INALLY, WE ARRIVE at the final chapter. Building on the importance of reflective leadership, this chapter explores the necessity of personal disruption for disruptive leadership. We'll delve into practices that encourage personal growth and self-transformation, investigating how personal disruption can lead to professional innovation and resilience.

In the warm hum of a café, where the world slows to the pace of sipped coffees and quiet conversations, William found himself at a solitary table set apart from the rest. It was here, amidst the aroma of roasted coffee and the subtle sight of steam rising from mugs, that the outer layer of a successful man began to peel away, revealing the quiet introspection beneath. This was no ordinary retreat, but a sanctuary where his veneer—built from years of societal and self-expectation—confronted the raw, unspoken questions of his being. In this space, the bustling world faded into the backdrop as William grappled with the depths of his identity, the ones not etched out in his many achievements but whispered in the silences between.

The atmosphere was thick with introspection as William, a seasoned supply chain executive, sat across from me, his executive coach. His eyes, usually brimming with analytical sharpness, now reflected a different kind of depth—one full of vulnerability and the earnest search for meaning. The corporate battlefield had left its mark, not just on his résumé but on his spirit. Here was a man at the crossroads of disruption, not just seeking to lead through change, but to live it.

William's story began on a familiar note. He told me about the everyday treadmill of life, where personal health and purpose had become casualties to routine. He spoke of a career that, despite its successes, felt devoid of connection to a deeper mission. He mourned the spark that once ignited his ambitions, now smouldering under the ashes of complacency.

Yet, buried beneath was an ember, a yearning to reignite that spark. William's confessions were not mere regrets but revelations. His unfinished law degree wasn't just a chapter left unturned; it was a symbol of unexplored paths and potentials. The notion of becoming a politician, once a dream to usher in change and do good, had transformed over time as he became cynical and disenchanted with the political system.

William's narrative spun a web connecting past and present, weaving through personal struggles such as a painful divorce that had estranged him from his children and tested his resilience. Yet, he had emerged; not unscathed, but certainly not defeated. His desire to be an entrepreneur—another path not taken—simmered within him, a blend of desire and fear laced with the seductive security of a steady pay cheque.

Our conversation took a turn, delving into the essence of identity beyond titles and roles. We explored the thought that the real question was not what he did or why he did it, but who he was at the core. It was about self-discovery as the first step towards self-transformation.

Drawing inspiration from stories of radical career shifts, we painted a landscape of possibilities. Each story was a testament to personal disruption, an illustration that the path to innovation and impact is paved with the courage to challenge one's own status quo. We spoke of the likes of Jack Ma, an English teacher who went on to found Alibaba Group and revolutionise e-commerce in China; Jeff Bezos, who left a lucrative career in finance to start Amazon from his garage, transforming retail forever. In Australia, we saw a remarkable example in Mark Holden, a former singer and television host of *Australian Idol*, who later pursued a career in law and became a barrister, proving that it's never too late to redefine oneself.

We also spoke about friends. There was Rodney, whose journey from the finance sector to Doctors Without Borders represented a pivot from corporate success to humanitarian fulfillment. Tarryn, once rooted in travel management, returned to university in her forties to fulfil a dream and a calling to become a nurse. Lawrence left a very senior and promising career in banking to spearhead a fund investing in founder-led businesses, aligning financial acumen with entrepreneurial passion.

'What would a life of consequence look like for you, William?' I asked, prompting a contemplation of legacy over longevity, of meaning over mere existence. The answer lay not in the external trappings of success, but in confronting the internal blockages that stifled his true potential.

Our session stretched on, peeling back layers of doubt and fear, inching closer to the core of his ambition.

We concluded with an action plan, not just with steps, but with a new mindset geared towards embracing disruption, both personally and professionally. It was not just about achieving goals, but about becoming someone who could reach them authentically and resiliently.

William left with more than a road map; he carried with him a renewed sense of self and the sparks of a personal revolution.

Breaking down to rebuild

The term 'personal disruption' seems fraught with challenges. It signifies upheaval, change and, most strikingly, uncertainty. This landscape, often perceived as foggy, is where growth becomes possible.

In the business context, disruption is a force that changes the game—a seismic shift that topples giants and elevates newcomers. Turning this lens inward leads to personal disruption. As disruptive innovation is essential to thriving in today's fast-paced business environment, personal disruption is an essential element of effective, forward-thinking leadership.

The need for personal disruption in disruptive leadership arises from the realisation that we are integral to the disruptive changes we champion. To lead effectively in disruptive times, we must be willing to disrupt ourselves.

Consider a seasoned executive who has always championed traditional marketing methods. Recognising the shift towards digital marketing, she decides to enrol in a digital marketing course, even though she is decades into her career. This act of stepping back into the learner's seat, challenging her own expertise and embracing a new frontier epitomises personal disruption.

Similarly, a manager who has always relied on hierarchical structures may begin to adopt a more collaborative approach, inviting input from all team members and dismantling the barriers of rank. This shift from a command-and-control mindset to one of collective contribution exemplifies the willingness to disrupt ingrained leadership styles.

Outside the workplace, think of an individual who embarks on a year-long sabbatical to travel and learn pottery, drawing parallels between moulding clay and shaping one's life, much like how Steve Jobs found inspiration in calligraphy. This pursuit of an unrelated skill, accompanied by self-reflection, symbolises personal disruption in its truest form. Lastly, think of a leader who, upon realising the importance of work-life balance for the wellbeing of her employees, decides to openly share her own struggles with burnout and implements flexible working hours in the company. By exposing her own vulnerabilities and acting upon them for the broader good, she showcases the essence of personal disruption.

This disruption transcends learning new skills or staying updated with trends, though these are part of it. It penetrates to the core of who we are, how we perceive ourselves and our roles. It's about questioning our assumptions, challenging our beliefs and reassessing our approaches.

Consider this: how can you champion disruption if you're unwilling to question your own status quo? Advocating for a culture of innovation and adaptability requires an openness to personal change. Personal disruption isn't just a catchy phrase; it's a fundamental requirement for effective leadership in a disruptive era.

Personal disruption embodies the willingness to step out of comfort zones and embrace unfamiliarity. It invites transformation, growth and the courage to pave new paths. In the face of uncertainty, the willingness to disrupt ourselves becomes the catalyst for personal and professional evolution, creating legacies that resonate and inspire.

Reframing perspectives: the neuroscience of personal disruption

As we navigate our self-disruption journey, we're often confronted with deeply rooted beliefs about ourselves. These beliefs can create barriers, limiting our potential and inhibiting our growth. How many times have we told ourselves, 'I can't do this,' or 'This is not my forte?' At the heart of personal disruption is the ability to challenge and reframe these beliefs. But why is reframing so crucial, and how does it tie into neuroscience?

Our brain is a fascinating entity, hardwired to establish patterns and streamline processes for efficiency. Think of it as a sophisticated computer system that constantly updates its software based on experiences. Every time we encounter a situation, our brain taps into this database of experiences, prompting us to react in familiar ways. This evolutionary feature saves time and energy. However, the downside is that these patterns can become rigid over time, leading to beliefs that may no longer serve us well.

Reframing is about creating a new narrative by challenging these outdated beliefs. For instance, let's take the belief, 'I'm not a leader.' By asking ourselves evidence-based questions like: 'Why do I think I'm not a leader?' or, 'Have there been instances where I displayed leadership qualities?' we can start identifying discrepancies in our original belief. This process allows us to update our mental database, introducing a new narrative that aligns more closely with our current self.

From a neuroscience perspective, this act of reframing strengthens new neural pathways in our brain. When we challenge a belief, we're essentially telling our brain to find alternative routes and create new connections. Over time, as we consistently reinforce this new narrative, our brain strengthens these connections, making them more dominant.

Another crucial aspect of reframing is its ability to enhance our concepts of control. Often, we may feel that situations are out of our hands or that external factors dictate our lives. By reframing, we shift the power back to ourselves. Instead of believing: 'I don't have control over this situation,' we can reframe it to: 'How can I influence the outcome of this situation?' Such a shift places us in the driver's seat, enabling us to approach challenges with a proactive mindset.

One more example could be the belief: 'I don't have the confidence.' By diving deep into the origin of this belief and challenging its validity, we can often find instances where we did exhibit confidence. Recognising these moments and giving them prominence helps create a new story: 'I have shown confidence in the past, and I can do it again.'

Reframing begins with recognising limiting beliefs, those self-inflicted constraints that stifle our growth. By deeply reflecting, we identify these inhibiting thoughts. The next step is to challenge these beliefs, diving into their origins and searching for contrary evidence. From this scrutiny emerges a new narrative, a fresh perspective that is more in tune with our current selves. To ensure this perspective takes root, it's essential to reinforce it consistently, further solidifying these new neural pathways in our brains. The transformation becomes evident when we witness subtle shifts in our mindset and actions. These small victories, born from reframing, deserve celebration, for they confirm the internalisation of our new, empowered narrative.

Reframing is not about deluding oneself but about updating our self-concept based on real, tangible evidence. It's a powerful tool in our personal disruption toolkit, enabling us to break free from self-imposed shackles and truly harness our potential. Reframing empowers us to think bigger, reminding us of our potential to influence, innovate and inspire. It enables us to break the confines of limiting beliefs and envision a legacy of monumental impact.

Discovering your strengths through self-disruption: redefining leadership impact

Self-disruption, at its heart, is an act of growth and adaptation. It's the commitment to constantly evaluate your leadership methodologies, reassess your beliefs and recalibrate your strategies. This introspection serves to ensure your practices are not just a product of past successes, but are also designed to propel future achievements.

One cornerstone in your self-disruption journey is the identification and nurturing of your passions. Not to be mistaken as mere hobbies, these passions encapsulate activities that genuinely excite you and stimulate your intellect. They captivate your attention to a point where time seems irrelevant. They are your unique sources of energy, your personal fountains of inspiration. When harnessed and aligned with your leadership role, these passions render your work fulfilling, driving you towards a purpose-infused existence.

Parallel to this process is the crucial task of acknowledging your strengths. These strengths encompass more than the skills you've acquired over the years; they include inherent talents, tasks you naturally excel at, your personal 'superpowers'. Recognising these abilities equips you to excel in your leadership role. Whether you're a natural problem-solver guiding your team through intricate problems or a communication master inspiring and motivating your team, leveraging these strengths is essential to your leadership.

While these elements are crucial, true self-disruption demands a third dimension: understanding the world's needs and expectations from you. This involves viewing the broader societal landscape, identifying the gaps your unique skill set can fill, and assessing how you can contribute to solving pressing issues. What problems in your sphere can you alleviate? Where can your skills, passions and strengths meet the world's needs? Introspecting and responding to these questions empowers you to adapt your leadership, ensuring its relevance and impact.

Your self-disruption journey is not an act of solitary growth or a self-centred evolution. It's about catalysing your transformation to meet real-world needs, which enriches the lives of those around you. The more effectively you align your passions and strengths with societal needs, the deeper and more profound your impact as a leader. Remember, every step in this journey of self-disruption takes you closer to becoming the leader you aspire to be, shaping a world that you envision.

Living a life of consequence: the gift of self-disruption

Self-disruption requires action, self-awareness and, above all, the courage to disrupt oneself. The title of this book, *Disruptive Leadership: How to Leave a Powerful Legacy in a Rapidly Changing World*, speaks to this journey. It's not about disrupting for the sake of chaos, but for the profound impact you can have on the world. Every day, every interaction, every challenge faced presents an opportunity to make an imprint.

We know being static is not an option. But neither is change for change's sake. Meaningful, lasting change—the sort that defines legacies—comes from an internal drive to be better, to do better, and to continually evolve. This is where self-disruption plays a vital role. It's the conscious decision to embrace growth, to seek out new experiences and knowledge, and to apply these learnings in service of a higher purpose.

At the beginning of this chapter, I said that we all have unique gifts and deserve to live a life of consequence. A life lived to its fullest potential is one where each day is seized, every challenge met head on, where generational traumas are confronted and societal expectations are questioned. It's about more than just dreaming or thinking; it's about doing. It is about being brave, letting go and believing in yourself—and, importantly, taking those actions.

Take the example of Jack Ma, the founder of Alibaba Group. In a world driven by technology and constant innovation, Ma embraced self-disruption by transitioning from an English teacher to a global business leader. His objective reflection on the limitations of existing Chinese enterprises in the digital economy prompted him to establish an internet company without any background in computing or e-commerce. Ma's willingness to disrupt his career-path and face the uncertainty of the tech industry reflects the spirit of 'living a life of consequence'. His story demonstrates that self-disruption and courage can lead to transformative changes, not just within an individual, but across the global business landscape.

When we step outside our comfort zones, when we dare to challenge our established patterns of thought and action, our brains literally reshape themselves. This is the essence of personal disruption. Instead of letting the world shape you, you proactively shape yourself and, by extension, the world around you.

A legacy is not a monument that we build at the end of our journey; it's the path we carve as we travel. Every time you decide to embrace change, every time you question the status quo, and every time you venture into the unknown, you're shaping your legacy.

Consider this: the impact you want to leave in the world is not a distant future endeavour. It's a present-day action. The choices you make now, the people you influence today, the values you uphold in this moment—these are the components of your legacy.

The legacy of consequence and impact is not about monumental shifts but the consistent, purposeful steps you take every day. It's in the conversations that uplift others, the challenges you face head on, and the authentic leadership you provide in every situation. Embrace this natural propensity, align it with purpose and vision, and you'll find yourself not just leading, but leaving a trail for others to follow.

The DISRUPTIVE LEADER Maturity Model

In this chapter, we introduce the Disruptive Leader Maturity Model. This model is where personal disruption meets the overarching theme of this book to produce a truly disruptive leader. This model shows how personal disruption and organisational disruption intersect and contribute to resilient, future-oriented leadership. Personal disruption relates to a leader's

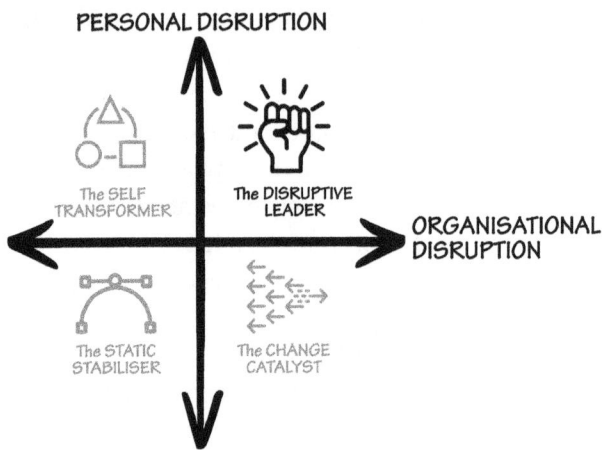

THE DISRUPTIVE LEADER

PERSONAL DISRUPTION

The SELF TRANSFORMER

The DISRUPTIVE LEADER

ORGANISATIONAL DISRUPTION

The STATIC STABILISER

The CHANGE CATALYST

capacity for self-evolution and growth, while organisational disruption addresses their skill in initiating and managing change within their organisation. Together, these elements form the essence of disruptive leadership and are crucial for creating a legacy in a world characterised by rapid change.

The Static Stabiliser: Leaders in this quadrant demonstrate resistance to both personal and organisational disruption. They may fear change, hold fixed mindsets, and establish an environment that impedes innovation. The impacts are stagnation, lack of growth, and an inability to leverage disruption as a catalyst for improvement. To evolve, these leaders should START embracing disruption on both personal and organisational levels, understanding that adaptation is vital in the disruptive era. They should STOP resisting change and recognise that growth comes from embracing, not avoiding, disruption.

The Self-Transformer: Here, leaders welcome personal disruption but struggle to drive disruption within their organisation. They may focus on personal growth and development, but overlook the necessity of channelling these changes to inspire their teams. This narrow focus can limit the organisation's potential to capitalise on disruption. Leaders in this quadrant should START sharing their journey of personal disruption and use their experiences to effectively inspire organisational change. They should STOP concentrating solely on personal growth and realise the need to drive organisational disruption as well.

The Change Catalyst: Leaders in this quadrant resist personal disruption but successfully instigate organisational change. They often neglect personal growth while prioritising the organisation's transformation. However, this imbalance can lead to inauthentic leadership and a potential disconnect with their team. Leaders here should START embracing personal disruption, recognising that authenticity and personal growth are crucial for longevity in leading organisational disruption. They should STOP neglecting personal disruption and understand its fundamental role in shaping effective leadership.

The Disruptive Leader: This is the ideal quadrant, where leaders embrace both personal and organisational disruption. They understand and appreciate the intrinsic link between personal transformation and the ability to inspire change within their organisation. This results in a dynamic and adaptable leadership style that fosters a culture of continuous change and growth. Leaders in this quadrant should CONTINUE their journey, constantly seeking growth opportunities and fostering an environment that encourages continuous disruption. They should keep sharing their personal disruption journey to inspire others.

Disruptive leadership in action

Embrace a culture of continuous self-questioning and adaptation: Leaders must develop a mindset that embraces personal disruption, challenging their beliefs and assumptions. This involves creating an organisational culture that values continuous learning, self-awareness and adaptability. Leaders must lead by example, fostering innovation and resilience, and inspiring others to perceive challenges as catalysts for growth. For instance, a CEO might openly share her decision to enrol in a cutting-edge technology course, demonstrating her commitment to continuous learning and inspiring her employees to do the same.

Encourage empathetic change management through personal disruption: Leaders who engage in personal disruption enhance their ability to guide teams through change-induced uncertainty. This involves practising empathy, understanding the emotional aspects of change, and fostering trust within the organisation. By linking personal growth with professional leadership, they create an environment of openness, nurturing continuous development. An example would be a manager who actively listens to employee concerns during a merger, empathises with their fears, and shares personal stories of adapting to change, illustrating the power of vulnerability and empathy.

Foster a supportive environment for exploration and innovation: Leaders must create an environment that encourages questioning the status quo and exploring novel avenues. By promoting an atmosphere where failure is viewed as a stepping stone for growth, they inspire creativity and innovation. This is achieved through supporting risk taking, nurturing a growth mindset, and recognising efforts that lead to professional innovation. For example, after a failed product launch, a director might hold a team workshop to dissect the lessons learned rather than placing blame, showcasing the value of failures as learning opportunities.

Promote resilience and authenticity through reflection and experiential learning: Leaders who embrace personal disruption acquire resilience and authenticity, equipping them to drive professional innovation. They must foster practices such as reflection, continuous learning and experiential learning to enhance self-awareness and growth mindset. By sharing their experiences and demonstrating resilience, they influence and inspire others within the organisation, laying the foundation for a resilient legacy. A leader might, for instance, hold monthly reflection sessions with their team, openly discussing challenges faced and resilience building strategies, thus promoting an authentic and transparent workplace culture.

Apply the Disruptive Leader Maturity Model to bolster leadership evolution: The Disruptive Leader Maturity Model, categorising leaders into four quadrants (Static Stabilisers, Self Transformers, Change Catalysts, Disruptive Leader), serves as a guiding tool for leadership growth. Leaders can utilise this model to assess their current quadrant and develop strategies to embrace both personal and organisational disruption. For example, Static Stabilisers might focus on valuing self-evolution, while Self Transformers may work to inspire their teams through their journey of personal disruption.

As we conclude our exploration of personal disruption and its necessity for transformative leadership, we end this final chapter of the book. In doing so, we also wrap up Part 5, acknowledging the harmonious balance between action and reflection in disruptive leadership. We've understood how driving action, reflective leadership and personal disruption create a holistic approach to leading in disruptive times.

CHAPTER INSIGHTS

- Personal disruption, essential for leadership in disruptive times, involves challenging personal status quo and demonstrating adaptability, nurturing a culture of innovation within an organisation.

- This readiness to question assumptions and beliefs enables leaders to understand the emotional aspects of change management, thereby guiding their teams empathetically through change-induced uncertainty.

- By challenging beliefs and promoting personal growth, personal disruption bolsters leadership authenticity, fostering trust and cultivating a culture of openness and continuous development.

- Personal disruption fuels professional innovation, creating an environment that encourages questioning the status quo and exploring novel avenues.

- With personal disruption, leaders acquire resilience and authenticity, equipping them to foster professional innovation and view failures as stepping stones for growth.

- Reflection, continuous learning and experiential learning are effective practices for fostering self-awareness and a growth mindset, encouraging personal disruption.

- Personal disruption necessitates resilience, enabling leaders to perceive challenges as catalysts for growth rather than obstacles.

- The process of personal disruption goes beyond personal growth; it involves leading by example, thereby influencing and inspiring others within the organisation.

THE PRIZES OF TRANSFORMA-TIONAL LEADERSHIP

In **Part 5: Transformational Leadership**, our narrative unfolds the essential components that shape leaders ready to tackle the challenges of the disruptive era. The guidance here is clear: success lies not just in recognising and embracing the critical principles of action, reflection and personal transformation. As leaders traverse this dynamic landscape, this roadmap serves as a blueprint, illustrating the path towards transformative leadership that will leave a lasting imprint, enduringly resonating through time. Through this journey, leaders are empowered to craft a legacy that will echo for generations, shaping a brighter, more resilient future.

Enacting Transformational Leadership

In an era of continuous disruption, the ability to initiate impactful actions and reflect upon them for valuable learning becomes integral to effective leadership. By embracing this approach, you will be able to drive tangible progression, learn from disruptive scenarios, and facilitate personal growth to enhance your leadership capabilities.

Strategic Actions Amidst Disruption

Transformational leaders recognise the necessity of swift and strategic action during disruptive times.

Through the adoption of calculated risks, prompt decision making, and effective implementation, you will instigate real changes and progress within your organisation. Your proactive approach will inspire your team to adapt and thrive in the face of disruption, fostering an environment that values initiative and result-oriented actions.

The Power of Reflective Leadership

Actions devoid of reflection can often lead to unforeseen pitfalls. However, by practising reflective leadership, you can extract valuable lessons from the turbulence of disruption. Reflecting on your actions, understanding their consequences, and gaining insights from these experiences can refine your future strategies and decisions. This cycle of action and reflection will enable you to continually fine-tune your leadership approach, reducing the likelihood of repeating past mistakes.

Embracing Personal Disruption

Transformational leadership involves a willingness to embrace personal disruption. By acknowledging personal growth and transformation as fundamental to your leadership role, you'll be able to match the pace of external change with internal evolution. This resilience and adaptability will serve as a robust foundation for overcoming the challenges that disruption inevitably presents.

Fostering a Culture of Transformation

Your actions and attitudes significantly shape your organisation's culture. By promoting a culture that values risk taking, embraces change, and encourages reflection and learning, you will empower your team to thrive in the face of disruption. This shift will not only drive your organisation's growth and innovation, but also create an environment where each member feels invested in and capable of contributing to the organisation's success. Your ability to foster this transformative culture will inspire trust and loyalty, paving the way for sustained success in a rapidly evolving business landscape.

IT IS NOT 'THE END', IT IS 'THE START'

THE ESSENCE OF disruptive leadership we've un-covered is far more profound than merely chal-lenging the norm; it requires embodying a mindset that thrives on innovation, values adaptability, and embraces the potential for learning hidden within every failure.

In our exploration, we've discovered the crucial role of action in disruptive leadership, which is less about movement and more about progress. After all, the loudest statements are made through our actions, not our words.

We also emphasised the invaluable role of regular reflection and continual learning in leadership. Reflection is our compass in times of change, while continuous learning fuels our growth. These are not optional extras, but the essence of impactful leadership.

Disruptive leadership, we've learned, is not a destination but an ongoing journey of growth, a pursuit of excellence and an enduring commitment to creating value. It is, above all, a commitment to *being* better, not just *doing* better.

Remember that your role as a disruptive leader is not merely to instigate change, but to be a beacon of hope. In a world of constant disruption, you have the capacity to be the calm in the storm, the light in the darkness. Your journey does not end here; in fact, it has just begun.

In guiding you through this exploration of disruptive leadership, my hope is that you will carry these insights with you as you continue your leadership journey. For a future not just different, but better.

We've reached the conclusion of our exploration, but remember, this isn't an end, but rather a beginning of your unique journey as a disruptive leader. Now it's time for a call to action, especially for those of you who are emerging leaders in these disruptive times.

Leadership is no longer about control. It's about influence and guidance. It's about fostering an environment where disruption and innovation are not just welcomed, but celebrated. It's about nurturing a culture of adaptability and a growth mindset, where failure isn't a dead end but a detour on the road to success.

In these times of rapid change and uncertainty, leaders who can navigate disruption, who can pivot and adapt, who can inspire and empower their teams, are not just desirable, they are indispensable. And that's the kind of leader you can choose to become.

But remember, leadership isn't a title. It's not a position of authority. It's a way of being. It's about stepping up, taking responsibility, making a difference. It's about courage, conviction, and a commitment to creating a positive impact, not just on your team or organisation, but on society at large.

The future is not yet written. It's up to us to shape it, to disrupt it, in ways that lead to a better tomorrow. The world needs disruptive leaders. It needs you.

Good luck, Have Fun, Be Kind and continue to Dream Big. Always remember—leadership is a privilege.

ABOUT THE AUTHOR

WITH OVER two decades of unparalleled international experience, Matthew has demonstrated exceptional leadership across pivotal roles in finance, commercial and executive functions. His journey began in Accounting and Finance, which laid a solid foundation for his eventual progression into Program Management and International Operations Management. Matthew later advanced to senior executive roles that included: serving as the Global Director of 4PL Operations at DSV, where he led the global supply chain for Adidas as part of their 4PL partnership; CEO of Cargo Services Australia, and Head of International Operations for Australian retailers Kmart and Target.

Matthew founded the Menark Group, a leading strategy and program delivery organisation specialising in driving business performance. The Menark Group is centred on enhancing commercial, operational and innovation capabilities across businesses.

With a global footprint, it operates in diverse markets, serving organisations looking to harness strategic insights and transformative frameworks to navigate today's complex business landscapes.

Matthew's profound understanding of dynamic business ecosystems is manifested in his international bestseller, *Fit for Disruption: How to Transform Your Business and Thrive in Times of Rapid Change*.

Beyond his corporate accomplishments, Matthew is a Course Facilitator (Contract) with Stanford University Graduate School of Business. Engaging with courses on strategy, innovation, organisational design, storytelling, critical analytical thinking and leadership, he merges his vast industry knowledge with executive educational pursuits, striving to mould leaders who lead with both empathy and conviction.

In 2024, Matthew embraces a new challenge as a Business Coach with the Stanford Institute for Innovation in Developing Economies, more commonly known as Stanford Seed. Based in India, this role epitomises his commitment to fostering global business growth and innovation. Stanford Seed is a Stanford Graduate School of Business led initiative that partners with entrepreneurs in emerging markets to build thriving enterprises that transform lives and communities. Seed's mission aligns seamlessly with Matthew's long-standing advocacy for business and entrepreneurship as a conduit for societal advancement and prosperity.

Matthew is a passionate advocate for the transformative power of business and entrepreneurship. He firmly believes in its potential to establish prosperous, harmonious and healthy societies. Matthew holds a Bachelor of Business (Accounting) from Monash University in Australia and has furthered his expertise with the Stanford LEAD program in Corporate Innovation.

www.ingramcontent.com/pod-product-compliance
Lightning Source LLC
Chambersburg PA
CBHW031838200326
41597CB00012B/195